T0367981

Cross-Functional
Inventory Research

World Scientific–Now Publishers Series in Business

ISSN: 2251-3442

Published:

World Scientific – Now Publishers Series in Business: **Vol.10**

Cross-Functional Inventory Research

Srinagesh Gavirneni

Cornell University, USA

Published by

World Scientific Publishing Co. Pte. Ltd.
5 Toh Tuck Link, Singapore 596224
USA office: 27 Warren Street, Suite 401-402, Hackensack, NJ 07601
UK office: 57 Shelton Street, Covent Garden, London WC2H 9HE

and

now publishers Inc.
PO Box 1024
Hanover, MA 02339
USA

Library of Congress Cataloging-in-Publication Data
Names: Gavirneni, Srinagesh, editor.
Title: Cross-functional inventory research / [editor], Srinagesh Gavirneni.
Description: New Jersey : World Scientific, [2016] |
    Series: World scientific-now publishers series in business ; volume 10 |
    Includes bibliographical references and index.
Identifiers: LCCN 2016026513 | ISBN 9789813144330 (hc : alk. paper)
Subjects: LCSH: Inventories. | Inventory control.
Classification: LCC HD40 .C76 2016 | DDC 658.7/87--dc23
LC record available at https://lccn.loc.gov/2016026513

British Library Cataloguing-in-Publication Data
A catalogue record for this book is available from the British Library.

Desk Editors: Herbert Moses/Philly Lim

Typeset by Stallion Press
Email: enquiries@stallionpress.com

Printed in Singapore

Published on the occasion of L. Joseph Thomas' retirement honoring his contributions to the Samuel Curtis Johnson Graduate School of Management, Cornell University, and the broader Operations Management community.

Contents

Foreword

L. Joseph (Joe) Thomas. A boy from a small town in southern Ohio. High school basketball star. All-state band on the trombone. Carnegie Tech Chemical Engineering grad, and straight on to Yale's Department of Industrial Administration (later Administrative Science, then folded into the School of Management) for his Ph.D. in Operations Research. I met him there in 1966 in an advanced statistics course. Right away, it was clear that Joe was someone special. Very friendly and hardworking, he always had time for others. And he had a wonderful fiancée, Marney, another Carnegie grad, who was working on her Ph.D. in some Ivy League school hidden away in a small town somewhere in "Upstate New York". I think it was called Ithaca.

In the 49 years since he joined the faculty at Cornell, Joe has served in many roles. He taught 13 different courses, served on endless committees, directed the Johnson School's Doctoral Program and Executive Education Programs, was appointed as Associate Dean for Academic Affairs three times, and got kicked upstairs to be the Anne and Elmer Lindseth Dean from 2007 to 2012.

Teaching is one of his favorite activities, and he does it extremely well. He has received several teaching awards, and he is always one of those most fondly remembered by alumni. I have watched him at many reunions, surrounded by former students who remember his wonderful classroom presence, and his ability to make courses interesting and even entertaining from time to time. Who do you know that can make students enjoy Statistics? Joe can.

The field of Production and Operations Management has been the focus of Joe's professional activities. His written contributions include 58 research articles, six books and contributions to books, and eight cases. He has been invited to make numerous research presentations at universities, international conferences, and other venues. He belongs to all of the professional societies related to Operations Management, and served many times as editor, referee, and conference organizer. Throughout his career, he has maintained close contact with what academics refer to as "the real world". (Is Academe unreal?) A number of businesses in the U.S. and abroad, as well as several nonprofit organizations, have sought his advice through consultancies and board memberships.

What I have been trying to convey is that Joe has influenced thousands of people in many ways, all beneficial, all generously given and gratefully received. To illustrate this further, I asked a few other people to tell something about Joe. Their comments and memories are summarized in the next few paragraphs, after which I will continue my remarks.

Steve Graves:

Joe has been an esteemed colleague for nearly 40 years. I got to know Joe's work from my advisor Warren Hausman, and always admired its style and contribution — his papers described interesting and important problems that were well motivated, and upon which Joe then generated applicable results and novel insights. Joe is a great role model for a younger researcher. I came to appreciate that Joe is not just an exceptional researcher, but also an exceptional person too: warm, open, selfless, and supportive. Joe is always interested in what you are doing, and always has good advice.

Ken Schultz:

Joe is one of the most decent people I've ever met. His moral standards are of the highest quality, and while he respects good research, how you lived your life was more important than how many papers you published.

I was about six months into my relationship with him before I heard him say anything negative about anybody else. I had just finished a Ph.D. course in the Economics department at Cornell. The final exam was a selection from the same eight questions every year. I, a lowly first year Ph.D. student, was feeling put upon. His comment: "Yes. I'm not quite sure why they do it that way," sent the correct message and left me nowhere to go but back to work.

His dedication to Cornell was unshakable. I remember being in his office when he got a call from Michigan about a chair and teaching position in their executive education program. Joe's side of the conversation went something like this:

"No, I appreciate it but we're pretty happy here in NY."

"Yes, I know you all have a very good program out there."

"Wow. That much money. Thank you, but as I said, we're quite happy here."

He never told me how much the offer was for, but I don't recall him saying "wow" all that often.

Wally Hopp:

As someone from outside Cornell, what impresses me most about Joe is what a marvelous citizen of the Operations Management community he has been. Even when he was dean, he somehow found time to attend professional events, give presentations, and write thoughtful letters on behalf of promotion and tenure candidates. I see Joe as the ultimate role model of the balanced academic. He serves many constituencies, always well, and always in the interest of people and his profession. I'm very grateful to have had him as a professional colleague for the past 30 years.

Candi Yano:

Joe Thomas has had a long-standing impact on the field of Operations Management in many ways. He was one of the pioneers in studying joint pricing-inventory problems over multiple time periods, and his seminal work has influenced many researchers in the now-popular area of Operations-Marketing interface models. His research on production planning under capacity constraints is also highly influential. For many years, I have used his papers in my graduate courses, not only to teach the students about the problem at hand, but also to expose them to different methodological approaches. Joe has also played a valuable role in editorial positions for several journals. Researchers appreciate his constructive comments and helpful style, which makes the revision process much easier and significantly improves the quality and contribution of the paper. Joe has had an influence on many of us in ways that he may not even know about and are too numerous to recount, but are very much appreciated.

Sridhar Tayur:

I took Joe's "Business Logistics" MBA class which gave me a good sense of how an effective MBA course can be taught. As a Ph.D. student in Engineering, that was very helpful. In particular, I liked how he handled the students' questions and also engaged them.

His good cheer at all times (in and out of class) and easy approachability make him a very rare person in academia. I recall one of his lines from our many interactions: "Avoid Type 3 error: Solving the wrong problem exactly." And: "There may have been a Type 4 error: solving the problem after it has passed."

I especially recall the "Just In Time" song during Red Barn annual party.

Larry Robinson:

I remember a few of his lines: "Good morning gentlemen, and I use the term loosely," and (to students): "My job is to talk, and yours is to listen. Let me know if you finish first." I remember sitting in on his logistics class once, and being amazed at his rapport with the class. At one point he said: "And that goes back to what Andrea said at the start of class." I might recall that someone said something about it in the right side of the classroom, but he remembered everyone and everything.

Doug Thomas:

I am not quite sure what to write, as my situation is a bit different than other contributors, since he is my father. I guess I'd say that, on a professional level, I learned from him (1) how to treat people, and (2) the joy of intellectual curiosity. He always seemed to me to treat everyone as if he sincerely cared about them.

Jack Muckstadt:

Over time, we wrote papers together, jointly taught a Cornell program called "Managing the Next Generation of Manufacturing Technology", coached our sons' basketball team, and, perhaps the most important factor in our 42 year friendship, we enjoyed and still do enjoy great wines and foods together.

I learned a lot about teaching nontechnical subjects and students by observing Joe's teaching style. I believe that Joe has proven to be one of Cornell's most effective instructors. Many thousands of students have benefitted from his explaining the theory and application of many topics pertaining to supply chain management.

Joe is a team player. He accepted the offer to serve the Johnson School as its dean not to promote himself but to lead and significantly improve the School and its standing. Our University is a better one due to his efforts.

We need to celebrate his outstanding career. He is a model for all of us. It has been a privilege to know him.

John McClain:

From these words of his friends and colleagues, you can see that Joe affects people in many ways, and always in a positive manner. Now I will close with some personal observations.

Joe and I have been friends since 1966, and colleagues in teaching, research, consulting, and textbook writing since 1969, when he was instrumental in bringing me to Cornell. Working with him is a pleasure. When we discussed research, ideas would flash back and forth so rapidly it was almost spooky. We even wrote an article during a flight to a conference, passing a sheaf of papers over the back of the seat. Joint teaching was a pleasure too. And Joe was always ready to help with course improvement. All of us in the Operations Management group found a willing ear and good advice when needed.

Academic life is not all work. The Cornell MBA students have an annual tradition known as the Follies. Although merciless and hilarious in poking fun at the faculty, the students generously allow the faculty 10 minutes. Joe and his family provided most of the faculty's contributions by writing new lyrics to songs that everybody already knew. For example, "Just In Time" is an old torch hit rewritten into a song about Production Management. "F is for Analysis of Variance" is about Statistics, written to the tune of "M-O-T-H-E-R". In recent years, other talented people have contributed new material, but the Thomas legacy lives on.

Joe and Marney love to bring friends together. Their annual Christmas Caroling Party, for example, began in the old fashioned way: cheery friends traipsing around the neighborhood singing. It evolved into a potluck at their home. After yummy food and desserts, everyone gathered around Joe and his piano. Children are always welcome, with fun stuff to do.

Joe and Marney host many other events at their home, for students, alums, colleagues, and friends. They are always warmly welcoming. Two highlights of a visit to the Thomas home are a visit to the fabulous wine cellar, and struggling to operate the very large, hand-cranked ice cream freezer.

* * *

In every way, being around Joe Thomas is a wonderful experience. I would like to close with the words of Jack Muckstadt: "He is a model for all of us. It has been a privilege to know him."

– John McClain

About the Contributors

Lucy Gongtao Chen is an Assistant Professor in the Department of Decision Sciences at NUS Business School, National University of Singapore. Her research is mainly in the areas of inventory management, supply chain management, the interface between operations and marketing, and the interface between operations and finance. Her research has appeared in journals such as *Management Science, Operations Research, Manufacturing and Service Operations Management, Production and Operations Management*, and *Journal of Operations Management*. She won an honorable mention in the 2007 M&SOM student paper competition.

Mohammad Delasay is a Post-Doctoral Fellow of Operations Management at the Tepper School of Business, Carnegie Mellon University. He received a Ph.D. in Operations Management from the University of Alberta. His research is in the application of queueing and stochastic models to design and improve the performance of service and healthcare systems, including emergency medical services and organ transplant centers. He has taught various undergraduate and MBA courses, including Operations Management, Statistics, and Simulation and Stochastic Modeling.

Armann Ingolfsson is an Associate Professor of Operations Management, the Roger H. Smith Professor of Business, and the Academic Director of the Centre for Excellence in Operations at the Alberta School of Business at the University of Alberta. He received a Ph.D. in Operations Research from MIT. His research interests focus on operations management in the service and health care sectors and developing methodology to analyze congested systems. He has published articles on these topics in *Management Science, Operations Research, Production and Operations Management,* and various other journals. He is the past Editor-in-Chief of INFORMS Transactions on Education and an Associate Editor for INFOR and the Journal for Quantitative Analysis in Sports. He has taught Operations Management, Analytics, and Statistics to undergraduate, MBA, executive education, and Ph.D. students. He is a past President of the Canadian Operational Research Society (CORS) and has served in various other roles for CORS.

Juan Li is a Quantitative Analyst at Google in operations decision support group. Her work includes using a wide selection of analytical tools including statistics, optimization and machine learning to analyze large amount of data from Google's IT infrastructure, and provide data driven decisions to improve operational resource efficiency. Prior to joining Google, Dr. Li worked at Xerox Innovation Group as a research scientist in data analytics area, where she worked on several projects to draw operational insight from machine sensor data. Dr. Li holds a B.A. in Mathematics from Smith College and a Ph.D. in Operations Research from Cornell University.

John McClain was in the U.S. Army for six months in 1960. Graduated at Washington State University in 1964 in Physics, followed by a Master's degree in Physics from Yale in 1965. Worked for Sikorsky Aircraft in Antisubmarine Warfare for two years, where McClain learned about Operations Research. Got a Ph.D. from Yale in O.R. in 1970 and joined the faculty of Cornell University's Business School, where I spent my entire academic career. In 1999, I was awarded the "Emerson Electric Chair in Manufacturing Management" (some say that Cornell gave me the "electric chair"). Some of McClain's activities include: Consultant to more than 20 different companies, hospitals and other organizations; President of the Manufacturing and Services Operations Management Society (MSOM); Author or co-author of more than 55 books, research articles and other scholarly publications, and five macro-enabled statistical tools using Microsoft Excel. McClain retired in July 2010.

Jack Muckstadt is the Acheson-Laibe Professor of Engineering Emeritus in Cornell University's School of Operations Research and Information Engineering and a Stephen H. Weiss Presidential Fellow. He served as the School's Director for nine years; he also established and was the first director of the Cornell Manufacturing Engineering and Productivity

Program. He is the co-director of Cornell's Institute for Disease and Disaster Preparedness. He has served as a member of the Board of Scientific Counselors to the Centers for Disease Control and Prevention. His teaching, research and consulting interests are in the areas of manufacturing systems and manufacturing logistics, supply chain systems, service parts management and, most recently, response logistics for mass casualty events and health system operations. He is a Fellow in two professional organizations. He was an officer in the U.S. Air Force for 21 years and, primarily working in the logistics field. He has consulted with numerous public and governmental organizations and focused on supply chain design, analysis, and operations. He holds a B.A. in Mathematics from the University of Rochester and an M.A. in Mathematics, an M.S. in Industrial Administration, and a Ph.D. in Industrial Engineering from the University of Michigan.

Huanhuan (Daphne) Qi is a Vice President in the Model Strategy and Data Analytics area at Northern Trust Company. Her primary responsibility is credit loss estimation using quantitative models with a focus on corporate default risk and loss prediction. Prior to this, she worked as a Senior Consultant at the Gap, Inc., developing optimization models to improve business operations for the company's supply chain. Her projects included demand forecasting and planning, as well as inventory and store delivery frequency optimization. She holds a B.A. in Applied Mathematics, a M.S. and Ph.D. in Industrial Engineering and Operations Research from the University of California, Berkeley. Her dissertation research focused on pricing strategies for supply chains involving both a retailer and a manufacturer, where both the retailers and consumer may stockpile when discounted prices are offered.

Lawrence W. Robinson is a Professor in the Operations, Technology, and Information Management group in the Johnson Graduate School of Management of Cornell University. He received his MBA and Ph.D. from the Graduate School of Business at the University of Chicago. His current research focuses on problems of operating in an uncertain environment, including examining the value of information sharing with order commitment in a supply chain, determining the optimal number of handicapped parking spaces, explaining the anchoring and insufficient adjustment bias in the newsvendor problem, and scheduling strategic patients at a doctor's office. He has published in a variety of journals, including *Operations Research, Management Science, Manufacturing and Service Operations Management*, and *Production and Operations Management*. He has been a Mobil Scholar, and has twice received the Executive MBA Globe Award for teaching excellence.

Robin Roundy has been a Professor of Mathematics at Brigham Young University since 2010. Prior to that, he was a Professor at Cornell University from 1983 to 2007, and served a mission for the Church of Jesus Christ of Latter-Day Saints from 2007 to 2010. He graduated magna cum laude from Brigham Young University. He received the Orson Pratt Award, which is given annually to the outstanding mathematics graduate. He then studied Operations Research at Stanford University, where he received his doctorate in 1984. In 1984, Professor Roundy won the Nicholson Student Paper Competition, sponsored by the Operations Research Society of America (ORSA). In 1985, he received a Presidential Young Investigator Award from the National Science Foundation. In 1988, he received the Fredrick W. Lanchester Prize of the Operations Research Society of America for the best paper of the year on Operations Research. He is the author of one of Management Science's 50 Most Influential Papers (2004). He is a two-time recipient of the S. Yau '72 Excellence in Teaching Award, and has won other teaching awards as well. He is a fellow of The Institute for Operations Research and the Management Sciences (INFORMS) and of The Manufacturing and Service Operations Management Society (MSOM).

Kenneth Schultz is an Associate Professor at the Air Force Institute of Technology. He received his Ph.D. from the S.C. Johnson Graduate School of Management at Cornell University where Dr. L. Joseph Thomas was his dissertation chair. He has taught at Cornell University, Indiana University and the University of Alberta. His work appears in *Management Science, Production and Operations Management* and the *Journal of Operations Management*. He is a leader in the area of Behavioral Operations Management working at improving the consideration of human behavior in Operations Management modeling. He was a founding member of and an officer in the INFORMS Section on Behavioral Operations Management and the POMS College of Behavior in Operations Management. His current research interests include how people behave within queues and pilot motivation to save fuel.

Sridhar Tayur is the Ford Distinguished Research Chair and Professor of Operations Management at Carnegie Mellon University's Tepper School of Business. He received his Ph.D. in Operations Research and Industrial Engineering from Cornell University and his undergraduate degree in Mechanical Engineering from the Indian Institute of Technology at Madras. He was the founder and CEO of the software company SmartOps (acquired by SAP) and is the founder of a social enterprise, OrganJet. SmartOps is the subject of a Darden Case Study and OrganJet of a HBS Case Study. He has published in *Operations Research, Management Science, Mathematics of Operations Research, Mathematical Programming, Stochastic Models, Queuing Systems, Transportation Science, POMS, IIE Transactions, NRLQ, Journal of Algorithms* and *MSOM Journal*, is co-editor of *Quantitative Models for Supply Chain Management*, and has served on the editorial boards of *Operations Research, MSOM Journal, Management Science* and *POMS*. He served as the President of MSOM Society. He has been a finalist for the Lanchester Prize and the Edelman Prize. He won the Healthcare Best paper Award by POMS in 2012 and the INFORMS Pierskalla Award in 2015. He also won the Undergraduate teaching Award, the George Leland Bach teaching award given by MBA students, the INFORMS Teaching Case award, and has been named as a 'Top Professor' by Business Week. He has won the Carnegie Science Center award for Innovation in Information Technology. He was named INFORMS Fellow in 2012. He served on the advisory board of CCG Inc., is on the advisory boards of TrueSpark, Zenrez and Vocal ID, on the Board of Directors of Orchestro and Transplant Interface and on the Board of Overseers at WGBH. In 2014, he made a $1 Million donation to CMU and in 2016 endowed an Institute Chair at IIT-Madras.

Doug Thomas is a Professor of Supply Chain Management at the Smeal College of Business at Penn State and Chief Scientist for Plan2Execute, LLC, a supply chain management consulting and software solutions provider. Prior to returning to graduate school, he worked for C-Way Systems, a software company specializing in manufacturing scheduling. In addition to his 16 years on the faculty at Penn State, Doug has had the pleasure of serving as a visiting faculty member at INSEAD (in Fontainebleau, France), the Johnson Graduate School of Management at Cornell University and The Darden School at the University of Virginia. His research interests include coordinating production and inventory planning across the extended enterprise and connecting decision models to logistics performance measurement. His work has appeared in several academic and practitioner journals in the areas of logistics and operations management, and he has co-authored a forthcoming book, *Inventory and Production Management in Supply Chains*, CRC Press. A frequent faculty leader in executive development programs, Doug has led numerous executive education sessions in Africa, Asia, Europe, and both North and South America. He hopes to make it to Australia at some point, but thinks leading an executive program in Antarctica is unlikely. He has testified as an expert witness and consulted for several large organizations on supply chain strategy including Accenture, CSL Behring, Dell, ExxonMobil, and Lockheed Martin Aerospace Corporation.

Candace ("Candi") Yano is a Professor in the Department of Industrial Engineering and Operations Research (IEOR) and the Gary and Sherron Kalbach Chair in Business Administration and Professor in the Operations and Information Technology Management Group at the Haas School of Business at the University of California, Berkeley, California. Prior to joining UC Berkeley, she was a Member of the Technical Staff at Bell Telephone Laboratories and a faculty member at the University of Michigan. She holds an A.B. in Economics, a M.S. in Operations Research, and a M.S. and Ph.D. in Industrial Engineering from Stanford University. Professor Yano's primary research interests are production, inventory and logistics management, particularly on how to deal with various sources of uncertainty in these contexts, as well as interdisciplinary problems involving manufacturing and marketing. She has served as the Editor-in-Chief of IIE Transactions and Department Editor (Operations and Supply Chains) for Management Science, as well as in various editorial capacities for Operations Research, Interfaces, Manufacturing and Service Operations Management, and Naval Research Logistics, among others. Professor Yano is a Fellow of the Institute for Operations Research and the Management Sciences (INFORMS) as well as the Institute of Industrial Engineers (IIE).

Rachel Q. Zhang is a Professor in Industrial Engineering and Logistics Management at the Hong Kong University of Science and Technology. She received her Ph.D. in Industrial Engineering and Management Sciences in 1994 from Northwestern University and was previously a faculty member in the Department of Industrial and Operations Engineering at University of Michigan, and the Johnson Graduate School of Management at Cornell University. Her research interests lie in the general area of operations management and the interface of operations, finance and marketing. Her research has appeared in such journals as *Operations Research, Management Science, Interfaces, IIE Transactions, Naval Research Logistics*, and *Advances in Applied Probability*. She received an honorable mention in the INFORMS Nicholson Paper Competition in 1994 and an early-career award (CAREER) from the US National Science Foundation in 1995. She co-chaired the MSOM Conference in June 2000, served as an MSOM cluster co-chair for the INFORMS National Meeting in Fall 1998, and the program chair for the 2006 IFORS conference. She also served as a member of the INFORMS Nicholson Competition Award Committee, the MSOM Student Paper Competition, Junior Faculty at INFORMS Paper Competition Committee, POMS SCM Student Paper Competition, and a panelist for the National Science Foundation in 2000. She also chaired the IIE Transaction (Scheduling and Logistics) Best Paper Award and the IIE Pritsker Doctoral Dissertation Award. She was the secretary of INFORMS Women in OR/MS during 1999–2000.

Chapter 1

Improvements in Inventory Management: Past Success and Future Opportunities

Douglas J. Thomas

Smeal College of Business
Penn State, USA

It is a privilege to contribute an essay in honor of the career and scholarly accomplishments of L. Joseph Thomas. While one needs to talk to only a few of his colleagues and former students to understand that his impact went far beyond his scholarly work, I feel comfortable in stating that he has positively influenced me in more ways and in greater magnitude than most. Nevertheless, in this chapter, I restrict my scope to a discussion of the field of inventory management, a field to which Professor Thomas has certainly made notable contributions, some of which I discuss below.

In this chapter, I briefly discuss and summarize the historical inventory management successes achieved collectively by academics and practitioners. This historical success has largely come from reductions in upstream inventories held by manufacturers. I conjecture that future improvements must largely come from downstream inventories, and I discuss three areas of challenge and opportunity: (1) Rapidly changing product and delivery variety offered to the customer, (2) information sharing between channel partners, and (3) aligning incentives between channel partners.

1 Introduction

Managing inventory well is important. The U.S. Census Bureau recently reported that U.S. firms hold $1.8 trillion in inventory across retailers, manufacturers, and wholesalers (U.S. Census Bureau, 2015b). Some recent studies have empirically verified the link between inventory management performance and firm performance that one would hypothesize based on our analytic inventory models. Hendricks and Singhal (2009) show that excess inventory announcements are met with negative stock market reaction, and Chen *et al.* (2007) also relate abnormal inventory levels to poor stock returns.

Many factors have continued to put upward pressure on firms' inventory levels, including increasing product variety, shortening product lifecycles, and an increase in global sourcing. A recent empirical study by Jain *et al.* (2013) indicates that firms that engage in more global sourcing do indeed have higher inventory levels. Firms with a wide range of products and/or short product lifecycles often have higher gross margin and greater demand uncertainty (Fisher, 1997), and an empirical study by Rumyantsev and Netessine (2007) concludes that more uncertainty, longer lead times and higher gross margin translate to higher inventory levels.

Despite these pressures, at an aggregate level, inventory levels have been dropping. Figure 1 shows the inventory-to-sales ratios over time for U.S. retailers, manufacturers, and wholesalers. Chen *et al.* (2005) report on inventory levels of U.S. firms between 1981 and 2000, noting that the average annual rate of inventory reduction over this period was 2%. Interestingly, much of this reduction came from a reduction in work-in-process inventory, whereas finished goods inventories did not decline. In a separate study, Rajagopalan and Malhotra (2001) find reductions in raw material and work-in-process inventory but mixed results on finished goods inventory for U.S. firms between 1961 and 1994.

The $1.8 trillion in inventory reported above is roughly equally split between manufacture, wholesale, and retail, but this distribution is a recent phenomenon. As indicated in Fig. 2, inventories have shifted downstream: in 1992, 46% of inventory was on manufacturers' books, down to 37% in 2014. Based in part on the scholarly work and data mentioned above, I draw one conclusion and state one conjecture.

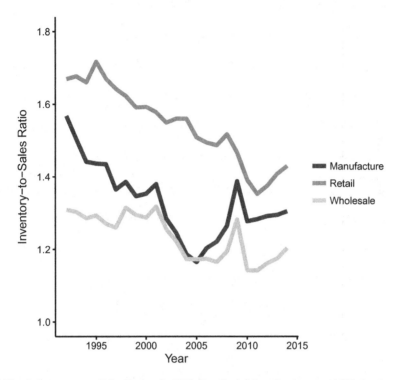

Fig. 1 Inventory-to-Sales Ratios for U.S. Retailers, Manufacturers, and Wholesalers
Source: U.S. Census Bureau. November 2015 Manufacturing and Trade Inventories and Sales report.

First, I conclude that many scholars and practitioners deserve credit for effectively "leaning out" manufacturing firms' raw material and work-in-process inventory levels. This improvement was certainly helped along by several influential books that continue to be on reading lists such as Goldratt and Cox (1986), Ōno (1988), and Womack *et al.* (1990), and influential academic work on managing work-in-process inventory including Conway *et al.* (1988) and Spearman *et al.* (1990) among others. Many of the insights from these and other academic works are nicely assembled and presented in Hopp and Spearman (2011).

Second, I conjecture that to continue this improvement in inventory management, future savings must largely come from downstream (i.e., finished goods and retail) inventories. Several recent studies have

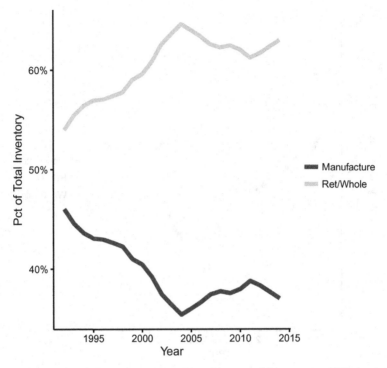

Fig. 2 Distribution of Inventory Between Manufacture and Downstream (Wholesale and Retail)
Source: U.S. Census Bureau. November 2015 Manufacturing and Trade Inventories and Sales report.

highlighted the importance of inventory management to the retail sector. Gaur *et al.* (2005) demonstrate strong correlation between good inventory performance (low inventory turnover) and high gross margin. Kesavan *et al.* (2010) show inventory (and gross margin) can be used to improve sales forecasts, and Kesavan and Mani (2013) show that inventory levels can help predict earnings. So, continued improvement in inventory management is important, particularly for downstream inventories, where I assert the largest savings opportunties exist.

In the remainder of this chapter, I discuss three areas that present challenges but also where I believe positive strides can be made in improving management of downstream inventories: (1) the rapidly changing customer offer, (2) information sharing between channel partners, and (3) incentive alignment between channel partners. In each area, I discuss some academic work to date and outline some possible areas of future research.

2 The Impact of New Customer Offerings

Customers want what they want, when they want, delivered how they want. Then, they want to be able to return it however they want. Results from a survey conducted by UPS (UPS, 2014) indicate that customers place particularly high value on being able to select both from a wide range of products and a wide range of shipping options. Online shopping continues to grow, with the percent of U.S. retail sales considered e-commerce growing from 2.8% in 2006 to 7.3% in 2015 (U.S. Census Bureau, 2015a).

Product variety has grown due to intense competition as well as significant growth in e-commerce sales. The introduction of the online channel allows firms to offer a "long-tail" of potentially high-variability, low-volume items that could not be profitably stocked in physical stores. This is good for customers, but challenging for those managing a supply chain. Brynjolfsson *et al.* (2003) estimated that in the bookselling sector in 2000, the additional product variety available to customers increased consumer welfare by close to $1 billion. While this increase in variety enhances welfare, it creates upward pressure on inventory levels needed to support this variety. In an empirical study of the retail sector, Rajagopalan (2013) concludes that retail firms with greater variety do indeed have higher inventory levels.

In addition to offering a wide variety of products, retailers are also trying many different approaches to try to meet customers' diverse *delivery* preferences across online and offline channels. The term "omnichannel" is now used to indicate a retailer's desire to offer their products to the customer wherever and however the customer wants. Bell *et al.* (2014) present a managerially-oriented discussion of omnichannel retailing with several examples of innovative customer offerings. The framework in Bell *et al.* (2014) distinguishes the customer experience in the dimensions of how customers acquire *information* about their intended purchase (by going to a store to examine the product or by researching online) and how the demand request is fulfilled (in store or online).

Recent discussions with retail executives[1] suggest that firms are moving rapidly to enhance customer offerings without necessarily understanding the inventory management consequences of those offerings. In particular, firms seem to be struggling with the following two questions:

(1) What delivery options should be made available and how should they be priced?

Customers will of course react to new delivery options. Gallino and Moreno (2014) report on the implementation of a buy-online, pick-up-in-store (BOPS) project. While one might expect this new online offering (BOPS) to increase online sales, the opposite happened, with store sales and traffic increasing and online sales decreasing. This phenomenon is largely attributed to customers using the information made available with BOPS to inform their decision of whether or not to go to the store, thus shifting some customers from online to the store.

Gallino *et al.* (2014) investigate the impact of a "ship-to-store" offering where customers can order from the full assortment available online and have the product shipped to a local store at no additional cost. They find that some demand for top-selling items typically carried in stores gets shifted to slower moving items. This may mean that customers who previously substituted a locally-stocked product for their preferred (but not locally-stocked) product, use the new ship-to-store option to get their desired product. This may increase customer satisfaction but shifting demand to the long tail of slow moving items increases the need for inventory system wide. The authors estimate an inventory increase of 2.7% is needed to support the ship-to-store initiative.

For online retailing, having a minimum purchase threshold to qualify for free shipping is common. As customers, we seem to like this option. The UPS survey mentioned above reports that 93% of respondents have taken action to qualify for free shipping. One specialty retailer revealed to me

---

[1]My thanks to members of the Retail Industry Leaders Association Supply Chain Leaders council, participants at the Supply Chain Leaders Forum at the Center for Supply Chain Research at the Smeal College of Business at Penn State and my faculty colleagues Jason Acimovic, Vidya Mani, and Chris Parker for many interesting discussions regarding omnichannel challenges.

that when they implemented a free shipping threshold, basket revenue did indeed increase, but they did not correctly forecast and stock the "small" items that customers frequently add to get to the threshold. This resulted in sufficient additional shipment expense (for split orders) such that the firm would have been better off not introducing the threshold or giving free shipping with no threshold. These examples suggest, not surprisingly, that customers will react to new delivery options in ways that have significant impact for managing system inventory. This leads to the second question.

(2) How should firms utilize their retail store space and inventory?

Due to the continued growth in online ordering and rising real estate costs, many retailers recently have closed retail locations as well as converting many locations to small-format stores. Such a store downsizing of course requires a reduction in the set of products offered. Mani *et al.* (2016) evaluate the impact of a major store-downsizing initiative for an office products retailer. They find that even within the relatively narrow category of office products, customers' willingness to substitute to a less-preferred item varies dramatically across product subcategories. Their analysis suggests that taking these substitution patterns into effect can increase same-store revenue by 6–10%. The findings here could complement the findings from the ship-to-store study mentioned by Gallino *et al.* (2014). For product categories where customers are often willing to substitute, it might be wise for a retailer to limit the set of products offered online (through ship-to-store, for example). Of course, as noted above, there will certainly be product categories where customer satisfaction is greatly enhanced by offering wide variety. Gao and Su (2016) provide insights in this direction based on an analytic model of BOPS where they show how product and market characteristics affect the attractiveness of blending online and offline channels.

In addition to rationalizing and re-sizing stores, firms must choose how to utilize store inventory to satisfy demand at other locations (either online or at other stores). Such an approach clearly has the opportunity to enable inventory efficiencies through demand pooling, but doing so creates several inventory management challenges. First, it has been well documented that store-level inventory accuracy can be poor (DeHoratius and Raman, 2008). Second, it is unclear how fulfillment costs (mostly order-picking and transportation costs) would compare with picking orders at a fulfillment center. If such tasks can be done by store associates during idle time, these costs may be low. If additional associates are needed, fulfillment costs may be higher. Third, many stores operate on "local" sales incentives, so how a store is credited (or not) for an online order will impact how promptly and accurately store-based fulfillment occurs. In conversations about omnichannel challenges, a specialty outdoor goods retailer shared that low-value online orders that stores were asked to fulfill were processed either after long delays or often not at all. A sporting goods retailer encountered similar issues and responded by increasing staff at the store and putting the additional staff in plain clothes so in-store customers would not distract them from their online order picking duties.

As these omnichannel and store format initiatives are a relatively recent phenomenon, there is not a great deal of academic work in this area. There are certainly opportunities to contribute to the academic literature as well as positively impact practice. I summarize this section as follows:

(1) New retail offerings such as store-format changes and new online/offline/hybrid channel offerings are coming fast, and these decisions are largely being made with customer satisfaction rather than inventory and fulfillment efficiency in mind.
(2) Customers' reactions to these offerings can be unpredictable and almost always have significant implications for inventory management.
(3) There are opportunites to make contributions by understanding how customers' variety, format, and channel preferences can be aligned with effectively managing inventory across the network of fulfillment centers and physical stores.

3 Information Sharing among Supply Chain Partners

Collaboration between channel partners is a great idea in principle but challenging to execute in practice. In a recent study based on surveys and interviews with purchasing managers, Fawcett *et al.* (2015) find that the majority of respondents see the potential value in collaboration but are disappointed in the realized results. Results of a survey with 374 supply chain professionals reported by O'Marah (2013) suggest that bilateral information sharing is critical to successful collaboration: 73% responded that customers need to share demand information with suppliers, and 83% responded that suppliers must share supply availability information.

Unlike the very recently emerging omnichannel area discussed in the previous section, there is a relatively strong body of academic work addressing the impact of information sharing between supply chain partners. Our profession has been quite effective at teaching the deletrious effects of poor information flows, often through the use of the beer game (Sterman, 1995), and there is a large body of literature on the "bullwhip" effect that arises in the beer game that I do not attempt to comprehensively discuss here. The interested reader is directed to Lee *et al.* (1997) who discuss rational decision factors that can exacerbate the bullwhip effect. Croson and Donohue (2006) complement this work by investigating the impact of behavioral factors on the bullwhip effect. Cachon *et al.* (2007) and Bray and Mendelson (2012) demonstrate the magnitude of the bullwhip effect in practice, with Bray and Mendelson (2012) reporting that improvements have been made: the magnitude of the bullwhip effect between 1995–2008 is substantially lower than the magnitude over 1974–2008.

Collaborative Planning, Forecasting, and Replenishment (CPFR) is a process that has emerged from industry, and is curated by the Voluntary Interindustry Commerce Standards organization (now merged with GS1 US, www.gs1us.org) to attempt to provide a standard process for collaboration that overcomes information-sharing challenges. A detailed process roadmap and several successful case studies are provided. In addition, there is also academic work on CPFR, complementing the aforementioned industry-based resources. Aviv (2001, 2007) analyzes the theoretical benefits of collaborative forecasting to both supplier and customer and these studies provide insights about the potential benefits of different kinds of information sharing arrangements.

Information sharing arrangements can include sharing only demand or forecast-related information as well as supply availability (i.e., capacity or inventory). The practice of Vendor-Managed Inventory (VMI) typically makes inventory information at a customer's location available to a supplier. See Waller *et al.* (1999) and Çetinkaya and Lee (2000) for discussions of VMI. Gavirneni *et al.* (1999) analyze the benefits of demand and inventory information sharing in a capacitated setting. Lee *et al.* (2000) show that the value of demand information sharing can be quite high when demands are serially correlated, and Cachon and Fisher (2000) investigate the value of information sharing between one supplier and multiple customers.

Collectively, these academic works, along with many others not discussed here, provide insights primarily addressing how firms should use shared information and what potential benefits might accrue. We have less academic work (the empirical bullwhip papers mentioned above notwithstanding) addressing what firms are doing in practice and how to overcome common barriers to collaboration. There have been some survey-based research efforts that establish the connection between a perceived collaborative capabilities and performance, such as Zhou and Benton (2007). One example of analysis of collaboration on operational data is Terwiesch *et al.* (2005) who examine the impact of forecasting sharing in the semiconductor industry. They find while substantial overall benefits could be achieved by effective information sharing, suppliers punish customers who provide noisy or poor forecasts with poor service, and suppliers who provide poor service receive inflated forecasts.

A survey of executives conducted by O'Marah (2014) reports trust (presumably lack of) as the top barrier to successful collaboration. Some recent research begins to lend some insight to this important barrier. Özer *et al.* (2011, 2014) behaviorally investigate subjects' willingness to share demand information (as a retailer) or believe shared demand information (as a supplier). They find that suppliers and retailers cooperate to some extent, but there is still evidence of forecast inflation (by retailers) and forecast discounting (by suppliers). These findings, combined with the findings from Terwiesch *et al.* (2005) discussed above suggest that while information sharing can work to some extent, there is most likely substantial room in practice to improve the efficacy of information-sharing arrangements.

Anecdotal evidence, surveys, and trade publications seem to suggest that while there are successful instances of information sharing, there are many barriers to adoption and much potential upside. I summarize this section as follows:

(1) Our field has provided valuable insights regarding how shared information should be processed and the potential value of effective information sharing.

(2) There are opportunities to contribute by empirically investigating information-sharing practices as well as further understanding (and helping to overcome) the key barriers that are preventing more widespread information sharing about channel partners.

4 Incentive Alignment among Supply Chain Partners

In the previous section, I discussed the information-sharing aspect of collaboration. Of course, for information sharing across channel partners to occur, incentives must be aligned. In fact, the SCM World survey mentioned above (where executives listed *trust* as the top barrier to successful collaboration) listed *misaligned incentives* as the second largest barrier. As with information sharing, there is a relatively large body of literature on aligning incentives in a supply chain. Cachon (2003) offers an excellent starting point on coordinating contracts, and the key ideas behind these coordinated contracts have made their way into the classroom, appearing in textbooks such as Chopra and Meindl (2007) and Cachon and Terwiesch (2009).

Coordinating contracts generally seek to alter the decision of at least one party in the supply chain from a decision that maximizes their self-interest to a decision that improves overall supply chain welfare. The terms of the coordinating contract typically dictate how the increased welfare is distributed between the two (or more) parties.

Before discussing the literature and future opportunities, I briefly discuss "push" and "pull" settings where coordinating contracts could be used to improve overall welfare. First, consider the "push" case, where a retailer facing uncertain demand must purchase goods in advance of a single selling season, and the supplier has posted a per-unit wholesale price presumably greater than his production cost. Because the retailer faces all of the excess supply risk but receives only some of the profit margin, she will buy and stock less than the ideal quantity from the supply chain perspective, an effect termed *double marginalization* (Spengler, 1950).

One coordinating contract that can be used to address the misalignment in this push setting is a buyback contract, where the supplier agrees to compensate the retailer for excess inventory at the end of the selling season. (Revenue sharing contracts work similarly in theory. See Cachon and Lariviere (2005)). Even though this involves a transfer payment from the supplier to the retailer for excess inventory, total welfare can be improved since the retailer should stock and sell more product.

There are comparable "pull" settings, where the supplier must maintain inventory to respond on-demand to retailer requests. In such a setting, it is the supplier who faces the excess inventory risk and needs to somehow be compensated for this risk. An advance-purchase discount contract, where the retailer commits to a minimum advance purchase quantity at a specified discount, can be used to address this setting. Cachon (2004) provides a thorough analysis and comparison of push and pull and advance purchase discount contracts. There has been a great deal of interesting work done on different kinds of coordinating contracts including revenue-sharing and buyback contracts discussed above, quantity-flexible contracts (Tsay, 1999), real options contracts (Barnes-Schuster *et al.*, 2002), target rebates (Taylor, 2002) and target limits for managing returns (Ferguson *et al.*, 2006).

A coordination mechanism commonly used in practice is a Service Level Agreement (SLA), where a customer sets minimum service level expectations and associated penalties for failing to meet these expectations for a supplier. Such agreements are common both in retail (Thomas, 2005; Craig *et al.*, 2015; Chen and Thomas, 2016) and in managing outsourced services (Hasija *et al.*, 2008; Baron and Milner, 2009; Milner and Olsen, 2008). In retail, the penalties associated with SLAs are often called *chargebacks*, and trade articles (Harrington, 2005; Cassidy, 2010; Gilmore, 2010) indicate that these chargebacks can be quite significant, suggesting that retailers are using these SLAs to try to coordinate the supply chain and improve product availability.

Some relatively recent work has examined the effectiveness of different kinds of SLAs on coordinating the supply chain. Liang and Atkins (2013) investigate a suppliers' optimal actions when there is a penalty for failing to meet an inventory availability target over a finite horizon. Sieke *et al.* (2012) examine a single-period performance measurement review and investigate how the supplier's optimal base-stock levels may change in the presence of flat-fee SLA noncompliance penalties.

Collectively, these works provide valuable insights for how firms can coordinate. I conclude this section with a discussion of four barriers that may be inhibiting better coordination in practice.

4.1 *Asymmetric Information*

We discussed the importance of information sharing in the previous section. We note here that a significant amount of the coordination work discussed above relies on the customer and supplier sharing common information. For example, the standard theoretical analysis of the wholesale price contract setting discussed above (Lariviere and Porteus, 2001) assumes that the supplier has accurate knowledge of the retailer's demand distribution and the retail selling price. Theoretical analysis of pull settings, where a retailer is proposing some kind of coordinating agreement, often assumes that the retailer has knowledge of the supplier's production cost. It is of course necessary to understand the full information setting first, but customers in practice are likely to be hesitant to fully share demand information (recall the forecasting-trust discussion from the previous section), and suppliers will almost certainly be hesitant to share their cost information. There has certainly been some notable work addressing the impact of information asymmetry on coordination (e.g., Corbett, 2001; Cachon and Lariviere, 2001; Li and Zhang, 2008), but I assert this remains a large barrier to improved coordination in practice.

4.2 *Suboptimal Decision Making*

It is well documented that, at least in laboratory settings, decision makers consistently make suboptimal inventory decisions. See Schweitzer and Cachon (2000), Bolton and Katok (2008), and Su (2008) for discussions of suboptimal inventory ordering. A supplier seeking to improve coordination by offering a buyback contract counts on the retailer ordering optimally or at least significantly increasing their order quantity. Unless the purchase quantities are specified in the contract, a supplier may be hesitant to offer something like a buyback contract since he could end up absorbing additional inventory risk with little or no benefit.

There is also behavioral evidence suggesting that subjects in a laboratory setting struggle to achieve gains from coordinating contracts. Katok and Wu (2009) study buyback and revenue sharing agreements, showing that subjects improve coordination but substantially less than predicted by theory. Davis *et al.* (2014) report similar suboptimal contract setting.

4.3   *Compliance with the Agreement*

While it can be shown that revenue sharing agreements and buyback contracts are equivalent under certain conditions, two additional challenges arise with revenue sharing agreements. First, the terms of trade are quite different, as coordinating revenue sharing agreements often call for a supplier to sell at or below their cost in exchange for a revenue share. I conjecture that in practice, few suppliers are willing to sign a contract to sell below cost no matter the other contract terms. Second, the retail revenue, of which the supplier is now getting a share, may not be observable to the supplier. The lack of bilateral observability can be a problem with SLA also. Gilmore (2010) reports that at one time it was common practice for at least one large retailer to issue chargebacks automatically under the assumption that all suppliers would be in violation of some aspect of the agreement.

There has been some theoretical work addressing the impact of whether or not actions are bilaterally verifiable. Cachon and Lariviere (2001) investigate a setting where customer and supplier actions may or may not be verifiable (called "forced" and "voluntary" compliance). The compliance regime, not surprisingly, has a substantial impact on the actions of the two firms and the resulting profit outcomes. Plambeck and Taylor (2006) investigate the impact of process visibility, showing such visibility improves coordination for two firms jointly producing where total output depends on both firms' actions but yield is uncertain.

4.4   *Multiple Products and Customers*

Much of the work on coordinating contracts addresses the situation with a single supplier, a single customer and a single product. In practice, supply chain partners could be dealing with hundreds if not thousands of different products and numerous trading partners. Since demand distributions, costs, prices, etc., could be quite different across these products, one might theoretically prefer different coordinating contract terms for different products and customers, but this is impractical. This means trading partners must try to find agreements that hopefully work across multiple products and partners, rather than finding ideal agreements for each setting. Chen and Thomas (2016) discuss several aspects of SLA from several U.S. retailers. Of the SLAs studied there, blanket agreements across products and customers are common. For example, Nordstrom's SLA simply specifies a flat penalty fee for an invoice and shipment mismatch: "Inaccurate ASN (856): Receipt quantities do not match ASN quantities: $150.00 per incident" (Nordstrom, 2015). In addition, these SLAs can also vary in how multiple products are treated. For example, Bonton's SLA does not permit a supplier to substitute products: "Style, size or color substitution will not be allowed under any circumstances on any replenishment order," (Bon-Ton, 2015) while "Burlington Stores allows a 10% fill rate variance per style," (Burlington, 2015). There is an opportunity to contribute by understanding how these (or alternate) approaches to multi-product, multi-partner coordination affect supply chain performance.

As information sharing and incentive alignment are both key elements to successful collaboration, it should not be surprising that I conclude this section and the previous section with similar points.

(1) Our field has provided valuable insights regarding how firms can align incentives to support better collaboration.
(2) There are opportunities to contribute by empirically investigating incentive-alignment practices as well as further understanding (and helping to overcome) the key barriers preventing improved coordination through incentive alignment.

5 Conclusions

I began this chapter by stating that the improvements in inventory management over the last several decades have come largely from better management of raw material and work-in-process inventories. For this positive inventory management trend to continue, improvements must now largely come from downstream inventories. To achieve this, downstream (i.e., retail) firms must understand and carefully select what product and delivery variety they offer to customers. They must also improve coordination among supply chain partners. Mostly, this means understanding and working to overcome the barriers to improved information sharing and improved incentive alignment.

Bibliography

Aviv, Y. (2001). The effect of collaborative forecasting on supply chain performance, *Management Science* **47**, 10, pp. 1326–1343.

Aviv, Y. (2007). On the benefits of collaborative forecasting partnerships between retailers and manufacturers, *Management Science* **53**, 5, pp. 777–794.

Barnes-Schuster, D., Bassok, Y. and Anupindi, R. (2002). Coordination and flexibility in supply contracts with options, *Manufacturing & Service Operations Management* **4**, 3, pp. 171–207.

Baron, O. and Milner, J. (2009). Staffing to maximize profit for call centers with alternate service-level agreements, *Operations Research* **57**, 3, pp. 685–700.

Bell, D. R., Gallino, S. and Moreno, A. (2014). How to win in an omnichannel world, *MIT Sloan Management Review* **56**, 1, p. 45.

Bolton, G. E. and Katok, E. (2008). Learning by doing in the newsvendor problem: A laboratory investigation of the role of experience and feedback, *Manufacturing & Service Operations Management* **10**, 3, pp. 519–538.

Bon-Ton (2015). Transportation and merchandise logistics standards. http://logistics. bonton.com.

Bray, R. L. and Mendelson, H. (2012). Information transmission and the bullwhip effect: An empirical investigation, *Management Science* **58**, 5, pp. 860–875.

Brynjolfsson, E., Hu, Y. and Smith, M. D. (2003). Consumer surplus in the digital economy: Estimating the value of increased product variety at online booksellers, *Management Science* **49**, 11, pp. 1580–1596.

Burlington (2015). Domestic vendor partnership manual, http://www.burlingtoncoatfactory. com/Repository/Vendor/Binder1.pdf.

Cachon, G. and Terwiesch, C. (2009). *Matching Supply with Demand*, Vol. 2 McGraw-Hill, Singapore.

Cachon, G. P. (2003). Supply chain coordination with contracts, in *Supply Chain Management: Design, Coordination and Operation*, A. G. De Kok and S. C. Graves (eds.), Handbooks in Operations Research and Management Science, Vol. 11, Elsevier, Amsterdam, pp. 227–339.

Cachon, G. P. (2004). The allocation of inventory risk in a supply chain: Push, pull, and advance-purchase discount contracts, *Management Science* **50**, 2, pp. 222–238.

Cachon, G. P. and Fisher, M. (2000). Supply chain inventory management and the value of shared information, *Management Science* **46**, 8, pp. 1032–1048.

Cachon, G. P. and Lariviere, M. A. (2001). Contracting to assure supply: How to share demand forecasts in a supply chain, *Management Science* **47**, 5, pp. 629–646.

Cachon, G. P. and Lariviere, M. A. (2005). Supply chain coordination with revenue-sharing contracts: Strengths and limitations, *Management Science* **51**, 1, pp. 30–44.

Cachon, G. P., Randall, T. and Schmidt, G. M. (2007). In search of the bullwhip effect, *Manufacturing & Service Operations Management* **9**, 4, pp. 457–479.

Cassidy, W. B. (2010). Wal-mart tightens delivery deadlines, *J. C. Com.* Available at: http://www.joc.com/economy-watch/wal-mart-tightens-deliverydeadlines_20100 2008.html

Çetinkaya, S. and Lee, C.-Y. (2000). Stock replenishment and shipment scheduling for vendor-managed inventory systems, *Management Science* **46**, 2, pp. 217–232.

Chen, C.-M. and Thomas, D. J. (2016). Inventory allocation in the presence of service level agreements, *Smeal College of Business Working Paper.*

Chen, H., Frank, M. Z. and Wu, O. Q. (2005). What actually happened to the inventories of american companies between 1981 and 2000? *Management Science* **51**, 7, pp. 1015–1031.

Chen, H., Frank, M. Z. and Wu, O. Q. (2007). US retail and wholesale inventory performance from 1981 to 2004, *Manufacturing & Service Operations Management* **9**, 4, pp. 430–456.

Chopra, S. and Meindl, P. (2007). *Supply Chain Management. Strategy, Planning & Operation*, Springer, NY.

Conway, R., Maxwell, W., McClain, J. O. and Thomas, L. J. (1988). The role of work-in-process inventory in serial production lines, *Operations Research* **36**, 2, pp. 229–241.

Corbett, C. J. (2001). Stochastic inventory systems in a supply chain with asymmetric information: Cycle stocks, safety stocks, and consignment stock, *Operations Research* **49**, 4, pp. 487–500.

Craig, N., DeHoratius, N., Jiang, Y. and Klabjan, D. (2015). Execution quality: An analysis of fulfillment errors in a retail distribution center, *Forthcoming, Journal of Operations Management*. Available at: ssrn: http://papers.ssrn.com/sol3/papers.cfm?abstract_id=2494516.

Croson, R. and Donohue, K. (2006). Behavioral causes of the bullwhip effect and the observed value of inventory information, *Management Science* **52**, 3, pp. 323–336.

Davis, A. M., Katok, E. and Santamaría, N. (2014). Push, pull, or both? A behavioral study of how the allocation of inventory risk affects channel efficiency, *Management Science* **60**, 11, pp. 2666–2683.

DeHoratius, N. and Raman, A. (2008). Inventory record inaccuracy: An empirical analysis, *Management Science* **54**, 4, pp. 627–641.

Fawcett, S. E., McCarter, M. W., Fawcett, A. M., Webb, G. S. and Magnan, G. M. (2015). Why supply chain collaboration fails: The socio-structural view of resistance to relational strategies, *Supply Chain Management: An International Journal* **20**, 6, pp. 648–663.

Ferguson, M., Guide Jr, V. D. R. and Souza, G. C. (2006). Supply chain coordination for false failure returns, *Manufacturing & Service Operations Management* **8**, 4, pp. 376–393.

Fisher, M. L. (1997). What is the right supply chain for your product? *Harvard Business Review* **75**, 2, pp. 105–116.

Gallino, S. and Moreno, A. (2014). Integration of online and offline channels in retail: The impact of sharing reliable inventory availability information, *Management Science* **60**, 6, pp. 1434–1451.

Gallino, S., Moreno, A. and Stamatopoulos, I. (2016). Channel integration, sales dispersion, and inventory management, *Sales Dispersion, and Inventory Management, Forthcoming in Management Science.*

Gao, F. and Su, X. (2016). Omnichannel retail operations with buy-online-and-pickup-in-store, *Forthcoming in Management Science.*

Gaur, V., Fisher, M. L. and Raman, A. (2005). An econometric analysis of inventory turnover performance in retail services, *Management Science* **51**, 2, pp. 181–194.

Gavirneni, S., Kapuscinski, R. and Tayur, S. (1999). Value of information in capacitated supply chains, *Management Science* **45**, 1, pp. 16–24.

Gilmore, D. (2010). Thinking about supply chain chargebacks, *Supply Chain Digest.*

18   *Douglas J. Thomas*

Goldratt, E. M. and Cox, J. (1986). *The Goal*, revised edn., North River Press, Croton-on-Hudson, NY.

Harrington, L. (2005). From cost to profit: Service parts logistics, *Inbound Logistics*.

Hasija, S., Pinker, E. J. and Shumsky, R. A. (2008). Call center outsourcing contracts under information asymmetry, *Management Science* **54**, 4, pp. 793–807.

Hendricks, K. B. and Singhal, V. R. (2009). Demand-supply mismatches and stock market reaction: Evidence from excess inventory announcements, *Manufacturing & Service Operations Management* **11**, 3, pp. 509–524.

Hopp, W. J. and Spearman, M. L. (2011). *Factory Physics*, Waveland Press, Mississippi.

Jain, N., Girotra, K. and Netessine, S. (2013). Managing global sourcing: Inventory performance, *Management Science* **60**, 5, pp. 1202–1222.

Katok, E. and Wu, D. Y. (2009). Contracting in supply chains: A laboratory investigation, *Management Science* **55**, 12, pp. 1953–1968.

Kesavan, S., Gaur, V. and Raman, A. (2010). Do inventory and gross margin data improve sales forecasts for US public retailers? *Management Science* **56**, 9, pp. 1519–1533.

Kesavan, S. and Mani, V. (2013). The relationship between abnormal inventory growth and future earnings for US public retailers, *Manufacturing & Service Operations Management* **15**, 1, pp. 6–23.

Lariviere, M. A. and Porteus, E. L. (2001). Selling to the newsvendor: An analysis of price-only contracts, *Manufacturing & Service Operations Management* **3**, 4, pp. 293–305.

Lee, H., Padmanabhan, P. and Whang, S. (1997). Information distortion in a supply chain: The bullwhip effect, *Management Science* **43**, 4, pp. 546–558.

Lee, H. L., So, K. C. and Tang, C. S. (2000). The value of information sharing in a two-level supply chain, *Management Science* **46**, 5, pp. 626–643.

Li, L. and Zhang, H. (2008). Confidentiality and information sharing in supply chain coordination, *Management Science* **54**, 8, pp. 1467–1481.

Liang, L. and Atkins, D. (2013). Designing service level agreements for inventory management, *Production and Operations Management* **22**, 5, pp. 1103–1117.

Mani, V., Thomas, D. J. and Bansal, S. (2016). Estimating substitution and basket effects in retail stores: Implications for assortment planning, *Working paper*.

Milner, J. M. and Olsen, T. L. (2008). Service-level agreements in call centers: Perils and prescriptions, *Management Science* **54**, 2, pp. 238–252.

Nordstrom (2015). Nordstrom expense offset policies, http://nordstromsupplier.com/.

O'Marah, K. (2013). Collaboration is like teenage you-know-what, *SCM World*.

O'Marah, K. (2014). The power of trust, *SCM World*.

Ōno, T. (1988). *Toyota Production System: Beyond Large-scale Production*, Productivity Press, NY.

Özer, Ö., Zheng, Y. and Chen, K.-Y. (2011). Trust in forecast information sharing, *Management Science* **57**, 6, pp. 1111–1137.

Özer, Ö., Zheng, Y. and Ren, Y. (2014). Trust, trustworthiness, and information sharing in supply chains bridging China and the United states, *Management Science* **60**, 10, pp. 2435–2460.

Plambeck, E. L. and Taylor, T. A. (2006). Partnership in a dynamic production system with unobservable actions and noncontractible output, *Management Science* **52**, 10, pp. 1509–1527.

Rajagopalan, S. (2013). Impact of variety and distribution system characteristics on inventory levels at US retailers, *Manufacturing & Service Operations Management* **15**, 2, pp. 191–204.

Rajagopalan, S. and Malhotra, A. (2001). Have US manufacturing inventories really decreased? An empirical study, *Manufacturing & Service Operations Management* **3**, 1, pp. 14–24.

Rumyantsev, S. and Netessine, S. (2007). What can be learned from classical inventory models? A cross-industry exploratory investigation, *Manufacturing & Service Operations Management* **9**, 4, pp. 409–429.

Schweitzer, M. E. and Cachon, G. P. (2000). Decision bias in the newsvendor problem with a known demand distribution: Experimental evidence, *Management Science* **46**, 3, pp. 404–420.

Sieke, M. A., Seifert, R. W. and Thonemann, U. W. (2012). Designing service level contracts for supply chain coordination, *Production and Operations Management* **21**, 4, pp. 698–714.

Spearman, M. L., Woodruff, D. L. and Hopp, W. J. (1990). Conwip: A pull alternative to kanban, *The International Journal of Production Research* **28**, 5, pp. 879–894.

Spengler, J. J. (1950). Vertical integration and antitrust policy, *The Journal of Political Economy*, **58**, pp. 347–352.

Sterman, J. D. (1995). The Beer Distribution Game, in *Games and Exercises for Operations Management*, J. Heineke and L. Meile (eds.), Prentice Hall, Englewood Cliffs, N.J., pp. 101–112.

Su, X. (2008). Bounded rationality in newsvendor models, *Manufacturing & Service Operations Management* **10**, 4, pp. 566–589.

Taylor, T. A. (2002). Supply chain coordination under channel rebates with sales effort effects, *Management Science* **48**, 8, pp. 992–1007.

Terwiesch, C., Ren, Z. J., Ho, T. H. and Cohen, M. A. (2005). An empirical analysis of forecast sharing in the semiconductor equipment supply chain, *Management Science* **51**, 2, pp. 208–220.

Thomas, D. J. (2005). Measuring item fill-rate performance in a finite horizon, *Manufacturing & Service Operations Management* **7**, 1, pp. 74–80.

Tsay, A. A. (1999). The quantity flexibility contract and supplier–customer incentives, *Management Science* **45**, 10, pp. 1339–1358.

UPS (2014). UPS pulse of the online shopper, https://www.ups.com/media/en/2014-UPS-Pulse-of-the-Online-Shopper.pdf.

U.S. Census Bureau (2015a). U.S. Census bureau news: Quarterly retail e-commerce sales, http://www.census.gov/retail/mrts/www/data/pdf/ec_current.pdf.

U.S. Census Bureau (2015b). U.S. Census bureau report on manufacturing and trade inventories and sales, https://www.census.gov/mtis/index.html.

Waller, M., Johnson, M. E. and Davis, T. (1999). Vendor-managed inventory in the retail supply chain, *Journal of Business Logistics* **20**, pp. 183–204.

Womack, J. P., Jones, D. T. and Roos, D. (1990). *Machine that Changed the World*, Simon and Schuster, NY.

Zhou, H. and Benton, W. (2007). Supply chain practice and information sharing, *Journal of Operations Management* **25**, 6, pp. 1348–1365.

Chapter 2

Inventory is People: How Load Affects Service Times in Emergency Response

Mohammad Delasay*, Armann Ingolfsson[†], and Kenneth Schultz[‡]

*Tepper School of Business, Carnegie Mellon University, Pittsburgh, Pennsylvania, United States
[†]Alberta School of Business, University of Alberta, Edmonton, Alberta, Canada
[‡]Air Force Institute of Technology Wright-Patterson AFB, United States

1 Introduction

In many service systems, the most important inventory in the system is people. Most queueing models assume that people and objects are interchangeable. While most people recognize the significant difference, the academic literature on how that difference manifests itself is still young. We analyze a large dataset of emergency medical service (EMS) responses in the city of Calgary to explore and understand how the inventory of patients in the system adapts as a function of load.

If variability is the enemy of managers, then people must be their bane. The problem with people is they are hard to predict. When your inventory consists of jelly beans (Sox *et al.*, 1991), you can pretty much expect that the inventory will not care how many other jelly beans are in the immediate vicinity or how long they have been in any particular box. That is not true with people. People react to the situation around them, and the range of reactions varies greatly. If the line is long, the reaction of the customer at the front of the line will be quite different from the server, which may be completely different from the person at the back of the line. Many people would postulate that emergency medicine is a science, and treatment should not vary based on the system load. Everyone should receive the same treatment. Many paramedics would argue that they are not scientists but caregivers. They would say good caregivers treat the entire situation and the situation includes how busy the system is.

It is this variability, complexity, and range of reactions that makes it difficult to include people in mathematical models. In 1998, Joe Thomas, working with students Ken Schultz and Dave Juran and his colleagues John Boudreau and John McClain (Schultz *et al.*, 1998), used an experiment to show that the predictions from standard queueing models failed to predict the behavior of a simple production system. In their experiment, the difference between a high and low inventory line changed idle time by 19%. However, output remained virtually unchanged. Following up on this analysis, Schultz (1997, Chapter 4) showed that most of the difference between model predictions and actual performance was due to the assumption that workers were independent of each other. The human operators changed their behavior as a result of the people around them and changes in the state of the system. Five years later, with the same colleagues and joined by Wally Hopp, Dr. Thomas wrote an influential paper in the Behavioral Operations Management literature (Boudreau *et al.*, 2003). They argued that most mathematical models, in order to preserve tractability, assume people are unimportant, deterministic, independent, stationary, or not part of the product.

Since then, many researchers have investigated how people are important, stochastic, interdependent, and nonstationary. In 2010, Drs. Schultz, Schoenherr, and Nembhard showed that interdependent workers on a radio line changed their work pace closer to the average pace of those around them (Schultz *et al.*, 2010). In 2010, Gans *et al.* showed that nonstationary call center agents reduce their average call time by 8.3% with every doubling of the cumulative number of calls handled. Gans *et al.* (2010) also showed that agents were stochastic, having widely different initial average call times, and that taking agent learning into account is important — ignoring learning caused simulated average customer wait to deviate by more than 20% in almost one third of their simulation experiments. Green *et al.* (2013) found that interdependent nurses are more likely to be absent when a hospital unit is understaffed, and that ignoring this interdependence in planning staffing levels could increase costs by 2–3%.

This large collection of empirical work is analyzed by Delasay *et al.* (2015). They show that there is no simple answer to the question "what is the load effect on service times?" The relationship is dependent on the reactions of the customers, the servers, and the networks to the system load, how long the load has been strong, and the changeover in type of service. They show 22 different mechanisms through which load type affects servers by changing either the speed or the amount of work. This conceptual model, the load effect on service times (LEST) framework, can be used to frame an investigation to predict how processing times, and therefore inventory, will respond to changes in load.

The effects of load on service times are important. Classical queueing theory tells us that the length of the line depends on the average and variability of the processing times. Figure 1 shows the relationship between average service times ($\pm$ 1 standard deviation) and the EMS system load, measured as the percentage of busy ambulances, in the city of Calgary. It certainly appears that the service time average and variability depend on load. In this chapter, we explore why one EMS crew's service time would be nonstationary and dependent on what other crews are doing. We have a long and rich literature exploring the effects of service time on server utilization in queueing systems. Figure 1 highlights the need to explore the opposite effect — that of load on service times.

We intend to add to the emerging literature on the effects of load on service time, using a large dataset of EMS calls in the city of Calgary. The effect of load is important for capacity planning: The average time to serve a patient can vary by up to 26%, depending on the system load (see Fig. 1).

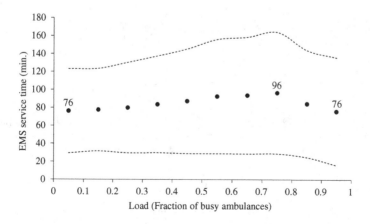

Fig. 1 Load-dependent EMS Service Times

For loads below 0.75, service slows down as load increases, but for loads above 0.75, service speeds up with load. The inverted-U relationship between load and service time that we see in Fig. 1 is not uncommon (Tan and Netessine, 2014; Batt and Terwiesch, 2016). The causes of the inverted-U relationship depend on the context, however, and we find that the causes in the EMS context differ from those identified in other settings.

We identify mechanisms that we believe are operative in this setting. Some of these mechanisms have been analyzed in previous empirical research. We show their effect in new settings and under different conditions. As a field, we must continue to document how, when, why, and how much these mechanisms are activated. We also identify new mechanisms as a result of applying the LEST framework to anticipate human reactions in an EMS system. In this way, we demonstrate how the LEST framework can be used to explore and understand a situation and reduce, at least by a little, the unpredictability of the human component in queueing systems.

2 The LEST Framework

The LEST framework describes mechanisms that link load effects to service time as a path in the network shown in Fig. 2. Each path begins with a load characteristic (changeover, which involves the load changing from zero to a positive value; load, which refers to the instantaneous value of

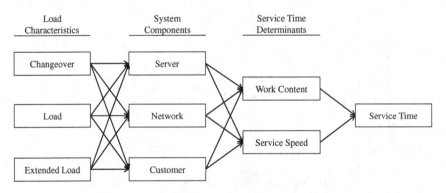

Fig. 2 The LEST Framework

the load; or extended load, which incorporates the history of the load), that influences a system component (a server, the network, or a customer) in a way that impacts a service time determinant (work content or service speed). Delasay *et al.* (2015) identify 22 such mechanisms, which are listed in Table 1. As a preview of our results, Table 5 lists 12 mechanisms that we identify as being operative in the EMS setting. Of the 12, 11 are listed in Table 1, but one mechanism (task transfer) is new. Another four mechanisms (network arrangement, geographical dispersion, geographical speedup, and

Table 1 Mechanisms

Load characteristics	System components		
	Server	Network	Customer
Changeover	Work content	Work content	Work content
	Physical setup (↑)	Network	Customer
	Forgetting (↑)	arrangement (↓)	early task
			initiation (↓)
	Service speed		
	Loss of rhythm (↑)		
Load	Work content	Work content	Work content
	Task reduction (↓)	Downstream	Bounce back (↑)
	Engagement (↑)	system	
	Server early task	congestion (↑)	
	initiation (↓)	Resource	
	Cognitive	sharing (↑)	
	sharing (↑)	Geographical	
	Workload	dispersion (↑)	
	smoothing (↓)		
	Service speed	Service speed	
	Social speedup	Geographical	
	pressure (↓)	speedup (↓)	
	Social loafing (↑)		
Extended	Work content	Work content	Work content
Load	Service	Network	Deterioration (↑)
	cancelation (↓)	chaos (↑)	
	Service speed		
	Learning		
	by doing (↓)		
	Fatigue (↑)		

network chaos) were first identified by Delasay (2014). The remaining eight mechanisms have been previously documented in non-EMS settings, as discussed in Delasay *et al.* (2015).

3   EMS Services

An EMS response to a medical emergency begins when a patient or bystander calls 911. An emergency medical dispatcher (EMD) answers and triages the call through a systematic medical interrogation to determine the patient's condition acuity. After gathering the required information, including the call address and the type of required equipment, the EMD dispatches an appropriately equipped ambulance to the incident scene.

The EMS ambulance service time begins when the ambulance receives the dispatch notification and it includes the five time intervals in Fig. 3:

— Chute time (T_{Chute}): The preparation and boarding time for the ambulance crew after receiving the dispatch notification.
— Travel time (T_{Travel}): From the dispatch location to the incident scene.
— Scene time (T_{Scene}): The time that ambulance crew are on scene providing medical care to a patient.
— Transport time ($T_{\text{Transport}}$): From the scene to a hospital, if the patient requires hospital transportation.
— Hospital time (T_{Hospital}): The offload time to transfer the patient to the emergency department (ED) after arriving to the hospital.

Ingolfsson (2013) reviews the literature on EMS planning and management, including empirical work investigating the five time intervals.

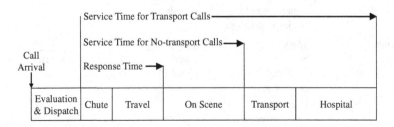

Fig. 3 EMS Service Time Intervals

We know of no previous work that focuses on mechanisms through which load impacts EMS service times, but Alanis *et al.* (2013) includes graphs that illustrate the association between EMS load and the five time intervals.

3.1 *Data, Explanatory Variables, and Descriptive Statistics*

Our analyses are based on a dataset of 108, 423 call records for the EMS system of the city of Calgary, Canada, in 2009. We focus on 92, 893 calls for which an ambulance was dispatched. The information for a call includes: (1) time stamps for the events in Fig. 3 generated by the EMD and paramedics, (2) coordinates for the ambulance dispatch location, call address, and hospital location, (3) call priority numbers assigned by the EMD (a number from 1 to 7 with 1 being assigned to Delta/Echo or the most critical priority calls), and (4) the number of busy and scheduled ambulances at the moment of call arrival. We use this information to extract the following variables for each call:

— The length of the EMS time intervals: T_{Chute}, T_{Travel}, T_{Scene}, $T_{\text{Transport}}$, and T_{Hospital}.
— Response and service times for no-transport ($T_{\text{Service, Notransport}}$) and transport ($T_{\text{Service, Transport}}$) calls:

$$T_{\text{Response}} = T_{\text{Chute}} + T_{\text{Travel}}$$

$$T_{\text{Service, Notransport}} = T_{\text{Chute}} + T_{\text{Travel}} + T_{\text{Scene}}$$

$$T_{\text{Service, Transport}} = T_{\text{Chute}} + T_{\text{Travel}} + T_{\text{Scene}} + T_{\text{Transport}} + T_{\text{Hospital}}.$$

— Travel (D_{Travel}) and transportation ($D_{\text{Transport}}$) distances, calculated based on shortest paths in the Calgary road network.
— Average travel speed (S_{Travel}) and average transportation speed ($S_{\text{Transport}}$), calculated as $S_{\text{Travel}} = D_{\text{Travel}}/T_{\text{Travel}}$ and $S_{\text{Transport}} = D_{\text{Transport}}/T_{\text{Transport}}$.
— Number of busy ambulances at dispatch (NB_{Dispatch}), scene arrival (NB_{Arrival}), scene departure ($NB_{\text{Departure}}$), and hospital arrival (NB_{Hospital}). We also compute the average number of busy ambulances $\overline{NB}$ at the four instants.
— Indicator $I_{\text{Transport}}$ for whether the patient is transported to hospital.
— Indicator I_{Urgent} for life-threatening calls (Delta/Echo priority).

— Indicator I_{Siren} for use of lights and sirens during travel to scene (corresponds to priority levels 1–4).
— Indicator $I_{Changeover}$ for an ambulance that responds from standby mode, that is, a regular service. We identify a service as regular (extended) if the time between the start of the service and the finish of the previous service by the same crew is more (less) than 10 minutes.
— EMS load at dispatch ($L_{Dispatch}$), scene arrival ($L_{Arrival}$), scene departure ($L_{Departure}$), and hospital arrival ($L_{Hospital}$), calculated as the proportion of busy ambulances:

$$L_i = NB_i/NS, i = \text{Dispatch, Arrival, Departure, Hospital,}$$

where NS is the number of scheduled ambulances. We also compute the average load $\overline{L}$ at the four instants.
— Extended load at the server level, EL_{Server}, quantified as the amount of time the responding ambulance has been continuously busy since their last changeover. In calculating EL_{Server}, we consider that an ambulance is continuously busy from one call to the next if the new dispatch notification is received in less than 10 minutes of the finish of the previous service.

Tables (2)–(4) provide descriptive statistics for these variables. The average durations for the time intervals range from 0.96 minutes (chute time) to 69.38 minutes (hospital time). The average total service time is 44.49 minutes for no-transport calls and 117.50 minutes for transport calls. The proportion of transport calls is 58%, so the average service time for all calls is 86.84 minutes.

Table 2 Descriptive Statistics for Service Time Intervals (min.)

Measure	T_{Chute}	T_{Travel}	T_{Scene}	$T_{Transport}$	$T_{Hospital}$
Mean	0.96	7.13	28.59	16.57	69.38
Median	0.73	5.78	23.35	14.57	56.97
Standard deviation	3.84	6.87	30.76	11.01	51.04
Coefficient of variation	4.00	0.96	1.08	0.66	0.74

Table 3 Descriptive Statistics for Service Time (min.)

Measure	$T_{\text{Service, Notransport}}$	$T_{\text{Service, Transport}}$
Mean	44.49	117.50
Median	34.58	105.9
Standard deviation	44.57	55.50
Coefficient of variation	1.06	0.47

Table 4 Descriptive Statistics for Explanatory Variables

Measure	NS	$\overline{NB}$	$\overline{L}$	D_{Travel} (km)	$D_{\text{Transport}}$ (km)
Mean	42.78	18.84	44%	3.89	13.27
Median	43.00	19.00	43%	3.11	12.47
Standard deviation	7.28	6.97	13%	3.07	6.94
Coefficient of variation	0.37	0.17	29%	0.79	0.52

4 Hypotheses and Results for EMS Service Time Intervals

In this section, we employ the LEST framework (Delasay *et al.*, 2015) to systematically investigate the mechanisms that cause each EMS service time interval to depend on EMS load. We consider each cell of the LEST framework and we identify how the corresponding system component and load characteristic are manifested for EMS service time intervals. Armed with this understanding, we propose mechanisms (previewed in Table 5) that relate the system component and the load characteristic to a service time interval. For each time interval, we aggregate the proposed mechanisms to generate hypotheses. We use multiple linear regression models to test our hypotheses.

4.1 *Chute Time*

Chute time is the first time interval and can be seen as the setup time for the EMS service.

Chute Time Mechanisms. Given that chute time can be seen as a setup time, we pay special attention to the server–changeover mechanisms

Table 5 Mechanisms for the Effect of EMS Load on Service Time

Load characteristics	System components		
	Server	Network	Customer
Changeover	Work content	Work content	
	Physical Setup	Network arrangement	
Load	Work content	Work content	
	Server early task initiation	Downstream system	
	Task transfer	congestion	
	Workload smoothing	Geographical dispersion	
	Service speed	Service speed	
	Social speedup pressure	Geographical speedup	
Extended load	Work content	Work content	Work content
	Fatigue	Network chaos	Deterioration

listed in Table 1. *Physical setup* could be at work for chute time. It is reasonable to believe that a regular service (where the ambulance is dispatched from standby mode, corresponding to $I_{Changeover} = 1$) will have a longer chute time than an extended service. Indeed, according to Aehlert (2011, p. 654), chute time for extended services is zero in most cases because the ambulance crew is already in the vehicle. Once identified, this mechanism seems obvious. An advantage of systematic use of the LEST framework is that such obvious mechanisms are not ignored.

Turning to server–load mechanisms, paramedics might engage in *server early task initiation*. Information about load may lead a crew to form an expectation about the likelihood of being dispatched in the near future. When the load is high, a crew may respond by initiating preparation tasks before receiving a dispatch notification.

Table 6 lists our proposed mechanisms for the chute time.

Chute Time Hypotheses. The physical setup and server early task initiation mechanisms lead directly to the following two hypotheses about chute time, which we test using Model (1):

Hypothesis 1: *Chute time increases with changeover.*

Table 6 Chute Time Mechanisms

Mechanism	Description
Physical setup	Regular service requires a longer setup than extended service.
Server early task initiation	During periods of high load, ambulance crews in standby mode initiate preparation tasks before receiving a dispatch notification.

Hypothesis 2: *Regular chute time decreases with load.*

$$T_{\text{Chute}} = \beta_0 + \beta_{I_{\text{Changeover}}} I_{\text{Changeover}} + \beta_{L_{\text{Dispatch}} \times I_{\text{Changeover}}} L_{\text{Dispatch}}$$
$$\times I_{\text{Changeover}} + \beta_{L_{\text{Dispatch}} \times (1 - I_{\text{Changeover}})} L_{\text{Dispatch}} \times (1 - I_{\text{Changeover}})$$
$$+ \beta_{NS} NS + \beta_{D_{\text{Travel}}} D_{\text{Travel}} + \beta_{I_{\text{Urgent}}} I_{\text{Urgent}} + \beta_{D_{\text{Travel}}}$$
$$\times I_{\text{Urgent}} D_{\text{Travel}} \times I_{\text{Urgent}} + \beta_{\mathbf{X}} \mathbf{X} + \epsilon. \tag{1}$$

In Model (1) and the other models of this section, $\mathbf{X}$ denotes a vector of control variables including day, time, and day and time interaction variables, ε is the error term, and "$\times$" represents interactions.

A significant positive coefficient for $I_{\text{Changeover}}$ supports Hypothesis 1 and provides evidence for the physical setup mechanism. A significant negative coefficient for $L_{\text{Dispatch}} \times I_{\text{Changeover}}$ supports Hypothesis 2 and provides evidence for the early task initiation mechanism for regular services. We include $L_{\text{Dispatch}} \times (1 - I_{\text{Changeover}})$ to check whether load has an effect on extended services. We include D_{Travel} in Model (1) because it may take longer for an ambulance crew to find the call address and to plan a route if the address is outside the unit's normal coverage region.

The estimation results for Model (1) in Table 7[1] provide support for both hypotheses. Average chute time is estimated to be 23 seconds longer for regular calls (providing evidence for physical setup) and an increase

---

[1] In Table 7 and other regression result tables, $***$, $**$, and $*$ denote statistical significance at the 0.1%, 1%, and 5% significance levels, respectively. Standard errors are shown in parentheses.

Table 7 Chute Time

Coefficient	T_{Chute} (min.) Model (1)
Intercept	$-1.29(1.11)$
$I_{\text{Changeover}}$	$0.39(0.16)^*$
$L_{\text{Dispatch}} \times I_{\text{Changeover}}$	$-0.42(0.16)^{**}$
$L_{\text{Dispatch}} \times (1 - I_{\text{Changeover}})$	$-0.13(0.31)$
NS	$0.04(0.02)$
D_{Travel}	$0.08(0.01)^{***}$
I_{Urgent}	$-0.01(0.08)$
$D_{\text{Travel}} \times I_{\text{Urgent}}$	$-0.04(0.01)^{***}$
R^2	0.0045
P-val.	$<2.2e - 16$

in load from 10% to 90% is estimated to shorten average chute time by 20 seconds for regular services (providing evidence for early task initiation). In contrast, load does not have a significant impact for extended services. We also see that average chute time increases by 4.8 seconds per kilometer of travel distance, which could be interpreted as a physical setup time that increases with distance. The distance effect is smaller for urgent calls. All of these effects are statistically significant.

4.2 Travel Time

Travel time has natural measures for work content and service speed: the travel distance and the average driving speed. Some of our proposed travel time mechanisms are about the distance and some are about the speed.

Travel Time Mechanisms. Table 8 summarizes our proposed mechanisms for the travel time.

Social speedup pressure: This is a potential server–load mechanism affecting driving speed. EMS systems are under pressure to meet response time targets. Paramedics' actions are tracked by computer-aided-dispatch systems and therefore, the paramedics are likely to feel pressure to speed up by driving faster as the EMS load increases.

Geographical dispersion: It is natural to view an EMS system and the EDs as the two nodes of a queueing network where the EDs are the

Table 8 Travel Time Mechanisms

Mechanism	Description
Social speedup pressure	Driving speed increases with EMS load.
Geographical dispersion	Travel distance increases with load.
Geographical speedup	Travel speed increases with distance.
Network chaos	Extended load increases travel times as the actual ambulance locations deviate from the planned locations.
Network arrangement	Travel distance is shorter for regular (not extended) services.

downstream nodes. We will exploit this view in Section 4.5 (hospital time). Here, we expand our perspective of network to include routes in the city road network. From this perspective, patients need simultaneous service from two servers (first, an ambulance and its paramedics, and second, from a route) during the travel and transport times. This perspective allows us to identify new network mechanisms. Travel time delays the start of medical care to a patient by an amount that depends on the travel distance. The travel distance depends on the dispatch policy and on the paramedics' selection of route to the call address.

Geographical dispersion causes longer travel distance when load is high. High EMS load means fewer available ambulances to cover a fixed geographic area (a city), which results in longer average travel distance. Geographic dispersion could also be relevant for other services, including repair and tow truck services, hospital porters, taxi and delivery services, and other emergency services (fire or police).

Geographical speedup: Geographical speedup mitigates geographical dispersion by enabling the paramedics to travel faster on longer trips that involve at least some highway or main artery travel (Budge *et al.*, 2010). Unlike geographical dispersion, geographical speedup impacts the service speed.

Network chaos: Ambulance locations are chosen to cover as many calls as possible within a target response time. If EMS load remains high for a long period, the actual locations of the available ambulances could deviate more and more from their planned positions, leading to suboptimal dispatch decisions and longer travel times. We call this the network chaos mechanism.

Network arrangement: As load returns to normal, or more specifically when an individual ambulance finishes service without being immediately dispatched to another call (i.e., a regular service), that ambulance can return to its planned location. Network arrangement causes travel distances to be shorter for regular (not extended) services.

Travel Time Hypotheses. Based on the mechanisms in Table 8, we develop three hypotheses for the travel time: one for the changeover effect, one for the load effect, and one for the extended load effect. The network arrangement mechanism directly leads to:

Hypothesis 3: *Travel time decreases with changeover.*

The social speedup pressure, geographical dispersion, and geographical speedup mechanisms all involve the effect of EMS load on the travel time. The two speedup mechanisms and the geographical dispersion mechanism predict opposite effects on the travel time. It is not clear which one — the increase in the work content or the increases in the service speed — will be the dominant effect. To clarify the interactions between these mechanisms, we use a simple model (Fig. 4) of the physics of ambulance travel time that was proposed by Kolesar *et al.* (1975) and formed the basis for a statistical model of ambulance travel times in (Budge *et al.*, 2010). The model assumes that (1) the ambulance accelerates at a constant rate a at the beginning of a trip and decelerates at the same constant rate a at the end of a trip and (2) if the trip is long enough, the ambulance reaches a constant cruising speed v during the middle of the trip. The two graphs of Fig. 4 illustrate a trip that is so short that the cruising speed is never reached and a trip that is long enough to reach the cruising speed.

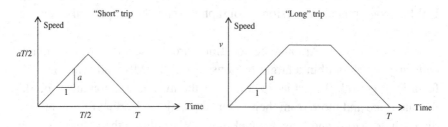

Fig. 4 Simple Model of the Physics of Ambulance Travel Time

From this model, one can derive the following Model (2) for the travel time T, the distance D, and the average speed $S = D/T$:

$$T = \begin{cases} \dfrac{2}{a}\sqrt{D} & D < \dfrac{v^2}{a}, \\[2ex] \dfrac{v}{a} + \dfrac{D}{v} & D \geq \dfrac{v^2}{a}. \end{cases} \tag{2}$$

Using the parameters of Model (2), we can specify the social speedup pressure, geographical dispersion, and geographical speedup mechanisms more precisely as follows:

— Social speedup pressure: Increased load increases the acceleration a, the cruising speed v, or both.
— Geographical dispersion: Increased load increases the distance D.
— Geographical speedup: Increased distance D increases the average speed D/T.

The model implies that the geographical speedup effect will occur, because we can derive:

$$S = \dfrac{D}{T} = \begin{cases} \dfrac{1}{2}\sqrt{aD} & D < \dfrac{v^2}{a}, \\[2ex] \left(\dfrac{v}{aD} + \dfrac{1}{v}\right)^{-1} & D \geq \dfrac{v^2}{a}. \end{cases}$$

Inspection of the two right-hand-side expressions for S shows that when D increases, S increases.

The remaining question is, what is the combined effect of social speedup pressure and geographical dispersion? That is, if load increases, causing a, v, and D all to increase, what happens to T? The answer is that it can go either way, as one can verify numerically using Model (2). If a, v, and D all increase by the same percentage, then T will remain unchanged for long trips but will decrease for short trips. If a and v increase by a larger (smaller) percentage than D, then T will tend to decrease (increase). Thus, it is not clear which mechanism (social speedup pressure or geographical dispersion) will dominate, and therefore we include all possibilities in the following hypothesis:

Hypothesis 4: (a) *Travel time increases with load.* (b) *Travel time decreases with load.* (c) *Travel time does not change with load.*

The network chaos mechanism, which involves the effect of extended load, leads directly to:

Hypothesis 5: *Travel time increases as high load periods last longer.*

We use Models (3)–(6) to test Hypotheses 3–5 and the supporting mechanisms:

$$T_{\text{Travel}} = \beta_0 + \beta_{I_{\text{Changeover}}} I_{\text{Changeover}} + \beta_{L_{\text{Dispatch}}} L_{\text{Dispatch}} + \beta_{NS} NS$$
$$+ \beta_{I_{\text{Urgent}}} I_{\text{Urgent}} + \beta_{I_{\text{Siren}}} I_{\text{Siren}} + \beta_{\mathbf{X}} \mathbf{X} + \varepsilon, \tag{3}$$

$$T_{\text{Travel}} = \beta_0 + \beta_{I_{\text{Changeover}}} I_{\text{Changeover}} + \beta_{L_{\text{Dispatch}}} L_{\text{Dispatch}} + \beta_{NS} NS$$
$$+ \beta_{I_{\text{Urgent}}} I_{\text{Urgent}} + \beta_{I_{\text{Siren}}} I_{\text{Siren}} + \beta_{D_{\text{Travel}}} D_{\text{Travel}} + \beta_{\mathbf{X}} \mathbf{X} + \varepsilon, \tag{4}$$

$$D_{\text{Travel}} = \beta_0 + \beta_{I_{\text{Changeover}}} I_{\text{Changeover}} + \beta_{L_{\text{Dispatch}}} L_{\text{Dispatch}} + \beta_{NS} NS$$
$$+ \beta_{I_{\text{Urgent}}} I_{\text{Urgent}} + \beta_{I_{\text{Siren}}} I_{\text{Siren}} + \beta_{\mathbf{X}} \mathbf{X} + \varepsilon, \tag{5}$$

$$S_{\text{Travel}} = \beta_0 + \beta_{I_{\text{Changeover}}} I_{\text{Changeover}} + \beta_{L_{\text{Dispatch}}} L_{\text{Dispatch}} + \beta_{NS} NS$$
$$+ \beta_{I_{\text{Urgent}}} I_{\text{Urgent}} + \beta_{I_{\text{Siren}}} I_{\text{Siren}} + \beta_{D_{\text{Travel}}} D_{\text{Travel}} + \beta_{\mathbf{X}} \mathbf{X} + \varepsilon. \tag{6}$$

In Model (3), a significant negative coefficient for $I_{\text{Changeover}}$ supports Hypothesis 3 and the sign and the significance of the coefficient for L_{Dispatch} determines which of the alternatives in Hypothesis 4 is supported. We expect the magnitude and significance of the coefficient for L_{Dispatch} to attenuate as we control for distance, in moving from Model (3) to (4).

In Model (5), a significant negative coefficient for $I_{\text{Changeover}}$ implies that average travel distance is shorter for regular services than for extended services, supporting network arrangement. A significant positive coefficient for L_{Dispatch} implies longer average travel distance under high load, which supports geographical dispersion.

In Model (6), a significant positive coefficient for L_{Dispatch} implies higher average speed under high load, supporting social speedup pressure.

Table 9 Travel Time

Coefficient	T_{Travel} (min.) Model (3)	T_{Travel} (min.) Model (4)
Intercept	7.75(2.46)**	3.69(2.39)
$I_{Changeover}$	0.26(0.07)***	0.43(0.07)***
$L_{Dispatch}$	4.20(0.21)***	0.04(0.20)
D_{Travel}		0.97(0.01)***
NS	0.03(0.05)	0.03(0.05)
I_{Urgent}	−1.42(0.05)***	−1.32(0.05)***
I_{Siren}	−4.55(0.11)***	−2.83(0.10)***
R^2	0.0487	0.2543
P-val.	<2.3e − 16	<2.3e − 16

Table 10 Travel Distance and Speed

Coefficient	D_{Travel} (km) Model (5)	S_{Travel} (km/min.) Model (6)	S_{Travel} (km/min.) Model (6), $D_{Travel} < 5$
Intercept	4.05(1.25)**	−7.41(7.83)	−4.87(5.16)
$I_{Changeover}$	−0.10(0.04)**	−1.24(0.24)***	−0.78(0.15)***
$L_{Dispatch}$	4.38(0.10)***	−0.50(0.67)	0.99(0.43)*
D_{Travel}		0.48(0.02)***	0.25(0.04)***
NS	0.01(0.03)	0.17(0.17)	0.14(0.10)
I_{Urgent}	−0.13(0.03)***	−0.09(0.17)	0.01(0.10)
I_{Siren}	−1.54(0.06)***	−0.09(0.35)	−1.04(0.25)***
R^2	0.0431	0.0063	0.0015
P-val.	<2.3e − 16	< 2.3e − 16	0.0003

A significant positive coefficient for D_{Travel} implies higher average speed for longer distances, supporting geographical speedup.

Tables 9–10 present the results for Models (3)–(6). Model (5) supports the network arrangement mechanism, which led us to Hypothesis 3. However, the significant positive coefficient of $I_{Changeover}$ in Model (3) does not support Hypothesis 3. One explanation would be that the regular service requires an acceleration phase before reaching a cruising speed phase, as in the simple model of the physics of ambulance travel time (Fig. 4), whereas the extended service could be initiated when the ambulance is already in the cruising speed phase. The resulting higher average speed for extended service could surpass the advantage of shorter average distance for regular service. The negative coefficient for $I_{\text{Changeover}}$ in Model (6) supports this argument.

Model (3) supports Hypothesis 4a, indicating a 0.42-minute increase in average travel time associated with a 10% increase in load. By comparing Models (3)–(5), we see that the increase in average travel time occurs primarily through geographical dispersion: A 10% increase in load leads to a 0.44-kilometer increase in average distance (Model (5)), which translates into a (0.44×0.97)-minute increase in average travel time (Models (4)–(5)), whereas the direct effect of a 10% increase in load on average travel time is not significant (Model (4)). The coefficients of determination (R^2) of Models (3) and (4) show that distance explains almost 20% of the variability in travel time.

Model (5) indicates that average distance increases with load and Model (6) indicates that average speed increases with distance. Taken together, these results support geographical speedup. In contrast, load does not have a significant effect on average speed in Model (6), thus failing to support social speedup pressure. However, we do see evidence of social speedup pressure in short trips, as shown in the last column of Table 10, where we re-estimate Model (6), including only the services with travel distances less than 5 kilometers.

4.3 Scene Time

In the field of prehospital care, there is an ongoing debate about the relative merits of the *scoop and run* (transport the patient to a hospital as quickly as possible) versus *stay and play* (paramedics initiate primary treatment and stabilize the patient on the scene before making the transport decision) strategies (Smith and Conn, 2014). Paramedics need to exercise discretion to decide not only on how much treatment to provide on scene but also whether to transport the patient to hospital, and in doing so they must consider such factors as the medical urgency, distance to the closest hospital, and their own qualifications and skill level. Because of the discretionary nature of the on-scene care, it is likely that EMS load also affects paramedics' decisions.

Table 11 Scene Time Mechanisms

Mechanism	Description
Task transfer	As load increases, up to a threshold, paramedics spend more time on scene in order to stabilize the patient on scene and avoid hospital transportation.
Workload smoothing	As load increases beyond a threshold, paramedics spend less time on scene in anticipation of short hospital times due to hospital surge capacity protocols.
Fatigue	If the paramedics have been busy for an extended period, then they take longer to complete their tasks on scene.
Deterioration	Increased load increases response time, which has an adverse effect on the patient's medical condition, which increase the required on-scene care time.

Scene Time Mechanisms. Table 11 summarizes our proposed mechanisms for the scene time. *Task transfer* and *workload smoothing* mechanisms are related to the effect of EMS system load on paramedics' on-scene decisions. *Fatigue* is the effect of extended load (how long the paramedics have been busy since their last service gap) on paramedics' behavior. *Deterioration* in patient health due to longer response times caused by high EMS load can also impact the scene time.

Task transfer and *workload smoothing*: If paramedics are aware of the system load (through radio communications, for example), then they may form expectations about the time they would need to spend in a hospital to offload the patient, if they transport the patient to a hospital. As we discuss in Section 4.5, *downstream system congestion* causes hospital time to increase with load up to a threshold, and to decrease with load beyond that threshold, because of surge capacity protocols. We postulate that predictability of the hospital time, based on the current EMS load, affects paramedics' decisions on the scene.

Specifically, when EMS load is below a critical threshold, paramedics spend more time on scene as load increases in order to stabilize the patient and to avoid hospital transportation, where they expect a long wait. We call this mechanism *task transfer*.[2] On the other hand, when EMS load

---

[2]This mechanism was referred to as *engagement* in Delasay (2014) and Delasay *et al.* (2015) but *task transfer* better captures the nature of this mechanism in an EMS setting.

increases beyond the critical threshold, paramedics may prefer to shorten the scene time and instead continue the care process in the ambulance, en route to a hospital, which we call *workload smoothing*, in the anticipation of short hospital times due to surge capacity protocols that come into effect in hospitals when EMS load is in critical situation.

Fatigue: We measure the extended load at the paramedic crew level as the total amount of time that the crew has been busy without a break between calls (we referred to this as extended service in Section 3.1). We expect that a fatigue mechanism could increase scene time for two reasons. First, scene time involves a demanding combination of physical and mental tasks. Second, paramedics have an opportunity to slowdown intentionally to take a break if needed.

Deterioration: Patients do not have direct information about load but they experience longer response time (chute time + travel time) when EMS system load is higher due to longer travel times, as supported in Hypothesis 4. Long response times can result in deterioration of a patient's medical condition (Feero *et al.*, 1995; Blackwell and Kaufman, 2002), which can increase the amount of time the paramedics need to spend on the scene.

Scene Time Hypotheses. Deterioration increases the scene time. Task transfer also increase the scene time, but only up to the critical load threshold. Workload smoothing causes the service times to decrease with load above the threshold. Taken together, we hypothesize:

Hypothesis 6: *Scene time increases with load below a critical threshold and decreases with load above the threshold.*

The fatigue mechanism leads directly to:

Hypothesis 7: *Scene time increases with extended load.*

We use Model (7) to test Hypotheses 6 and 7.

$$T_{\text{Scene}} = \beta_0 + \beta_{L^2_{\text{Arrival}}} L^2_{\text{Arrival}} + \beta_{L_{\text{Arrival}}} L_{\text{Arrival}} + \beta_{EL_{\text{Server}}} EL_{\text{Server}}$$
$$+ \beta_{T_{\text{Response}}} T_{\text{Response}} + \beta_{NS} NS + \beta_{I_{\text{Urgent}}} I_{\text{Urgent}}$$

$$+ \beta_{I_{\text{Transport}}} I_{\text{Transport}} + \beta_{L_{\text{Arrival2}} \times I_{\text{Urgent}}} L^2_{\text{Arrival}} \times I_{\text{Urgent}}$$

$$+ \beta_{L_{\text{Arrival}} \times I_{\text{Urgent}}} L_{\text{Arrival}} \times I_{\text{Urgent}} + \beta_{\mathbf{X}} \mathbf{X} + \varepsilon. \quad (7)$$

A significant positive coefficient for L_{Arrival} and a significant negative coefficient for L^2_{Arrival} support the concave relation between load and scene time that is postulated in Hypothesis 6 and for the underlying task transfer and workload smoothing mechanisms. To isolate the effect of the deterioration mechanism, we control for response time in (7). A significant positive coefficient for T_{Response} would support deterioration. A significant positive coefficient for EL_{Server} supports Hypothesis 7 and fatigue. We include interaction terms $L^2_{\text{Arrival}} \times I_{\text{Urgent}}$ and $L_{\text{Arrival}} \times I_{\text{Urgent}}$ in Model (7) in order to check whether the proposed mechanisms are more pronounced for less urgent patients, where the opportunities for discretion might be greater.

Table 12 presents results for Model (7). The results support the concave relation between load and scene time (Hypothesis 6) and provide evidence for the task transfer, workload smoothing, and deterioration mechanisms. Figure 5 plots estimated average scene time versus load for transported urgent and nonurgent services based on the results in Table 12 and with

Table 12 Scene Time

Coefficient	T^{Scene} (min.) Model (7)
Intercept	$-1.95(8.91)$
L^2_{Arrival}	$-29.47(4.79)^{***}$
L_{Arrival}	$26.40(4.42)^{***}$
EL_{Server}	$0.01(0.00)^{***}$
T_{Response}	$0.50(0.01)^{***}$
NS	$0.63(0.23)^{**}$
I_{Urgent}	$3.93(1.83)^{**}$
$I_{\text{Transport}}$	$-12.28(0.20)^{***}$
$L^2_{\text{Arrival}} \times I_{\text{Urgent}}$	$28.37(9.24)^{**}$
$L_{\text{Arrival}} \times I_{\text{Urgent}}$	$-24.15(8.41)^{**}$
R^2	0.0647
P-val.	$<2.3e - 16$

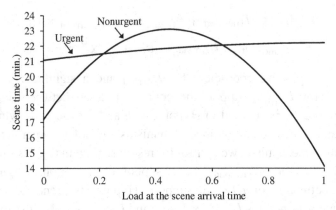

Fig. 5 Scene Time versus Load based on Model (7); $NS = 42.79$, $T^{\text{Response}} = 8.09$ min., and $EL_{\text{Server}} = 6.75$ min.

all independent variables except load, urgency, and transport set to their average values. We see that the impact of load on average scene time is indeed much more pronounced for nonurgent calls. Model (7) also supports the fatigue mechanism and its effect on increasing scene time due to the extended load.

4.4 Transport Time

Like travel time, transport distance and driving speed are the natural measures for the work content and service speed of the transport time interval. However, we do not expect the geographical dispersion and geographical speedup mechanisms to be relevant for transport time, for the following reasons. Travel time is from A (dispatch location) to B (call location), where A is impacted by load but B is not. Transport time, in contrast, is from B (call location) to C (the closest hospital to B), and we do not expect B and C to be impacted greatly by load.

In some EMS systems, an ED can request to divert incoming ambulances to neighboring hospitals during periods of overcrowding. This phenomenon is known as "ambulance diversion" (Deo and Gurvich, 2011; Gurvich *et al.*, 2014). In such systems, one would expect the average transport distance to the closest hospital that is not on diversion to increase with load — similar to the network chaos mechanism for travel time. This does not apply directly in Calgary because the system is centrally managed and individual hospitals do not have the freedom to decide to go on diversion.

We estimated Models (3)–(6) with travel time replaced with transport time. As expected, we did not observe statistically significant impacts of load on transport time.

4.5 *Hospital Time*

Hospital time is the final and the longest EMS service time interval.

Hospital Time Mechanisms. Hospital time is the contact point between EMS and the ED. Therefore, we pay special attention to the network mechanisms listed in Table 1, especially the downstream system congestion mechanism. We propose no changeover mechanisms for hospital time. Table 13 summarizes our proposed mechanisms for hospital time.

Downstream system congestion: Congestion in the ED is likely to impact the hospital time interval through the downstream system congestion mechanism (Forster *et al.*, 2003; Asaro *et al.*, 2007; Hillier *et al.*, 2009). EMS load is positively correlated with the ED load. EMS patients add workload to an ED and a congested ED causes ambulances to back up to offload patients, resulting in longer hospital time.

Social speedup pressure: We expect the effect of downstream system congestion to be mitigated at high loads. Paramedics and ED staff are likely to feel pressure to shorten hospital time when the EMS load is close to its limit. Some jurisdictions have formal protocols that prescribe actions that must be taken to expedite patients when EDs and EMS systems are under high load (Handel *et al.*, 2010; Villa-Roel *et al.*, 2012). For example in Edmonton and Calgary, Alberta, Canada, "ED surge capacity protocols"

Table 13 Hospital Time Mechanisms

Mechanism	Description
Downstream system congestion	ED congestion causes hospital time to increase with load.
Social speedup pressure	When EMS load is very high, ED staff and paramedics speed up the admission of ambulance patients.
Fatigue	Extended load increases the amount of overwork and slows the work of paramedics at the hospital.

require EDs to accelerate admission of ambulance patients when fewer than seven ambulances are available for service in the city (Alberta Health Services, 2010).

Fatigue: We expect that the fatigue mechanism increases hospital time for the same reasons that we mentioned for scene time. First, the interval involves a demanding combination of physical and mental tasks. Second, paramedics have an opportunity to slow down intentionally to take a break if needed.

Hospital Time Hypotheses. Based on the downstream system congestion and social speedup pressure mechanisms, we hypothesize:

Hypothesis 8: *Hospital time has a concave relationship with load.*

The fatigue mechanism leads directly to:

Hypothesis 9: *Hospital time increases with extended load.*

We use Model (8) to test Hypotheses 8 and 9. A significant negative coefficient for L^2_{Hospital} supports the concave relation between the hospital time and load as proposed in Hypothesis 8. A significant positive coefficient for EL_{Server} supports Hypothesis 9 and the fatigue mechanism.

$$T_{\text{Hospital}} = \beta_0 + \beta_{L^2_{\text{Hospital}}} L^2_{\text{Hospital}} + \beta_{L_{\text{Hospital}}} L_{\text{Hospital}}$$

$$+ \beta_{EL_{\text{Server}}} EL_{\text{Server}} + \beta_{NS} NS$$

$$= \beta_{I_{\text{Urgent}}} I_{\text{Urgent}} + \beta_{L^2_{\text{Hospital}} \times I_{\text{Urgent}}} L^2_{\text{Hospital}} \times I_{\text{Urgent}}$$

$$+ \beta_{L_{\text{Hospital}} \times I_{\text{Urgent}}} L_{\text{Hospital}} \times I_{\text{Urgent}} + \beta_{\mathbf{X}}\mathbf{X} + \varepsilon. \qquad (8)$$

The results of Model (8), as presented in Table 14, support the concave relation between load and hospital time (Hypothesis 8). Figure 6 shows the estimated relationship between load and average hospital time, for urgent and nonurgent calls, with all other independent values set to their average values. As shown, the effect of social speedup pressure is more pronounced for nonurgent patients, although the differences are not statistically significant (see the coefficients of the two interaction variables in Table 14). The results in Table 14 do not support Hypothesis 9 and

Table 14 Hospital Time

Coefficient	T_{Hospital} (min.) Model (8)
Intercept	30.55(19.65)
L^2_{Hospital}	−44.79(10.04)***
L_{Hospital}	75.74(9.38)***
EL_{Server}	−0.01(0.01)
NS	0.05(0.51)
I_{Urgent}	11.27(3.97)**
$L^2_{\text{Hospital}} \times I_{\text{Urgent}}$	37.16(19.60)
$L_{\text{Hospital}} \times I_{\text{Urgent}}$	−31.76(18.02)
R^2	0.0508
P-val.	$< 2.2e - 16$

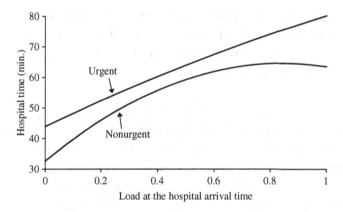

Fig. 6 Hospital Time versus Load based on Model (8); $NS = 42.79$

the fatigue mechanism about the effect of extended load on increasing the hospital time.

5 Conclusion and Future Directions

Inventory is people. People react to the situation around them in complicated ways. We use the LEST framework to understand some of those complicated interactions to help predict how service times react to changes in load.

A better understanding of variations in service time is important to capacity and scheduling of service operations and queues. Academics already have a fairly good understanding of how service times affect utilization. We inform our understanding of how utilization affects the service time.

In Fig. 1, we showed how EMS service times are concave with load. In this paper, we have shown how that concavity develops from a complicated mix of multiple facets of care delivery with both behavioral and technical responses to changes in load. We used the LEST framework to explore these complexities. We have found changeover, load, and extended load responses. We have seen responses in servers, networks, and one in the customers. We have seen changes in both speed and work content. Some of the mechanisms in operation here are, once identified, rather obvious. Others are less so. We use the nature of the service encounter to breakdown the service into component parts and we use the LEST framework to guide our exploration into potential mechanisms.

We have identified 12 different mechanisms applying to EMS response times that are both logical and supported by our dataset. Eight mechanisms were previously identified as shown in Delasay *et al.* (2015). Four mechanisms have not been previously examined.

(1) *Physical setup* increases the work content under changeover when paramedics respond after having had a break between missions.

(2) *Network arrangement* reflects the work reduction on changeover corresponding to ambulances being well dispersed.

(3) *Server early task initiation* reflects paramedics being more prepared to respond when they know the system is under load.

(4) *Task transfer* is the tendency of paramedics to do more tasks on scene and delay transport to the hospital (stay and play) as load increases up to a threshold.

(5) *Workload smoothing* comes into play above a threshold as paramedics do fewer tasks on the scene as load extends beyond a threshold in order to begin transfer to the hospital.

(6) *Fatigue* occurs when servers under load for an extended period of time-slowdown.

(7) *Deterioration* is the possibility that delays in response time will accompany additional work requirements upon arrival on the scene.

(8) *Geographical dispersion* acknowledges that workload increases under load as fewer available ambulances are more widely dispersed.

(9) *Social speedup pressure* is the response felt by servers to respond quickly as travel distances increase with load.

(10) *Geographical speedup* reflects server speed increasing as longer distances allow increased use of faster roads when load is high.

(11) *Network chaos* is the tendency of the system to move towards a worse response position when load is high for an extended period.

(12) *Downstream system congestion* occurs when hospital congestion, correlated with high ambulance load, delays transfer at the hospital.

These mechanisms affect processing times in almost all stages of the response process. Average chute time decreases by 23 seconds if no changeover is required and, as load increases, chute times decrease. Effects of load on travel time are more complicated. While average distance (work) increases with load, average speed increases with distance. These effects combine so that a 10% increase in load is accompanied by a 0.42-minute increase in average travel time. The relationship between load and scene time is concave and more significant for nonurgent calls. For nonurgent calls, scene time increases from 17 minutes to 22 minutes as load increases up to 55% and then, it drops to 14 minutes as load gets close to 100%. We find no effects on transport time. Hospital time is also concave with load for nonurgent care with a tipping point around a load of 80%. The average hospital time increases from 33 minutes to 65 minutes when load increases from 10% to 80% due to downstream system (ED) congestion.

These findings will be of interest to EMS managers in identifying and understanding how their systems respond to load. The concave nature of the response curve suggests an identifiable tipping point beyond which system response begins to deteriorate. Managers should be able to find the tipping point using local historical data and consider policies to mitigate the negative effects.

This work also helps us to gain a better understanding of these 12 mechanisms and how they affect response times. If we wish to generalize the common effects of load on service time, much more empirical exploration of the mechanisms involved is required. We, as a field, need to continue to record empirical evidence of different mechanisms before we can begin the process of generalization.

A third contribution of this work is demonstrating how the LEST framework can be used to understand the relationships of load and time. The framework allows us to take a very complicated problem and break it down into its component parts. We can help both researchers and managers explore the relationship of load and time by giving them the framework under which the larger topic can be split and questions directed at the component parts. Providing structured questions is one of the strongest contributions any theory can make.

Bibliography

Aehlert, B. (2011). *Paramedic Practice Today: Above and Beyond* (Vol. 2), Jones & Bartlett Publishers, MA.

Alanis, R., Ingolfsson, A. and Kolfal, B. (2013). A Markov chain model for an EMS system with repositioning, *Production and Operations Management* **22**, 1, pp. 216–231.

Alberta Health Services. (2010). Emergency department surge capacity protocols. Available from www.albertahealthservices.ca/3167.asp. Last accessed 17 June 2015.

Asaro, P. V., Lewis, L. M. and Boxerman, S. B. (2007). The impact of input and output factors on emergency department throughput, *Academic Emergency Medicine* **14**, 3, pp. 235–242.

Batt, R. and Terwiesch, C. (2016). Early task initiation and other load-adaptive mechanisms in the emergency department, *Management Science*, Forthcoming.

Blackwell, T. H. and Kaufman, J. S. (2002). Response time effectiveness: comparison of response time and survival in an urban emergency medical services system, *Academic Emergency Medicine* **9**, 4, pp. 288–295.

Boudreau, J., Hopp, W., McClain, J. O. and Thomas, J. L. (2003). On the interface between operations and human resource management, *Manufacturing & Service Operations Management* **5**, 3, pp. 179–202.

Budge, S., Ingolfsson, A. and Zerom, D. (2010). Empirical analysis of ambulance travel times: the case of Calgary emergency medical services, *Management Science* **56**, 4, pp. 716–723.

Delasay, M. (2014). Essays on queueing systems with endogenous service times, PhD thesis.

Delasay, M., Ingolfsson, A., Kolfal, B. and Schultz, K. (2015). Load effect on service times, *Working paper*.

Deo, S. and Gurvich, I. (2011). Centralized vs. decentralized ambulance diversion: A network perspective, *Management Science* **57**, 3, pp. 1300–1319.

Feero, S., Hedges, J. R., Simmons, E. and Irwin, L. (1995). Does out-of-hospital EMS time affect trauma survival? *The American Journal of Emergency Medicine* **13**, 2, pp. 133–135.

Forster, A. J., Stiell, I., Wells, G., Lee, A. J. and Van Walraven, C. (2003). The effect of hospital occupancy on emergency department length of stay and patient disposition, *Academic Emergency Medicine* **10**, 2, pp. 127–133.

Gans, N., Liu, N., Mandelbaum, A., Shen, H. and Ye, H. (2010). Service times in call centers: Agent heterogeneity and learning with some operational consequences, *Institute of Mathematical Statistics Collections* **6**, pp. 99–123.

Gurvich, I., Deo, S. and Park, E. (2014). Does limiting time on ambulance diversion reduce diversions? Signaling equilibrium and the network effect, *Working paper*.

Green, L. V., Savin, S. and Savva, N. (2013). Nursevendor problem: Personnel staffing in the presence of endogenous absenteeism, *Management Science* **59**, 10, pp. 2237–2256.

Handel, D. A., Ginde, A. A., Raja, A. S., Rogers, J., Sullivan, A. F., Espinola, J. A. and Camargo, C. A. (2010). Implementation of crowding solutions from the American college of emergency physicians task force report on boarding, *International Journal of Emergency Medicine* **3**, 4, pp. 279–286.

Hillier, D. F., Parry, G. J., Shannon, M. W. and Stack, A. M. (2009). The effect of hospital bed occupancy on throughput in the pediatric emergency department, *Annals of Emergency Medicine* **53**, 6, pp. 767–776.

Ingolfsson, A. (2013). EMS planning and management, in *Operations Research and Health Care Policy*, G. S. Zaric (ed.), Springer, New York, pp. 105–128.

Kolesar, P., Walker, W. and Hausner, J. (1975). Determining the relation between fire engine travel times and travel distances in New York City, *Operations Research* **23**, 4, pp. 614–627.

Schultz, K. L. (1997). Analysis of serial production systems using simulation and behavioral experiments, PhD dissertation, Cornell University.

Schultz, K. L., Juran, D. C., Boudreau, J. W., McClain, J. O. and Thomas, L. J. (1998). Modeling and worker motivation in JIT production systems, *Management Science* **44**, 12, pp. 1595–1607.

Schultz, K. L., Schoenherr, T. and Nembhard, D. (2010). An example and a proposal concerning the correlation of worker processing times in parallel tasks, *Management Science* **56**, 1, pp. 176–191.

Smith, R. M. and Conn, A. K. (2009). Prehospital care Scoop and run or stay and play? *Injury* **40**, pp. S23–S26.

Sox, C., McClain, J. L. and Thomas, J. (1991). Jellybeans: Storing capacity to satisfy customer demands within a specified time limit, *Working Paper*, JGSM-Cornell University.

Tan, T. F. and Netessine, S. (2014). When does the devil make work? An empirical study of the impact of workload on worker productivity, *Management Science* **60**, 6, pp. 1574–1593.

Villa-Roel, C., Guo, X., Holroyd, B. R., Innes, G., Wong, L., Ospina, M., Schull, M., Vandermeer, B., Bullard, M. J. and Rowe, B. H. (2012). The role of full capacity protocols on mitigating overcrowding in EDs, *The American Journal of Emergency Medicine* **30**, 3, pp. 412–420.

Chapter 3

Inventory Control Under Financial Turbulence

Lucy Gongtao Chen[*,¶], Lawrence W. Robinson[†,‖], Robin O. Roundy[‡,**],
and Rachel Q. Zhang[§,††]

*Department of Decision Sciences, NUS Business School,
National University of Singapore, Singapore, 119245
¶bizcg@nus.edu.sg

† Johnson Graduate School of Management Cornell University, Ithaca, NY 14853
‖ lwr2@cornell.edu

‡ Department of Mathematics, Brigham Young University,
Provo, UT 84602
** robin@mathematics.byu.edu

§ Department of Industrial Engineering and Logistics Management,
Hong Kong University of Science and Technology Clear Water Bay,
Kowloon, Hong Kong
†† rzhang@ust.hk

In global supply chains, both the operational costs and discount factors of a firm can be strongly affected by unpredictable national and international economic forces. In this chapter, we investigate the impact of these financial uncertainties on inventory decisions by modeling the operational costs, discount factors, and demands as stochastic processes that evolve as financial uncertainties are realized over time. To illustrate the benefits of incorporating stochastic discount factors, we conduct a case study of four types of Mexican firms who conduct sizeable business with the U.S. With a discount factor model fitted to data, we conduct a numerical study and show that both the business type and the stockout protocol strongly affect the optimal inventory decisions, and that the cost penalty for ignoring the dynamic nature of the financial environment can exceed 36%.

1 Introduction

In this chapter, we consider inventory decisions for firms who conduct business internationally. The firm may buy raw material and produce a product abroad (or domestically), and then sell it domestically (or abroad). In anticipation of near-term instabilities such as wars, political events, and economic cycles, firms need to understand the impact of such risks and adjust their major operational decisions (e.g., production planning and inventory decisions) accordingly. Most of the inventory research to date has assumed that the operational costs as well as the discount factors are fixed and known in advance. However, it has long been recognized in the finance literature that risks in both international and domestic markets can significantly affect a firm's operational costs as well as the appropriate discount factor for evaluating its future cash flows. According to studies on international asset pricing (such as Stulz, 1994), both national market indices (e.g., interest rates and domestic market returns) and international market indices (e.g., exchange rates and international market returns) are appropriately modeled as random variables. As a result, both the operational cost parameters (e.g., inventory holding costs, backorder costs, and purchasing prices) and discount factors should be treated as stochastic processes that evolve as these financial indices are realized over time.

Researchers in Operations have of course recognized the risks associated with inventory. Some have incorporated risky future cash flows into decision-making in inventory models with deterministic demand. For instance, Beranek (1967) investigated the impact of the timing of the loan repayments on inventory carrying costs and hence the optimal ordering policy. Grubbstrom (1980) illustrated ways to correctly determine the capital costs of work-in-progress and finished goods inventories and derived the relationship between the payment structure and the stocks of finished goods and work-in-progress.

Other work has incorporated the risks of holding inventory into the opportunity cost of capital within a stochastic demand model. Anvari (1987) and Kim and Chung (1989) both showed that the level of inventory determines the risk and hence the opportunity cost of capital. They concluded that the opportunity cost of capital for investments in inventory is an increasing function of the inventory level, and is higher for firms facing more risky demand. Kim and Chung (1989) also showed that the optimal inventory level decreases as the demand volatility increases. Singhal *et al.* (1994) analyzed the effect of risks on lot sizes and reorder points. They showed when the replenishment lead times are relatively short, then an increase in demand riskiness leads to a lower reorder point and a smaller lot size. However, when lead times are long, an increase in demand riskiness still decreases the reorder point, but may result in a larger lot size. They also concluded that cost minimization models with a fixed opportunity cost of capital have a large penalty in overall costs, relative to models that adjust the opportunity cost of capital to reflect the riskiness of cash flows.

Several inventory researchers have used both operational and financial hedging to ameliorate the risks associated with demand and exchange rates. Van Mieghem (2003) studied ways to mitigate risks in capacity investment by using operational and financial hedging. Van Mieghem (2007) studied three canonical networks: a product-dedicated network, a sequential network featuring resource-sharing, and a parallel network that allows for resource substitution. He showed that resource levels may actually increase under a general utility function with risk-aversion, and that the optimal levels of flexible technology, substitutable inventory, and resource imbalance will increase with risk aversion under operational hedging. Gaur and Seshadri (2005) used options to construct an optimal hedging transaction that minimizes profit variance and increases the expected utility for a risk-averse decision maker, when demand is correlated with the price of a financial asset. They showed that this ability to hedge will cause a risk-averse decision-maker to order more inventory. At a more macrolevel, Axarloglou and Kouvelis (2001) investigated the ownership structure of a firm's foreign subsidiaries who supply a foreign market, and showed that exchange rates are an important factor for this decision. However, they did not address how firms should adjust their inventory replenishment policies when facing potential financial turbulence in the near future.

Along the similar line is the work by Ding *et al.* (2004) and Kazaz *et al.* (2005). Both papers examined the impact of exchange-rate changes on the optimal capacity investment decision in a global manufacturing network. While Kazaz *et al.* (2005) mainly looked at the operational hedging, Ding *et al.* (2004) explored integrated operational and financial hedging and found that firms that use financial hedging are less sensitive to demand and exchange rate volatilities, and are able to exercise greater control over its profit variance. While these papers carefully consider the impact of exchange-rate changes on inventory decision-making, they do not examine the impact of volatility, as we do in this chapter. And while these papers study a one-period problem, we look at a finite horizon problem, which is more appropriate when financial turbulence occurs frequently and lasts for several periods.

This chapter builds upon Chen *et al.* (2015), which incorporates financial uncertainties into a single-product, periodic-review, finite-horizon stochastic inventory system by allowing both the discount factors and operational costs to be stochastic and to evolve over time as financial information is realized. Chen *et al.* (2015) provides sufficient conditions under which (s, S) inventory policies are optimal. These conditions may fail in the presence of financial turbulence. In such cases, our numerical examples demonstrate that, in the absence of a fixed ordering cost, it may be optimal never to order, or to order only when the inventory level is *above* a certain level. Even when an order-up-to policy remains optimal, the order-up-to inventory levels can be drastically different from those that do not consider financial instability.

More importantly, we propose a risk-factor model for the stochastic discount factors, and analyze the significance of the financial turbulence in inventory replenishment decisions for four different types of firms under three different stockout protocols. In the case of cyclic periods of significant financial risks (such as the Mexican presidential elections), we develop a methodology that uses historical data to generate a model of discount factor evolution. We illustrate the loss of ignoring the dynamic nature of the financial environment through an example of four types of Mexican firms who conduct sizeable business with the U.S. The likelihood of financial instability increases dramatically during the months before and after Mexican presidential elections. A numerical case study based on Mexican financial data shows that both the business type and stockout protocol have large and disparate impacts on inventory decisions, and that the cost penalty for ignoring the stochastic nature of the financial environment can be quite severe (cost penalties of up to 36%).

When the discount factor evolves with the financial environment, it needs to be modeled as a stochastic process, which puts tremendous burden on inventory decision-making due to the curse of dimensionality. However, our numerical study shows that the cost penalty is negligible if we replace the stochastic discount factor by its mean.

Since discount factors reflect decision makers' and investors' attitudes towards risk, as shown by our study, different stochastic discount factors can lead to very different inventory decisions and financial positions. A firm's decisions must reflect their investors' attitude towards risk, especially during volatile financial periods. Our work provides models and analyses that will enable firms who operate internationally to better understand and control risks and to improve their profitability when facing financial instability.

The chapter is organized as follows. In Section 2, we briefly summarize the model and structural results in Chen *et al.* (2015), which provides the theoretical foundation for this chapter. In Section 3, we use empirical studies on asset pricing to identify financial risk factors that affect discount factors and operational costs in a global setting, and propose models for estimating the stochastic discount factors that are to be updated as financial information is revealed. In Sections 4 and 5, we conduct a numerical case study on the optimal ordering policy and calculate the cost penalties for ignoring the dynamic nature of the discount factors and costs. We summarize the chapter in Section 6.

2 Problem Formulation and Structural Results

In this section, we summarize the model and structural results in Chen *et al.* (2015), which provide a theoretical foundation for our analysis in this paper. For conciseness of exposition, we will be brief. Readers can refer to Chen *et al.* (2015) for more details.

2.1 *Model Description*

We consider a single-product, periodic-review inventory system. The firm makes the purchasing decisions and payments to the suppliers at the beginning of each period. Demand then occurs and the firm delivers the available inventory to customers. Revenues are realized, and the firm incurs holding and stockout costs for inventory and unsatisfied demand, respectively.

We study both the backorder case and the lost sales (LS) case. Under backorder, we consider two cases: (i) the "pay-to-order" (PTO) case, in which the customers pay when they place their orders, and (ii) the "pay-to-delivery" (PTD) case, in which they pay when their orders are delivered. In both cases, we assume that corporate policy requires demand to be met as soon as inventory is available. Customers pay for the product in their domestic currency, and all costs and revenues are converted to the firm's domestic currency at the time at which they are incurred. For example, for a Chinese firm importing goods from the U.S., the costs incurred in the U.S. are immediately converted from U.S. dollars to Chinese yuan, and Chinese customers pay for the product in yuan. On the other hand, for a Chinese firm exporting goods to the U.S., many of the firm's costs are incurred in China, and are denominated in terms of yuan. The revenues from customers and all costs incurred in the U.S. are immediately converted from U.S. dollars to Chinese yuan.

For ease of exposition, we adopt the same notation as in Chen *et al.* (2015), where

T = the length of the planning horizon,

t = the period index, starting with period 1,

L = replenishment lead time (assumed to be zero in the LS case),

x_t = inventory position at the beginning of period t, before ordering,

y_t = inventory position at the beginning of period t, after ordering,

D_t = demand during period t,

$D_{t,w} = \Sigma_{j=t}^{w} D_j$, total demand from period t through period w,

$\mathbf{D}_{t:w} = (D_t, D_{t+1}, \ldots, D_w)$, vector of demands from periods t through w,

$\mathbf{Z}_t$ = vector of financial information available at the beginning of period t,

$\mathbf{z}_t$ = a realization of $\mathbf{Z}_t$,

$\mathbf{Z}_{t:w} = (\mathbf{Z}_t, \ldots, \mathbf{Z}_w)$, vector of financial information for periods t
through w.

Note that we use boldfaced letters to represent vectors, the dimensions
of which will be clear from the context. The financial information vector $\mathbf{Z}_t$
may include exchange rates, stock market indices, interest rates, etc., all of
which evolve over time. We assume that $\{\mathbf{Z}_t,\ 1 \leq t \leq T + 1\}$ is a Markov
chain, and is not necessarily time-homogeneous. We use the time index t
to refer to the current time period, so that $\mathbf{z}_\tau$ has already been observed for
$\tau \leq t$.

We recognize that both fixed and variable ordering costs are incurred at
the beginning of a period, and hence model them as functions of the realized
financial information. On the other hand, holding costs, backorder costs,
and revenues are likely to be incurred at various times throughout each
time period; so we model them as functions of both $\mathbf{z}_t$ and $\mathbf{Z}_{t+1}$. Discount
factors convert the future cash flows to the current period, and hence are also
modeled as functions of both the current and future financial information.
As such, we have the following cost/price parameters and discount factors,
same as in Chen *et al.* (2015):

$$K_t(\mathbf{z}_t) = \text{fixed ordering (and/or setup) cost at the beginning}$$
$$\text{of period } t,$$

$$c_t(\mathbf{z}_t) = \text{variable purchasing (and/or production) cost at the}$$
$$\text{beginning of period } t,$$

$$v(\mathbf{Z}_{T+1}) = \text{unit salvage value for on-hand inventory at the end}$$
$$\text{of the planning horizon,}$$

$$h_t(\mathbf{z}_t, \mathbf{Z}_{t+1}) = \text{holding cost for carrying one unit of inventory from}$$
$$\text{period } t \text{ to } t + 1, \text{ valued at the end of period } t,$$

$$\pi_t(\mathbf{z}_t, \mathbf{Z}_{t+1}) = \text{penalty cost (including the goodwill cost) for}$$
$$\text{one unit of backorders or lost sales at the end}$$
$$\text{of period } t, \text{ valued at the end of period } t,$$

$$p_t(\mathbf{z}_t, \mathbf{Z}_{t+1}) = \text{selling price in period } t, \text{ valued at the end}$$
$$\text{of period } t,$$

$\beta_t(\mathbf{z}_t, \mathbf{Z}_{t+1})$ = discount factor to convert cash flows at the end of
   period t to equivalent flows at the beginning
   of period t,

$\beta_{t,w}(\mathbf{z}_t, \mathbf{Z}_{t+1:w+1}) = \beta_t(\mathbf{z}_t, \mathbf{Z}_{t+1})\Pi_{j=t+1}^{w}\beta_j(\mathbf{Z}_j, \mathbf{Z}_{j+1})$, discount factor to
   convert cash flows at the end of period w to
   equivalent flows at the beginning of period t.

   To simplify the presentation, we will often write K_t, c_t, h_t, p_t, π_t, D_t, β_t, $\beta_{t,w}$, and v, making the dependencies on the financial information vectors implicit. We also define $A^+ = \max\{0, A\}$, $A^- = (-A)^+$, $A \wedge B = \min\{A, B\}$, $A \vee B = \max\{A, B\}$, and

$$\delta(a) \doteq \begin{cases} 1 & \text{if } a > 0, \\ 0 & \text{otherwise.} \end{cases}$$

2.2 Model Formulation

The dynamic programming formulation for the expected discounted cost at the beginning of period t, $1 \le t \le T - L$, can be written as

$$f_t(x_t, \mathbf{z}_t) = -c_t x_t + \min_{y_t \ge x_t}\{K_t\delta(y_t - x_t) + V_t(y_t, \mathbf{z}_t)\}, \tag{1}$$

$$V_t(y_t, \mathbf{z}_t) = c_t y_t + E_{\mathbf{D}_{t:t+L}, \mathbf{Z}_{t+1:t+L+2}}\big[\beta_{t,t+L}\widehat{G}_t(y_t, \mathbf{z}_t, \mathbf{Z}_{t+1:t+L+2}, \mathbf{D}_{t:t+L})$$

$$+ \beta_t f_{t+1}(\gamma(y_t - D_t), \mathbf{Z}_{t+1})\big], \tag{2}$$

where $\gamma(x) \doteq x$ under backlogging, and $\gamma(x) \doteq x^+$ under lost sales. Note that $\widehat{G}_t(y_t, \mathbf{z}_t, \mathbf{Z}_{t+1:t+L+2}, \mathbf{D}_{t:t+L})$, the modified one-period cost in period $t + L$, is given by

$$\widehat{G}_t(y_t, \mathbf{z}_t, \mathbf{Z}_{t+1:t+L+2}, \mathbf{D}_{t:t+L}) = h_{t+L}\,(y_t - D_{t,t+L})^+$$

$$+ \hat{\pi}_{t+L}\,(y_t - D_{t,t+L})^- - p_{t+L}\,D_{t+L},$$

where

$$\hat{\pi}_t = \pi_t + \begin{cases} p_t, & \text{if LS,} \\ p_t - \beta_{t+1}p_{t+1} & \text{if PTD,} \\ 0, & \text{if PTO,} \end{cases}$$

with $\beta_{T+1} = 1$. Note that in the PTD case, the penalty cost $\hat{\pi}_t$ can be negative for some realizations of the financial information vectors.

We assume that at the end of the horizon, all outstanding backorders are filled via a zero-lead-time purchase made at the end of period T at the unit cost of $c_{T-L+1}(\mathbf{Z}_{T+1})$. (The time index $T - L + 1$ is chosen for notational convenience.) In the PTD case, the end-of-horizon revenue is taken at the beginning of period $T+1$ at $p_{T+1}(\mathbf{Z}_{T+1})$ per unit, which is already included in $\widehat{G}_{T-L}$. Therefore, the end-of-horizon cost that initiates the recursion in (1) and (2) is given by

$$
\begin{aligned}
f_{T-L+1}&(x_{T-L+1}, \mathbf{z}_{T-L+1}) \\
&= E_{D_{T-L+1,T}, \mathbf{Z}_{T-L+2:T+1}} \Big\{ \beta_{T-L+1,T} \Big[- v \cdot (x_{T-L+1} - D_{T-L+1,T})^+ \\
&\quad + \begin{cases} 0, & \text{if lost sales,} \\ c_{T-L+1} \cdot (x_{T-L+1} - D_{T-L+1,T})^-, & \text{if backorder} \end{cases} \Big] \Big\}.
\end{aligned} \tag{3}
$$

2.3 Structural Results

Let

$$
\mathcal{A}_t = \mathcal{A}_t(\mathbf{z_t})
$$

$$
= \begin{cases} c_t + E_{\mathbf{Z}_{t+1:t+L+2}}\big\{ - \beta_{t,t+L} \cdot \hat{\pi}_{t+L} + \beta_t [- c_{t+1} \\ \quad + \mathcal{A}_{t+1}^+(\mathbf{Z}_{t+1})] \big\} & \text{if backorder,} \\ c_t - E_{\mathbf{Z}_{t+1:t+L+2}}(\beta_{t,t+L} \cdot \hat{\pi}_{t+L}), & \text{if lost sales;} \end{cases} \tag{4}
$$

$$
\mathcal{B}_t = \mathcal{B}_t(\mathbf{z_t}) = c_t + E_{\mathbf{Z}_{t+1:T+1}} \Big[\sum_{j=t+L}^{T} \beta_{t,j} \cdot h_j - \beta_{t,T} \cdot v \Big], \tag{5}
$$

for $1 \leq t \leq T - L$, with $\mathcal{A}_{T-L+1} = 0$. The following Theorem 1 (Chen *et al.* 2015) describes the sufficient conditions under which (s, S) policy is optimal.

Theorem 1. *An (s, S) policy is optimal in period t, if*

1. *$\mathcal{B}_j > 0$ for all realizations $\mathbf{z}_j$ and all $j = t, \dots, T - L$,*
2. *$\mathcal{B}_{T-L} - \mathcal{A}_{T-L} \geq 0$ for all possible realizations $\mathbf{z}_{T-L}$, and*

3. *for all realizations* $\mathbf{z}_j$ *and all* $j = t, \ldots, T - L - 1$,

   (a) $h_{j+L} + \hat{\pi}_{j+L} \geq 0$ *under backlogging and* $h_j + \hat{\pi}_j - c_{j+1} \geq 0$ *under lost sales; and*

   (b) $K_j(\mathbf{z}_j) \geq E_{\mathbf{Z}_{j+1}}\big[\beta_j(\mathbf{z}_j, \mathbf{Z}_{j+1}) \cdot K_{j+1}(\mathbf{Z}_{j+1})\big]$.
   If in addition $\mathcal{A}_t < 0$, *then* $s > -\infty$.

The implications of these conditions are thoroughly discussed in Chen *et al.* (2015). While Condition 1 prevents an infinite ordering quantity, Condition 2 ensures the K_t-convexity of the cost function in the last period. Note that both these conditions will hold with appropriate end-of-horizon values $v(\mathbf{Z}_{T+1})$ and $c_{T-L+1}(\mathbf{Z}_{T+1})$, the forms of which can be found in Chen *et al.* (2015).

3 Modeling the Stochastic Discount Factors β_t

In Section 2, we have briefly summarized the model and main results in Chen *et al.* (2015), which we will build upon by further investigating the impact of the financial uncertainties. We start by introducing in this section methods to explicitly model the stochastic discount factors β_t introduced in Section 2. For completeness, we first present two basic models and then review the conventional approaches for pricing financial securities.

Estimating the discount factor β_t is very challenging, as it necessarily includes subjective beliefs about future cash flows. There are two different types of discount factors: a project-specific discount factor and a firm-wide discount factor. In recognition of the specific risks that a particular project faces, the project-specific discount factor is generally incorporates a premium over the firm-wide discount factor. But since the risks associated with managing the inventories of established products are considered to be standard (and diversifiable) for the firm, a firm-wide discount factor is used in practice. Hence, we focus on firm-wide discount factors and drop the word "firm-wide" for ease of presentation.

There are several simple ways to model discount factors. The simplest one, which has been used in many inventory models, is to assign it a constant value that applies to the entire time horizon under consideration (e.g., $\beta_t(\mathbf{z}_t) = 0.95$ for all t and all $\mathbf{z}_t$). A generalization of this approach allows the discount rates to vary over time, although they are still assumed to be known in advance (i.e., β_t can vary over t, but not with $\mathbf{z}_t$). A third approach, rarely seen in the inventory literature, is to model the discount factor as a deterministic function of the current financial information. In this approach, $\beta_t(\mathbf{z}_t)$ is known at the beginning of period t, and is a function of $\mathbf{z}_t$ rather than of $(\mathbf{z}_t, \mathbf{Z}_{t+1})$ as we assume it to be. For example, one might simply define $\beta_t(\mathbf{z}_t) = 1/[1 + R_t(\mathbf{z}_t)]$, where $R_t(\mathbf{z}_t)$ is the expected return of the firm in period t. As a second example, a firm conducting international business might let $\beta_t(\mathbf{z}_t) = \frac{1}{1+i_t^d} = \frac{e_t}{r_t^F(1+i_t^f)}$ where i_t^d is the domestic interest rate, e_t is the exchange rate, i_t^f the interest rate in the foreign country, and r_t^F the forward exchange rate for $t+1$ given in period t. In that case, $\mathbf{z}_t = (i_t^d)$ or $\mathbf{z}_t = (e_t, i_t^f, r_t^F)$; see Ross *et al.* (2001). Although this state-dependent approach takes financial information into account, it does not fully capture the stochastic nature of the discount factors.

3.1 *Pricing a Security*

Within the finance literature, the discount factor $\beta_t(\mathbf{z}_t, \mathbf{Z}_{t+1})$ for period t is usually interpreted as the reciprocal of one plus the required rate of return of the firm in period t, which is clearly random at the start of period t. Although how to practically measure the intrinsic return of a firm is still an active research question, the standard academic approach is to estimate it as the relative price change of the firm's common stock over the period. Therefore, in this section, we review the two most prominent methodologies for asset pricing.

The Capital Asset Pricing Model (CAPM) and Arbitrage Pricing Theory (APT) are two most popular models for security pricing. The CAPM specifies the asset's expected return to be an affine function of the overall market risk. APT, in contrast, assumes that a stock's return is a linear function of macroeconomic factors, some of which may be unique to that firm. So APT differs from CAPM in its assumptions and in its explanation of the factors associated with the risk of an asset. In our modeling of discount factors, we will identify risk factors based on empirical studies of asset prices, and adopt an APT-type model.

In international markets, research results reveal that exchange rate exposure does not, on average appear to justify a risk premium in the U.S. stock market (Jorion, 1990; 1991), although it does earn a significant risk premium in other markets, especially in developing countries (Bailey and Chuang, 1995). In the context of international asset pricing, the degree of market segmentation is an important issue. For assets in a market that is fully integrated with the world market, national market risks might diminish while world market risk increases. This leads to the necessity of determining whether the national market is isolated enough from the world market to merit an additional risk premium. Political risk is another potential source of uncertainty (Dumas, 2003). Generally, when pricing a security using the APT approach, one first identifies the set of possible risk factors, and then tests their statistical significance.

3.2 Modeling the Discount Factors

We propose three simple models for obtaining the discount factors, all of which are APT-type linear models. The first model relates a firm's return R_t to some set of relevant risk factors $\mathbf{g}_t(\mathbf{z}_t, \mathbf{Z}_{t+1})$, which are functions of relevant financial information $\mathbf{z}_t$ and $\mathbf{Z}_{t+1}$. The other two models relate the discount factor β_t to risk factors directly.

(1) In the first model, we set

$$R_t = \mathbf{a}^T \mathbf{g}_t, \tag{6}$$

and $\beta_t = 1/(1 + R_t)$. Here, $\mathbf{a}^T = (a_0, a_1, \ldots, a_N)$ is a vector of constants that are estimated from historical data, and $\mathbf{g}_t = (1, g_{1t}, \ldots, g_{Nt})^T$ are the risk factors.

(2) The second model directly models β_t as a linear function of these same financial risk factors, as

$$\beta_t = \mathbf{b}^T \mathbf{g}_t, \tag{7}$$

where $\mathbf{b}^T = (b_0, b_1, \ldots, b_N)$ is a vector of constants.

(3) Instead of applying the APT model directly to the discount factors in an additive fashion, the third model uses a multiplicative model for the discount factors by assuming a log-linear relationship between β_t and

the financial risk factors, as

$$\log(\beta_t) = \mathbf{c}^T \log(\mathbf{g}_t), \tag{8}$$

for some constant vector $\mathbf{c} = (c_0, c_1, \ldots, c_N)^T$. Here, $\log(\mathbf{g}_t) = (1, \log(g_{1t}), \ldots, \log(g_{Nt}))$.

Following the suggestions of Bailey and Chuang (1995), we propose the following five risk factors for Mexican firms that conduct business with U.S. firms:

$g_{1t}(\mathbf{z}_t, \mathbf{Z}_{t+1}) = \dfrac{Z_{1,t+1}}{z_{1,t}} =$ relative change of the exchange rate at period $t + 1$ over period t,

$g_{2t}(\mathbf{z}_t, \mathbf{Z}_{t+1}) = \dfrac{Z_{2,t+1}}{z_{2,t}} =$ one plus world market return for period t,

$g_{3t}(\mathbf{z}_t, \mathbf{Z}_{t+1}) = \dfrac{Z_{3,t+1}}{z_{3,t}} =$ one plus Mexican market return for period t,

$g_{4t}(\mathbf{z}_t) = z_{4t} =$ Mexican domestic interest rate at the beginning of period t,

$g_{5t}(\mathbf{z}_t) = z_{5t} =$ U.S. interest rate at the beginning of period t,

with $\mathbf{Z}_t$ being given by

$Z_{1t} =$ exchange rate at the beginning of period t,

$Z_{2t} =$ world market index at the beginning of period t,

$Z_{3t} =$ Mexican market index at the beginning of period t,

$Z_{4t} =$ Mexican domestic interest rate at the beginning of period t,

$Z_{5t} =$ U.S. interest rate at the beginning of period t (foreign to Mexico).

Although Bailey and Chung (1995) also considered political risk factors, we consider only factors that reflect economic risks, because the political risks will be embedded in the economic factors. For example, in recent decades, political turbulence surrounding presidential elections in Mexico actually changes the national economy (FOCAL, 1999), which is reflected in the consensus estimates of economic risks.

3.3 *Modeling the Evolution of β_t*

In order to calculate the discount factor β_t, we need to model the evolution of the risk factors g_{it} over time. Standard approaches to time series modeling are applicable. The first step in modeling g_{it} is to test for autocorrelation. If there is no autocorrelation, the sequence $\{g_{it}:t = 1, 2, \ldots\}$ can be modeled as observations from an *i.i.d.* random variable. Because we have seen that sample autocorrelation functions often have an exponentially decreasing appearance, we consider the simple additive AR(1) model, using

$$g_{i,t+1} = \phi_0 + \phi_1 g_{it} + \xi_{it}; \qquad (9)$$

in the log-linear version of the AR(1) model we have instead

$$\log(g_{i,t+1}) = \alpha_0 + \alpha_1 \log(g_{it}) + \log(\eta_{it}). \qquad (10)$$

Here, both the $\{\xi_{it}\}$ and $\{\log(\eta_{it})\}$ are *i.i.d.* random variables with mean 0. Note that when the g_{it}'s are *i.i.d.*, ϕ_1 (or α_1) is zero.

4 Case Study

There are a great many different types of variability affecting financial markets, a company's global supply chain, and its operations (e.g., its cost structures, lead times, and demand characteristics). Thus, a comprehensive numerical study is well beyond the scope of this chapter. In this section, we instead analyze an illustrative case study. Our case study considers four different types of Mexican firms, differentiated by the (simple) architectures of their supply chains, which operate in the U.S. and/or Mexico. They are a *Local Firm*, an *Importer*, an *Exporter*, and a Mexican-owned *Subsidiary* that operates in the U.S. Here, Mexico is referred to as the domestic country and the U.S. as the foreign country. These firms anticipate and respond to an observed fact that was the underlying motivation for this research: that Mexican financial markets are much more turbulent in the months surrounding their presidential elections. We examine how the inventory decisions made by these firms change because of financial uncertainty during the months surrounding each election.

The purpose of this numerical study is three-fold. First, we study how firms should adjust their inventory replenishment decisions in expectation of the financial uncertainty during the months surrounding an upcoming election. Second, we examine what ordering policies are optimal when conditions in Theorem 1 fail to hold. And third, we study the cost penalty of ignoring the dynamic nature of the financial environment.

We test three different inventory control policies. The first one is the *optimal policy*, computed via dynamic programming (DP). In the DP model, the state variable contains all of the currently-available financial information that might affect current and future discount factors and exchange rates (see Section 4.2). The second policy was motivated by conversations with Latin American managers. They monitor exchange rates very carefully and do not hesitate to adjust their inventory management policies when they anticipate a swing in near-term exchange rates. However, they seem to be unconscious of the fact that discount factors should impact their operational decisions in the short-to-medium term. This observation led us to the *constant-discount-factor policy*, which fully understands and reacts to the probabilistic model that governs future exchange rates, but which optimizes its actions under the simplifying assumption that the discount factor will remain constant (at its historical average) over the planning horizon. The third policy is motivated by the possibility that a time-varying deterministic discount factor, if selected properly, may work as well as a stochastic one. Under this policy, we use the mean of the stochastic discount factor in each period, referred to as the *average-discount-factor policy*. Since an (s, S) policy may not be optimal under any of the above three control policies, complete enumeration is used to minimize the DP.

In this section, we first give a brief discussion on the financial environment surrounding Mexican presidential elections. In Sections 4.2 and 4.3, we discuss technical aspects of our numerical test environment, including the tests of statistical significance that we performed on our risk factors, the distributional assumptions regarding the financial variables, and the operational costs. Section 4.4 summarizes our test environment. In Section 4.5, we discuss the degree to which the conditions for the optimality of (s, S) policies hold within our test environment. We also optimize the operations of the four types of firms, examine optimal inventory policies and costs when the impact of financial turbulence is properly accounted for (and when it is not), and explore general implications for global supply chain management.

4.1 *The Financial Environment*

The periods of economic turbulence that Mexico has gone through in the last few decades are reflected in the fluctuation of its exchange rates. The monthly change in the exchange rate between the Mexican peso and the U.S. dollar between February 1976 and February 1995 is plotted in Fig. 1. (Our data period ends in February 1995 to eliminate the potential noise caused by the difference in the exchange rate regimes. Although Mexico changed to the floating regime in December 1994, we kept the data for the next two months in order to maintain two complete election cycles. The inclusion of two months under the new regime should have little or no impact on our study.) Sharp spikes, representing sharp devaluations of the Mexican peso and economic crises, are clearly evident. Most of these spikes occur during a time period starting four months before the presidential election and ending two months after the presidential inauguration (March 1976–February 1977, and every six years thereafter), called the *electoral season*. The months in an electoral season are called *election months*; all other months are called *regular months*. We define quarters to start in the months March, June, September, and December, and differentiate between *election quarters* and *regular quarters*.

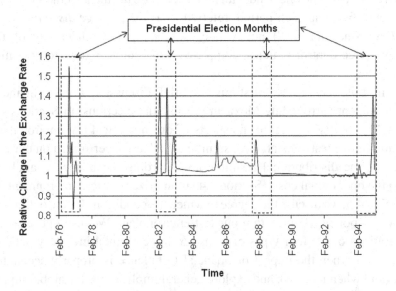

Fig. 1 Relative Change in the Exchange Rate

Table 1 Predicting the Quarterly Discount Factor β_t: Coefficients

	Constant (c_0)	Change in the Exchange Rate (c_1)	Mexican Market Return Plus One (c_3)
Election Quarters	−0.0065	1.13	−0.596
Regular Quarters	0.0272	—	−1.280

As exchange rates change, the costs and prices of goods will move as well, so that it is important for firms to anticipate these changes and plan ahead. For instance, a Mexican importer may want to increase her order quantity if she expects that the peso will soon be devalued. During times of financial turbulence in Mexico, banks tend to dramatically decrease the number of loans that they approve. The Mexican Cetes (analogous to the U.S. treasury bill) rate jumps sharply in an effort to defend the peso devaluation. However, this rate cannot be considered as a valid benchmark for costs of capital, since there is a very real chance that the government would default. This probably explains why the domestic interest rate g_{4t} is not statistically significant (see Section 4.2).

4.2 The Risk Factors: Selection and Evolution

In this section, we summarize our approach to selecting and modeling the evolution of the risk factors over time. (More details are available upon request.) We start by determining the significance of the five risk factors in Section 3.2 using the log-linear model for the discount factor, $\log(\beta_t) = \mathbf{c}^T \log(\mathbf{g}_t)$. We then create a statistical model that captures the evolution of the discount factors. To estimate the parameters $\mathbf{c}$ of the log-linear model, we use historical data on the return of one Mexican firm, the DESC group, which has four divisions that have business in both Mexico and the U.S.: chemical, automotive, food, and real estate. Stepwise regression showed that the exchange rate risk (g_{1t}) and Mexican domestic market risk (g_{3t}) were the two significant factors for the election quarters, and that g_{3t} was the only significant factor for the regular quarters, both at the 95% level. Table 1 gives the resulting coefficients $\mathbf{c}$ for the quarterly discount factor.

Table 2 Mean and Standard Deviation of the Discount Factor over Time

Quarter	1	2	3	4	5	6	7
Mean	0.952	0.952	1.215	1.215	1.215	1.215	0.952
Standard Deviation	0.647	0.647	0.311	0.311	0.311	0.311	0.647

We now model the evolution over time of the risk factors g_{1t} and g_{3t}, following the approach of Section 3.3. Based on statistical tests of autocorrelation, we model g_{3t}, and g_{1t} during election quarters as *i.i.d.* random variables. During regular quarters, we model the change in the exchange rate g_{1t} using the standard logarithmic AR(1) autoregressive model $\log(g_{1,t+1}) = \alpha_0 + \alpha_1 \log(g_{1t}) + \log(\eta_{1t})$; see (10). We assume that the $\log(\eta_{1t})$'s are *i.i.d.* with mean 0. Using regression, we find that $\alpha_0 = 0.004057$ and $\alpha_1 = 0.8183$, showing that $\log(g_{1t})$ is a stable process.

To complete the model, we need distributions for the following four *i.i.d.* random variables: η_{1t} and g_{3t} during regular quarters, and g_{1t} and g_{3t} during election quarters. We achieve this by discretizing the logarithms of these random variables and creating histograms. Because of the curse of dimensionality common to dynamic programming, we choose to simulate a problem of seven periods (quarters). In order to see the different behavior in regular quarters and election quarters, it is necessary to have at least one regular quarter bracketing the election quarters. Further, because the end-of-horizon condition guarantees normal behavior in the first nonelection quarter after the election, we expect to see standard inventory control for all regular quarters following that one. Thus, we decided to extend our dynamic program to include an additional regular period before the election season, rather than after it. Our numerical results confirm that the effects of financial turbulence began to show up in the second normal quarter, which would have not been observed if only one regular quarter had been included before the election (in a six period problem). Table 2 provides the mean and standard deviation of the stochastic discount factor $\beta_t = \beta_t(z_t, Z_{t+1})$ for each quarter t. Here, quarters 1, 2, and 7 are regular quarters, and quarters 3–6 are election quarters.

4.3 The Operational Costs

Operational costs and revenues can be affected by many factors. For our case study, we will assume that the costs and selling prices have known values which, over the planning horizon, are constant in the markets in which they occur. For tractability, we will ignore the fixed ordering costs. Thus, Condition 3(b) in Theorem 1 is automatic. Conditions 1, 2, 3(a) and the unlabeled condition $\mathcal{A}_t < 0$ are sufficient to guarantee the convexity of the value functions and the optimality of a finite order-up-to policy.

The costs incurred in Mexico are denoted as (c, h, π, p), while those in the U.S. are referred to as (c', h', π', p'). We assume that in each quarter the firm converts all costs and revenues into Mexican pesos immediately. Consequently, the values of the dollar-denominated costs and prices are proportional to the exchange rate z_{1t} in a given quarter t. Table 3 lists the cost parameters used for the four Mexican firms. Note that by assumption, the variable ordering costs are incurred in the market where a product is made, but the holding costs, stockout costs and revenues are realized in the market where the product is sold.

4.4 Summary of the Test Environment for the Case Study

In this case study, we consider four hypothetical Mexican firms, differentiated by their supply chain architecture. The Local Firm operates entirely in Mexico, the Importer manufactures (or procures) in the U.S. and sells in Mexico, the Exporter manufactures (or procures) in Mexico and sells in the U.S., and the Subsidiary is Mexican-owned and operates in the U.S.

In our numerical test environment, we use the risk factors g_{1t} (relative change in the exchange rate at quarter $t + 1$ versus quarter t) and g_{3t} (one

Table 3 Cost Parameters for the Four Firms

	c_t	h_t	π_t	p_t
Local Firm	c	h	π	p
Importer	$c'z_{1t}$	h	π	p
Exporter	c	$h'Z_{1,t+1}$	$\pi'Z_{1,t+1}$	$p'Z_{1,t+1}$
Subsidiary	$c'z_{1t}$	$h'Z_{1,t+1}$	$\pi'Z_{1,t+1}$	$p'Z_{1,t+1}$

plus Mexican market return for quarter t). The risk factor g_{1t} during the regular quarters evolves according to the logarithmic autoregressive AR(1) model of (10), using the coefficients and the distribution for the noise factor $\log(\eta_{1t})$ described in Section 4.2. The risk factor g_{3t} during regular quarters, and the risk factors g_{1t} and g_{3t} during election quarters, follow the *i.i.d.* distributions described in Section 4.2.

In each quarter, the risk factors g_{1t} and g_{3t} determine the exchange rate directly and govern the discount factors as in (8), using the coefficients that were obtained in Section 4.2. The exchange rate affects the cost parameters as outlined in Table 3. The fixed costs are set to zero. The other cost parameters are $c = 2$, $h = 0.1$, $\pi = 0.8$, $p = 6$, $c' = 0.2$, $h' = 0.01$, $\pi' = 0.08$, and $p' = 0.6$.

Our case study considers a 7-quarter problem with zero lead time ($L = 0$), zero starting inventory ($x_1 = 0$), and a discrete uniform demand distribution over $[0, 5]$ in each quarter. The demands are stochastically independent of the financial variables. The electoral season consists of quarters 3 through 6, which have elevated financial instability. Quarters 1, 2, and 7 are regular quarters that have lower financial volatility. At the conclusion of quarter 7, any remaining on-hand inventory will be sold back to the supplier at the salvage value $v(\mathbf{Z}_8)$. If there is negative inventory, the firm is required to fill all backordered demand by a purchase at the unit price $c_{T-L+1}(\mathbf{Z}_8)$, and receives revenue in the PTD case. The salvage value $v(\mathbf{Z}_8)$ and the purchase price $c_{T-L+1}(\mathbf{Z}_8)$ at the end of quarter 7 are determined as specified in Chen *et al.* (2015). In Section 4.5 below, we test two inventory control policies, the optimal policy and the constant-discount-factor policy, which we described in the third paragraph of Section 4. We will discuss the third inventory policy, the average-discount-factor policy, in Section 4.6.

4.5 *Impacts of the Stochastic Discount Factor*

In this section, we will test the conditions in Theorem 1, and characterize the structure of the value function V_t and the optimal inventory decision when the value function is not convex. We also investigate the loss from using constant discount factors for the inventory control policies in financially turbulent environments.

We limit our model testing to situations where the cost parameters $v(\mathbf{Z}_{T+1})$ and $c_{T-L+1}(\mathbf{Z}_{T+1})$ ensure the value function V_t is convex in the final quarter, and only test the convexity of V_t over the first six quarters. To avoid the trivial case of ordering an infinite amount of inventory and salvaging it at the end of the horizon, we will select the salvage value function $v(\mathbf{Z}_{T+1})$ so that $\mathcal{B}_t > 0$. Thus, we only need to test two conditions in Theorem 1: $h_t + \hat{\pi}_t \geq 0$ under backlogging, and $h_t + \hat{\pi}_t - c_{t+1} \geq 0$ under lost sales, with $\mathcal{A}_t < 0$.

As one will see later, the value function is always convex in the PTO case, and so an order-up-to policy will be optimal. This is generally true in the LS case, except for the Importer after the electoral season. For the PTD case, convexity will almost certainly fail at least in one period, except for the Importer. When convexity does fail, the value functions have a specific structure that has interesting operational implications.

4.5.1 *The Condition* $\mathcal{A}_t < 0$

Recall that this condition is not required for a base-stock policy to be optimal, in the absence of fixed ordering costs. It ensures that when a base-stock policy is optimal, the order-up-to level is finite, which holds automatically in the LS case. For the backorder cases, we chose $c_{T-L+1}(\mathbf{Z}_{T+1})$ so that the condition holds for the final quarter, and we test the condition for quarters 1 through 6. In the PTO case, the condition holds for all firms and all states. In the PTD case, the value functions may be convex, increasing, or up-down-up. The condition $\mathcal{A}_t < 0$ holds as long as the value function is convex, and fails when the value function is increasing or up-down-up.

4.5.2 *The Condition* $h_t + \hat{\pi}_t \geq 0$ *under PTO*

Without fixed costs, this condition guarantees the convexity of the value function V_t and the optimality of an order-up-to policy. This will always hold under the PTO stockout protocol, so that we can now consider the ordering behavior of the four firms. Recall that the maximum demand in a quarter is five and that the lead time is zero. Thus, only financial considerations would cause the optimal echelon inventory to ever exceed five. Also note that under PTO, firms do not have control over the timing of revenue realization. Therefore, the impact of stochastic discount factors

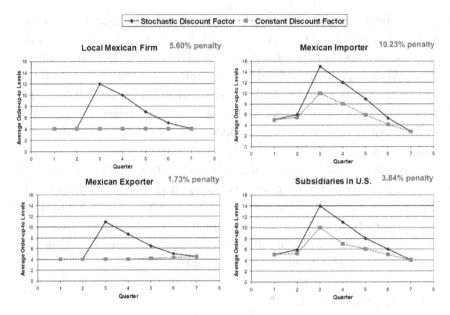

Fig. 2 Average Order-up-to Levels under PTO

on inventory decisions arises from the costs (measured in pesos), not the revenues.

Figure 2 shows the mean optimal order-up-to levels over all the financial states in each period for the four firms under PTO. As one can see, the optimal order-up-to levels are much higher than those obtained using a constant discount factor for all firms. As the electoral season draws to a close, the reasons for these discrepancies disappear, and the optimal order-up-to levels drop towards the levels that one would expect to see under a constant discount factor. These swings in the order-up-to levels are the result of three different causes, listed in the order of their apparent importance.

- **Large Discount Factors Impact Acquisition Costs** for all four firms. During the electoral season, there is a high possibility that financing becomes more costly. That makes a peso more valuable later on in the electoral season. That is, it is cheaper to buy earlier on, so that all the firms will order significantly more inventory at the beginning of quarter 3. Note that large discount factors are solely responsible for the Local Firm to stockpile inventory, with an order-up-to level in quarter 3 of approximately 12 units, versus four units with a constant discount factor (Fig. 2).

- **Devaluation Impacts Acquisition Costs.** There is a high possibility of a devaluation of the peso during the electoral season, making production in the U.S. more expensive. For the Importer and the Subsidiary, this creates another incentive to stock up on inventory before the election season begins. Figure 2 seems to indicate that this factor increases the order-up-to levels of the Importer and the Subsidiary in quarter 3 by approximately three units (comparing the rightmost column of Fig. 2 to the left column).

- **Devaluation Impacts Holding Costs.** A devaluation of the peso would increase the cost of holding inventory in the U.S. This gives the Exporter and the Subsidiary an incentive to decrease their inventory levels. Figure 2 indicates that this factor decreases the order-up-to levels of the Exporter and the Subsidiary in quarter 3 by approximately one unit (comparing the top row of Fig. 2 to the bottom row).

4.5.3 *The Condition $h_t + \hat{\pi}_t \geq 0$ under PTD*

In the PTD case, the condition $h_t + \hat{\pi}_t \geq 0$ always holds in quarters 1 and 6, but never in quarters 2–5. In other words, the condition fails when any of the parameters in $\hat{\pi}_t = \pi_t + p_t - \beta_{t+1} p_{t+1}$ has an index in an election quarter. When the condition fails, we observe that the value function V_t falls into one of the following three different categories: (1) V_t is monotonically increasing, called *Increasing*, in which case no order is placed; i.e., an order-up-to policy with $S = -\infty$ is optimal. (2) V_t is convex but not monotone, called *Convex*, in which case an order-up-to policy with a finite S is optimal. (3) V_t first increases, then decreases, and then increases again, called *Up-down-up*, in which case there exist two local minima: $-\infty$ and a finite one with $-\infty$ as the global minimum. This implies that the optimal policy is not in a simple order-up-to fashion and that one orders only when inventory is not too high or low. When an order is placed, the order-up-to level is finite.

Table 4 shows the percentage of states in each quarter when the cost function is Increasing, Convex, and Up-down-up for the four different firms,

Table 4 Percentage of the States Having Different Types of Cost Functions under PTD and the Finite Local Minimizer (the finite inventory level that locally minimizes an Up-down-up function)

Type of Firm	Cost Functions	Quarters t						
		1	2	3	4	5	6	7
Local Firm	Increasing	0	100%	0	0	0	0	0
	Convex	100%	0	0	0	0	100%	100%
	Up-down-up	0	0	100%	100%	100%	0	0
	Finite Local Minimizer	—	—	12	10	7	—	—
Importer	Increasing	0	50%	0	0	0	0	0
	Convex	100%	10%	100%	100%	87.24%	100%	100%
	Up-down-up	0	40%	0	0	12.76%	0	0
	Finite Local Minimizer	—	16	—	—	9	—	—
Exporter	Increasing	100%	100%	100%	99.92%	26.02%	0	0
	Convex	0	0	0	0	0	100%	100%
	Up-down-up	0	0	0	0.08%	73.98%	0	0
	Finite Local Minimizer	—	—	—	9	6	—	—
Subsidiary	Increasing	100%	100%	0	0	0	0	0
	Convex	0	0	0	0	0	100%	100%
	Up-down-up	0	0	100%	100%	100%	0	0
	Finite Local Minimizer	—	—	15	12	9	—	—

under PTD. For the Up-down-up functions, we also list the local finite order-up-to levels (Finite Local Minimizer) in cases where orders are placed. Figure 3 shows the average optimal inventory levels in each period at the four firms under PTD. In the case of Up-down-up value functions, the inventory level used to calculate the "Average Order-up-to Levels" in Fig. 3 refers to one of the two local minimizers, whichever produces the lowest value function for given system states. As we will see later, in our study with starting inventory level zero as specified in Section 4.4, the local minimizer that optimizes the value function is often $-\infty$, which in Fig. 3 is represented by the lowest possible inventory state value in every period t [$-5t$].

As one can see, the ordering decisions under PTD are quite different from those under PTO and are more complex because the ordering decisions

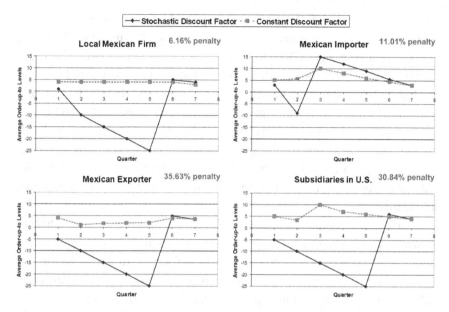

Fig. 3 Average Order-up-to Levels under PTD

affect the timing of the cash inflows in addition to the operating costs. For all the firms except the Importer, the dominant strategy is to delay incomes until the last quarter of the electoral season in order to maximize the revenues due to high discount factors. This strategy is especially important to the Exporter and the Subsidiary due to exchange rate increase. The importance of deferring revenue dominates other considerations, such as the attractiveness of buying inventory when it is cheap (before the electoral season begins), and the cost of carrying the inventory.

In this context, Table 4 shows that for the Local Firm and the Subsidiary, the value function is Up-down-up in most quarters during the electoral season and in most states. That means that there exists some threshold: an inventory level at which the value function is increasing and is equal to the local minimum. If the inventory level is above the threshold, then the system follows an order-up-to policy under which an order is placed to raise the inventory level up to the finite local minimizer. Furthermore, Table 4 indicates that the order-up-to level (i.e., the Finite Local Minimizer) is chosen according to the same logic that governs the PTO case: purchase the inventory before the discount factor causes the effective procurement cost to rise. On the other hand, if the net inventory level is below the threshold then there are existing backorders (or the potential to accumulate backorders), and the optimal policy will be to not order anything until quarter 6 in order to maximize the revenue from these backorders. For the Local Firm and the Subsidiary, comparing the finite local minimizers from Table 4 and the optimal inventory levels in Fig. 3, it is clear that in periods 1 and 2, the optimal policy controls the inventory so that the net inventory level will almost always be below the threshold during the electoral season, and both purchases and revenues will be deferred. For the Exporter, Up-down-up value functions are less prevalent because the exchange rates create an added incentive to delay the revenue.

An Importer operating under the PTD stockout protocol uses a hybrid strategy. It is primarily influenced by the factor that dominated optimal policies in the PTO case (buy inventory before the discount factor and exchange rate cause acquisition costs to rise), and the factor that determined behavior for the other three firms in the PTD case (delay income to maximize its value). However, the economics of buying in the U.S. and selling in Mexico result in a very different balance between these factors. In quarter 2, the importance of delaying income dominates, and no purchase is made. But when the electoral season begins (the beginning of quarter 3) the balance shifts, the combined impact of the discount factor and the exchange rate on acquisition costs starts to dominate, and the Importer buys large amounts of inventory while it is still relatively inexpensive. In Table 4, we see that the value functions are almost all convex, an indication of the fact that this strategy is consistently followed in nearly all states and time periods.

4.5.4 *The Condition* $h_t + \hat{\pi}_t - c_{t+1} \geq 0$ *under Lost Sales (LS)*

Table 5 lists the percentage of states in each quarter for which the condition $h_t + \hat{\pi}_t - c_{t+1} \geq 0$ fails to hold for the LS case. In our computational experiments under LS, the cost functions were always quasi-convex, so that an order-up-to policy was always optimal. These experiments are admittedly limited, but seem to indicate that at least when $K_t = 0$, order-up-to policies are likely to be optimal in many lost sales settings.

Table 5 Percentage of States in which $h_t + \hat{\pi}_t - c_{t+1} \geq 0$ Fails for the LS Case

Quarters t	Local Firm	Importer	Exporter	Subsidiary
1–3	0	0	0	0
4	0	0	0	0
5	0	12.04%	0	0
6	0	24.52%	2.74%	0

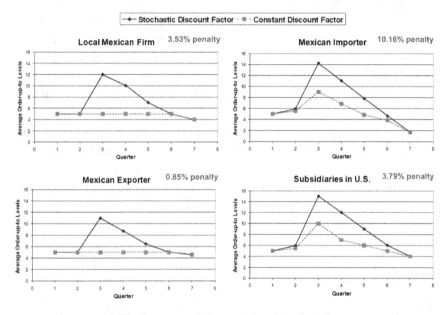

Fig. 4 Average Order-up-to Levels under LS

Figure 4 shows the order-up-to levels for the four firms under lost sales. As with the PTO protocol, under lost sales the firm does not control the timing of revenue realization. Thus, the inventory decisions and the explanations for them are similar to the PTO case. There are two interesting differences. First, since unsatisfied demand is lost, firms have a stronger incentive to stock inventory, as shown by the typical decision of the constant-discount-factor model to stock to a level of 5, rather than 4 as in the PTO case. Second, during the electoral season devaluations may have rendered the Importer's business unprofitable by increasing the cost of acquiring inventory in the U.S. Consequently, in quarter 7, the Importer has an order-up-to level of zero in 33% of the states. In the backorder cases, the Importer must meet all of the demand, so this does not happen.

4.5.5 *Cost Penalty of using a constant discount factor*

In this section, we explore the implications of using sub-optimal constant-discount-factor inventory control policies in environments with financial turbulence.

Figure 5 shows the cost penalty of using a constant discount factor, defined to be the relative difference in actual costs between inventory policies that are optimal for (assumed) constant and stochastic discount factors. We can see that the penalty is most significant for the Exporter and the Subsidiary in the PTD case, which can be as high as 36%. Under the PTD stockout protocol, the timing of cash inflows can be controlled through effective inventory management, which is not possible under the PTO and LS protocols, and which amplifies the effect of the stochastic discount factors. The Local Firm and the Importer are less sensitive to these discount factors than the Exporter and the Subsidiary whose revenue is in U.S. dollars, which is likely to gain value during elections. Other than the

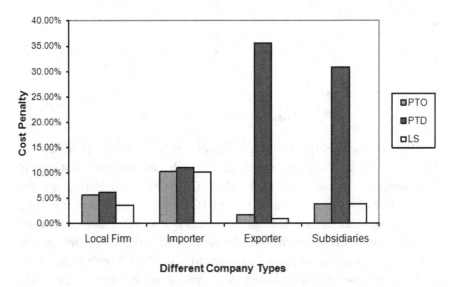

Fig. 5 Cost Penalty for using a Constant Discount Factor

Exporter and the Subsidiary under PTD, in general, the Importer incurs the highest cost penalty due to high purchasing costs incurred in U.S. dollars during the election quarters.

4.6 *Average-Discount-Factor Policy*

Section 4.5 analyzed the implications of using a constant discount factor when the real financial environment is volatile and nonstationary. In this section, we compare the optimal inventory policies and costs with the average-discount-policy, where the stochastic discount factors are replaced by their means, in order to determine the cost penalty when the variability of the discount factors is partially counted for.

Figure 6 shows the relative cost penalty from using the average discount factor. The cost penalty is close to zero for all four firms under the three stockout protocols. We also found that the average-discount-factor inventory replenishment policy is almost the same as the optimal policy. (Details are omitted for conciseness of exposition, and are available upon request.) Therefore, it appears that the nonstationarity of the stochastic discount factors is a more important factor than their inherent variability.

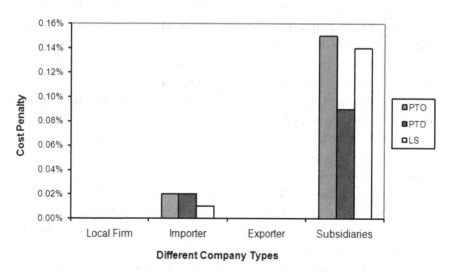

Fig. 6 Cost Penalty for using an Average Discount Factor

5 Numerical Case Study: More on Stochastic Discount Factors

Note that the mean of the stochastic discount factors presented in Table 2 can be greater than one, indicating that investors are willing to accept the negative return of the firm. While investors generally can perform better by putting their money in a risk-free asset instead, it may not be unreasonable for them to leave money with a firm in Mexico, especially during the turbulent times captured in our data. During those election quarters, currency crisis occurred and the rate on the Mexican government's Cetes bills spiked sharply. However, this rate was by no means "risk free," as the Mexican government had a significant likelihood to default on them, as happened in 1982 and 1994.

Investors have several options, each reflecting a different risk attitude. Investors may choose to invest their money in a firm even though the firm may generate negative returns. After all, money stashed under mattresses may get robbed or stolen, and money invested in government bonds may lost through default. Investing in firms may result in smaller losses; such an option is consistent with the use of a stochastic discount factor greater than one. Investors might choose to invest in firms that will not lose money in expectation. In this case, the stochastic discount factor will be bounded from above by 1. The third option is that investors still naively use the government "risk-free" rate as a hurdle rate for their investment. In this case, the stochastic discount factor should be bounded from above by $1/(1 + R_f)$, where R_f is this "risk-free" rate.

Our goal is to compare these policies against one another and identify the cost penalty from adopting a sub-optimal policy. There are three different investment outlooks (each reflecting a different risk attitude), and two sub-optimal policies (constant and average discount factor policies) for each, for a total of six combinations. Since our numerical study shows that the performance of the average-discount-factor policy is very close to the optimal one regardless of investors' risk attitude, we omit the details associated with the average-discount-factor policy. Furthermore, since the optimal policies are quite similar when the stochastic discount factor is bounded from above by 1 and $1/(1 + R_f)$, respectively, we will focus on the comparisons between the constant-discount-factor policy and the optimal policy when the stochastic discount factor is

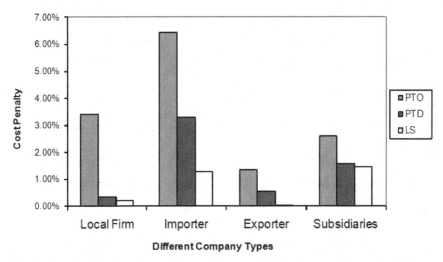

Fig. 7 Cost Penalty for using a Constant Discount Factor when the Stochastic Discount Factor is Bounded from above by $1/(1 + R_f)$

bounded from above by $1/(1 + R_f)$, and compare the results with those in Section 4.

We calculate the historical "risk-free" rates in Mexico (details are omitted and are available upon request) and model them as random variables following different distributions in the regular and election quarters. As expected, the results are less dramatic with the bounds.

Figure 7 shows the cost penalty of using a constant discount factor. The cost penalty is noticeably smaller compared to that in Fig. 5, with a maximum value of 6.5%, since the bounds with the stochastic discount factor is closer to the constant discount factor. Furthermore, the cost penalty for the Exporter and Subsidiaries under the PTD stockout protocol is no longer significant. It appears that when the discount factor is bounded, profit delay is no longer an attractive option. Rather, the larger concern will be the higher dollar-denominated purchasing cost for the Importer and Subsidiaries.

Figure 8 shows the average order-up-to levels under PTO. In contrast to the previous case in Section 4, here all the firms tend to order less than with a constant discount factor. This is because the bounded discount factor is generally smaller than the constant discount factor. Further, bounding

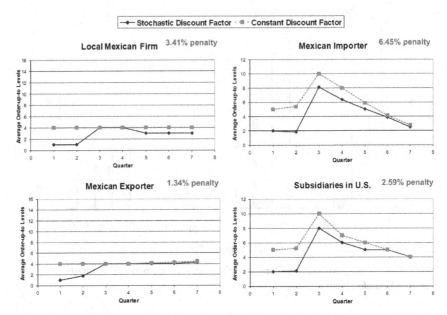

Fig. 8 Average Order-up-to Levels under PTO when the Stochastic Discount Factor is Bounded from above by $1/(1 + R_f)$

the stochastic discount factor reduces the difference between its values in the regular and election quarters, making it closer to the constant discount factor. Hence, firms do not stock up as observed in Section 4.5. Figure 10 shows the average order-up-to levels under LS. The behavior (and the rationale behind it) is similar to those under PTO.

Figure 9 shows the average order-up-to levels under PTD. Similar to under PTO, all firms order less than if a constant discount factor is used except for the Exporter, due to its high dollar-dominated backorder cost. In contrast to Fig. 3, none of the four firms delays the realization of the revenue (except for the Exporter and the Subsidiary in quarter 2), due to smaller discount factors due to the bounds. In quarter 2, due to the mild backorder cost and the potentially higher revenues in the future, the Exporter and the Subsidiary will prefer to delay revenue realization. However, when the election starts in quarter 3, the high dollar-denominated backorder cost, coupled with a smaller discount factor that reduces the benefit of delaying revenue recognition, motivates stockpiling rather than backlogging.

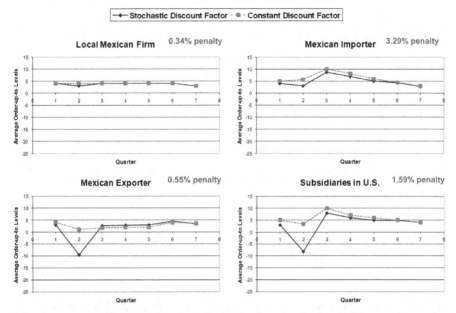

Fig. 9 Average Order-up-to Levels under PTD when the Stochastic Discount Factor is Bounded from above by $1/(1 + R_f)$

In summary, differing investor attitudes towards risk call for very different inventory decisions, and can lead to very different financial positions. It is therefore critical for firms to understand the investors' behavior and risk attitude in financially turbulent environments, and to make operational decisions accordingly.

6 Conclusion

In this chapter, we challenge the use of constant discount factors and known operational costs in traditional inventory models. In environments where there are foreseeable intervals of economic volatility, we propose a data-driven approach for modeling the distribution of the stochastic discount factors, and their evolution over time. Our approach is based on the arbitrage pricing theory, and the commonly-held relationship from the finance literature that the (firm-wide) discount factor should equal the reciprocal of one plus the rate of return of the firm.

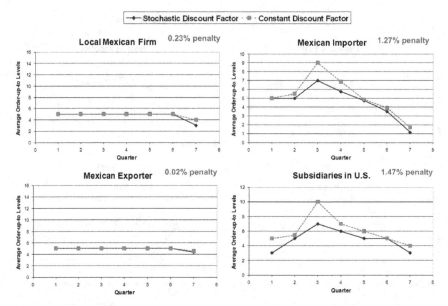

Fig. 10 Average Order-up-to Levels under LS when the Stochastic Discount Factor is Bounded from above by $1/(1 + R_f)$

We present a case study based on four Mexican firms that are affected by the financial instability that often surrounds presidential elections in Mexico. During the electoral season, the discount factor has a mean that is greater than one, meaning that the internal rate of return has a negative mean. This is because in Mexico, capital often becomes very expensive or temporarily unavailable during periods of financial turbulence; hence, a peso in the future may well be worth more than a peso today. The four types of firms all reacted to the potential for financial turbulence very strongly, and in very different ways. We observed the stockpiling of large amounts of inventory (under PTO and LS protocol), and the use of deliberate inventory shortfalls as a means of deferring revenue for extended periods of time (under PTD protocol). The primary drivers of this behavior are the potential for currency devaluations, and the discount factors.

In traditional inventory models, when unfilled demand is backordered, it does not really matter whether the client pays when the order is placed or when the inventory is delivered; any difference can be compensated for by adjusting the backorder cost. But when discount factors and other financial information are stochastic and nonstationary, revenue timing can make a substantial difference. Suppliers who are paid when the inventory is delivered can use inventory management to control the timing of their cash inflows — sometimes with great effect. From the buyer's perspective, a PTO protocol creates a much more desirable set of supplier incentives than a PTD discipline does.

When facing a negative return, investors normally can do better by leaving money in a risk-free asset. In Mexico's case, although during the crisis period the reported government rate is not really risk-free due to the elevated risk of government default, some investors might still choose this rate as a benchmark, or might choose to invest only in firms that do not lose money. We therefore also discuss the cases where the stochastic discount factor is bounded from above by 1 or by $1/(1 + R_f)$ where R_f is the announced "risk-free" rate. We observe that inventory decisions can be very different than if the stochastic discount factor is unbounded. It is therefore important to understand investors' risk attitude during financial crises, as our study shows that the cost penalty under different risk attitudes can be very different, especially for the Exporter and Subsidiary under PTD stockout protocol.

We also study the case where the mean of the stochastic discount factor which differs from period to period is used to compute the optimal policy. It turns out that the mean can capture the dynamic financial environment quite well, and therefore can be a good proxy to use to compute the optimal policy.

A comprehensive study of inventory management in the presence of predictable periods of financial turbulence would be very valuable. In addition to a much more comprehensive set of scenarios, there are other very important considerations that remain to be studied. For example, we have assumed that under the PTD protocol, demand is met whenever inventory is available. Companies that are more concerned with profit than service might make a different decision. We also assumed that all costs and revenues have constant values in the local currency, and that they are converted to the firm's domestic currency at the time they are incurred (see Section 4.3). Once again, different assumptions could be modeled. Finally, when there are cyclic time intervals that oscillate between periods of high and low financial risk (like the Mexican presidential elections) we have shown how to use historical data to obtain an evolutionary model of discount factors. However, for one-time events (such as the Iraq War), the question of how to model the dependence of discount factors on financial variables is of course much harder.

This chapter focuses on how firms should react operationally to financial uncertainties. While many financial instruments can be used to hedge financial risks, hedging through inventory management may play an important role in some financial environments. For global firms facing predictable financial instabilities in the near future, this hedging may bring in significant savings by using a stochastic discount factor rather than a constant discount factor.

Bibliography

Anvari, M. (1987). Optimal criteria and risk in inventory models: The case of the Newsboy problem, *The Journal of Operational Research Society* **38**, 7, pp. 625–632.

Axarloglou, K. and Kouvelis, P. (2001). Exchange rates and ownership structure of foreign subsidiaries: An empirical investigation, *Olin Business School Working Paper* 2002-03-010.

Bailey, W. and Chuang, Y. (1995). Exchange rate fluctuations, political risk, and stock returns: Some evidence from an emerging market, *Journal of Financial and Quantitative Analysis* **30**, 4, pp. 541–561.

Beranek, W. (1967). Financial implications of lot-size inventory models, *Management Science* **13**, 8, pp. 401–408.

Canadian Foundation for the Americas (FOCAL) (1999). Mexico's presidential election, *FOCAL Policy Paper (FPP-99-04)*.

Chen, L. G., Robinson, L. W., Roundy, R. O. and Zhang, R. Q. (2015). New sufficient conditions for (s, S) policies to be optimal in systems with multiple uncertainties, *Operations Research* **63**, 1, pp. 186–197.

Ding, Q., Dong, L. and Kouvelis, P. (2007). On the integration of production and financial hedging decisions in global market, *Operations Research* **55**, 3, pp. 470–487.

Dumas, B. (2003). Which "going price" is right? *INSEAD Quarterly* **6**, pp. 19–21.

Gaur, V. and Seshadri, S. (2005). Hedging inventory risk through market instruments, *Manufacturing & Service Operations Management* **7**, 2, pp. 103–120.

Grubbstrom, R. W. (1980). A principle for determining the correct capital costs of work-in-progress and inventory, *International Journal of Production Research* **18**, 2, pp. 259–271.

Jorion, P. (1990). The exchange rate exposure of U.S. multinationals, *Journal of Business* **63**, 3, pp. 331–345.

Jorion, P. (1991). The pricing of exchange rate risk in the stock market, *Journal of Financial and Quantitative Analysis* **26**, 3, pp. 363–376.

Kazaz, B., Dada, M. and Moskowitz, H. (2005). Global production planning under exchange-rate uncertainty, *Management Science* **51**, 7, pp. 1101–1119.

Kim, Y. H. and Chung, K. H. (1989). Inventory management under uncertainty: A financial theory for the transactions motive, *Managerial and Decision Economics* **10**, 4, pp. 291–298.

Ross, S. A., Westerfield, R. W. and Jaffe, J. F. (2001). *Corporate Finance*, McGraw-Hill, Irwin.

Singhal, V. R., Raturi, A. S. and Bryant, J. (1994). On incorporating business risk into continuous review inventory models, *European Journal of Operational Research* **75**, 1, pp. 136–150.

Stulz, R. M. (1994). International portfolio choice and asset pricing: An integrative survey, *NBER Working Paper No. 4645*.

Van Mieghem, J. A. (2003). Capacity management, investment and hedging: Review and recent developments, *Manufacturing & Service Operations Management* **5**, 4, pp. 269–302.

Van Mieghem, J. A. (2007). Risk mitigation in newsvendor networks: Resource diversification, flexibility, sharing, and hedging, *Management Science* **53**, 8, pp. 1269–1288.

Chapter 4

Optimizing Retailer Procurement and Pass-Through of Trade Discounts When Retail Discounts Affect Reservation Prices and Stockpiling

Candace Arai Yano* and Huanhuan Daphne Qi[†]

*Department of Industrial Engineering
and Operations Research and Haas School of Business
University of California, Berkeley, Berkeley, CA 94720
†Northern Trust, 50 S. LaSalle St., Chicago, IL 60603

1 Introduction

Manufacturers offer trade discounts to retailers, hoping that retailers will pass the savings on to their customers, thereby increasing the manufacturer's market share and possibly also increasing his profit. Empirical research (e.g., Besanko *et al.*, 2005) suggests, however, that manufacturers rarely pass the entire discount to customers, and sometimes do not pass through any of it at all.

In this chapter, we focus on low- to moderately-priced, discretionary, consumable products that customers will purchase if the price is "low enough," but for which they will forego consumption (or consume an alternate default product) otherwise. For such products, retail discounts have a strong impact on demand. We study the retailer's problem of determining his jointly optimal pass-through and procurement strategy when intermittent retail price discounts affect customers' reservation prices and may lead them to stockpile. Intermittent price discounts are known to have an adverse effect on reservation prices (or synonymously, willingness-to-pay), which we refer to as the (negative) brand equity effect, but they allow retailers to reach customers who are unwilling to buy at the regular price. Furthermore, all customers may stockpile, which reduces the retailer's costs by shifting the cost of holding inventory to the customers. When a manufacturer offers a trade discount, the retailer may offer even deeper discounts, which will magnify both the beneficial and adverse effects mentioned above. We seek a strategy for the retailer that achieves the best tradeoff. We also discuss implications for the manufacturer's choice of trade discounts in view of the retailer's optimal reaction to these discounts.

We show that, not surprisingly, including brand equity effects leads the retailer to discount less than when considering customer stockpiling alone. What is surprising, however, is that the brand equity effect sometimes causes a threshold effect: below the threshold, the pass-through is zero and at the threshold, the pass-through jumps noticeably. This phenomenon arises only in the presence of the brand equity effect and not when only stockpiling behavior is considered. Furthermore, rarely does the retailer pass on a substantial portion of the discount. The retailer's reaction to a trade discount depends, in part, on the retailer's (optimal) discounting strategy in the absence of trade discounts. Consequently, manufacturers need to understand the retailer's discounting strategy in the absence of a trade discount and to evaluate how large a trade discount will be needed to induce a reaction on the part of the retailer that is profitable for the manufacturer when brand equity effects and stockpiling are present.

The remainder of this chapter is organized as follows. Section 2 contains a review of the literature. In Section 3, we provide a formal statement of the problem, and formulations of the customers' problem of when and how much to purchase and a general version of the retailer's problem of choosing a discounting and ordering strategy. In Section 4, we derive detailed results and a solution procedure for the retailer's problem assuming a uniform distribution of customer reservation prices. Section 5 presents the results of an extensive numerical study of how the retailer's pass-through changes with the manufacturer's trade discount, and characteristics of situations that lead to high or low pass-through rates. We conclude in Section 6.

2 Literature Review

We review the literature on several topics that are closely related to our study: (i) formation of customers' reference prices and their effect on purchasing decisions, (ii) consumers' reaction to promotions, including stockpiling, (iii) how retail price promotions affect immediate and long-term demand, (iv) retailer discounting policies, and (v) retailers' optimal pass-through of manufacturers' trade deals. The literature on each of these topics is extensive. For brevity, we restrict our review to models involving a single product. We focus primarily on providing rationale for our modeling assumptions and on describing normative models that address key aspects of the scenario that we consider. In addition, because our model includes only one manufacturer and one retailer, with only a few exceptions, we restrict our attention to the literature on bilateral monopoly scenarios.

2.1 *Reference Prices*

Consumers evaluate prices against the standard of a reference price (Monroe, 1973). Researchers have analyzed the effects of both internal reference prices (from a customer's memories of actual prices) and external reference prices (observed prices, such as displayed "regular prices") on consumer purchase behavior. Reference price models have been extended to include other factors such as price trend and promotion frequency. Many studies indicate that inclusion of reference prices improves predictions of purchase probabilities, and that consumers have asymmetric responses to perceived gains (offered price less than the reference price) and losses (offered price greater than the reference price) (cf. Winer, 1986). Other streams of work investigate how reference prices affect purchase quantity and purchase timing decisions. The literature on reference prices is extensive. We refer the reader to Briesch *et al.* (1997), Lowengart (2002), and Mazumdar *et al.* (2005), and references therein.

There is considerable literature on how discounts affect reference prices; the link to reservation prices is more indirect. Jedidi and Jagpal (2009) provide an insightful review of the literature on willingness-to-pay measures, but they do not discuss how discounts affect willingness-to-pay. Reference prices and reservation prices are different concepts, and some research (e.g., Gabarino and Slonim, 2003) suggests that they are distinct and are based on different inputs and perceptions. But Blattberg *et al.* (1995) state in a matter-of-fact manner (and without references), "If a product is heavily promoted (meaning discounted deeply and promoted frequently), the consumer's reference price of the product decreases. The consumer will then buy less of the product at regular price because his or her reservation price has decreased correspondingly." Other researchers (e.g., Briesch *et al.*, 1997) have used estimated reference prices in various choice models as if they were reservation prices. It appears to be common wisdom that retail discounts affect consumers' reference and reservation prices in much the same way.

This raises the question of how discounts affect reference (or reservation) prices. Briesch *et al.* (1997) evaluate five different models to estimate consumer's utilities for various brands and conclude that an exponentially weighted average of a brand's own prices appears to perform the best overall among the five. Krishna and Johar (1996) suggest that the average of the retailer's offered prices (across all periods) is a good estimate of the customer's reservation price. We use this representation in our model. It is simpler than an exponentially weighted average but still captures the first-order effects of discounts on customers' reservation prices.

2.2 *Empirical Findings on the Effects of Retail Price Promotions*

In the literature, various impacts of price promotions on consumer purchasing decisions, such as brand choice, stockpiling, and consumption acceleration, have been reported. See Currim and Schneider (1991) for a taxonomy of customer purchase strategies in response to promotions. Researchers draw different conclusions about the magnitudes of effects, but generally conclude that that brand switching and stockpiling (purchase acceleration) are the two strongest effects (cf. Gupta, 1988; Bell *et al.*, 1999; van Heerde *et al.*, 2003). Our model is a single-product model, so we do not discuss the literature on brand choice effects here. We refer the reader to Raju *et al.* (1990), Raju (1995), Sun *et al.* (2003) and the references in van Heerde and Neslin (2008) for examples of research on the effect of price promotion on brand choice.

In our model, the retailer can decide the timing and depth of price discounts. Kumar and Pereira (1995) investigate the effect of scheduling of price promotions in consecutive weeks. Their empirical findings reveal a strong effect (mostly negative) of consecutive-period promotions on sales, whether the promotions are for the same or competing brands.

A stream of empirical research examines the effect of promotions on consumers' stockpiling behavior. Beasley (1998) reports that consumers' stockpiling decisions depend on their household deal-proneness, inventory level, and the depth of discount. A study by Aggarwal and Vaidyanathan (1993) suggests that short-term promotions encourage stockpiling, but long-term promotions (e.g., manufacturer's coupons) do not. A study by Mela *et al.* (1998) indicates that increasing promotional activity over the years has cultivated consumers' tendency to purchase more during promotions and less during nonpromotional periods. This is consistent with findings on the impact of references prices on consumer stockpiling. Bell and Bucklin (1999) find that consumers stockpile if they perceive a price gain (which is more likely when there is a price promotion) and postpone a purchase if they perceive a loss. Krishnamurthi *et al.* (1992) also find that a price gain has a positive effect on purchase quantities. Slonim and Gabarino (2009) present empirical results indicating that observed purchase behavior is due to a combination of reference price effects and stockpiling. Huchzermeier *et al.* (2002) develop an empirical model to estimate demand for situations in which a product comes in different sizes and the retailer may offer price promotions at different times for different sizes. They also develop an approach to jointly optimize price promotions and inventory decisions.

Researchers report mixed results on whether stockpiling in response to promotions accelerates consumption; the effect appears to be category-specific (see Ailawadi and Neslin, 1998; Chandon and Wansink, 2002; Bell *et al.*, 2002; Ailawadi *et al.*, 2007). Researchers have also studied whether consumers' stockpiling during promotions is offset by lower post-promotion purchases. Hendel and Nevo (2003) report affirmative evidence. Studies on the long-term effects of promotions generally conclude that they have little or no persistent impact on sales volume in a mature market (cf. Dekimpe and Hanssens, 1999; Nijs *et al.*, 2001; Pauwels *et al.*, 2002).

2.3 Normative Models of Consumer or Retailer Response to Price Promotions

Here, we consider articles on buyers' responses to suppliers' explicit decisions to offer temporary discounts. In principle, the models described here could apply to either a customer purchasing from a retailer or a retailer purchasing from a manufacturer, assuming each of these dyads is operating in isolation. We do not discuss situations with price changes due to exogenous factors. Articles that also consider the downstream party's discounting decisions (where applicable) are discussed later.

Interestingly, there are two nearly distinct research streams on buyers' responses to suppliers' temporary discounts. Operations management articles typically assume that the timing of temporary discounts is random; they focus on determining the structure of the optimal inventory policy. See Silver *et al.* (1993), Gurnani (1996), Gavirneni (2004), Chaouch (2007), and Berling and Martinez-de-Albeniz (2011) and references in these articles for representative research. Marketing articles, on the other hand, typically pose the question as one of how the depth and frequency of discounts influence the buyer's ordering decisions, particularly stockpiling and overall purchases. Raju (1995) reviews the literature on this topic up to the early 1990s. See also Ho *et al.* (1998) and references therein.

2.4 Retailer's Discounting Policy

Normative models on retailers' discounting policies can be divided according to whether they consider reference price effects. We first discuss articles that do not consider these effects.

Blattberg *et al.* (1981) consider a model in which a retailer optimizes his ordering frequency and the magnitude of a discount to offer upon receipt of each order. There are two customer segments; only one segment stockpiles with the degree of stockpiling depending upon the customer's inventory holding cost and reservation price, and the offered discount price. In the model, the retail discounts are a means for the retailer to pass inventory holding costs to customers. Jeuland and Narasimhan (1985) study a variant of the Blattberg *et al.* model, allowing for greater customer heterogeneity. They primarily view discounts as a device for price discrimination, but they do derive the retailer's optimal depth of discount and discount frequency for their model. Bucovetsky (1983) studies a discrete-time equilibrium model in which the (monopolist) retailer optimizes the time series of prices and customers optimize how much to purchase in each period (including stockpiling). He characterizes the equilibrium pricing strategy under rational expectations and explores the dispersion of prices. Su (2010) considers a similar situation but with customers who differ with respect to consumption rate, valuation of the product, fixed cost of making a purchase, and inventory holding cost. He shows that the retailer's equilibrium strategy is either to offer a constant price or to offer a discount at constant intervals.

Sivakumar (1996) uses simulation to explore the effects of frequency and depth of promotion. He concludes that for high-priced brands, retailers should offer large discounts infrequently but for low-priced brands, it is better to offer small discounts frequently. Kurata and Liu (2006) compare an every-day-low-price policy and a high-low price policy in a two-stage supply chain where the cost of additional inventory needs due to promotions may be considered. They derive optimal promotion decisions under the assumption of a Markov-switching promotion regime.

We now turn to articles that consider the effects of reference prices. Achabal *et al.* (1990) develop an optimization model to determine the retailer's frequency and depth of discounts and inventory levels in normal and promotional weeks. In their model, demand is affected by both the offered price and the retailer's inventory level. The sales lift depends upon both the discount percentage and the time between discounts; the latter captures the effect of discounts on reference prices. Geng *et al.* (2010) consider a model in which the retailer chooses a discount frequency and depth of discount. The reference price in their model is the frequency-weighted mean of the offered prices, and their (linear) demand function differs depending upon whether the offered price is above or below the reference price.

Greenleaf (1995) develops a dynamic programming model to determine the optimal timing and depth of recurring promotions when demand is affected by asymmetric reference price effects. He models the reference price as an exponentially-weighted average of past prices plus a random error term, and allows certain parameters, such as production costs, to vary with time. Kopalle *et al.* (1996) present a dynamic programming model for the retailer's problem of setting prices over an infinite horizon when the customers' reference price is an exponentially weighted average of past prices and demand depends upon both the price itself and the direction and magnitude of the difference between the offered and reference prices. They show that the optimal pricing policy consists of cycles. More recent work under more general assumptions has been done by Popescu and Wu (2009) and in continuous-time settings by Fibich *et al.* (2003; 2005). See Arslan and Kachani (2011) for a survey of the broader literature on dynamic pricing with reference price effects.

There is also a stream of empirical research that explores the broader question of the retailer's choice of pricing strategy which includes, for example, the option between everyday low price and high-low pricing. Recent articles include Shankar and Bolton (2004), Nijs *et al.* (2007), and Ellickson and Misra (2008), which include many relevant references.

2.5 Retailer's Pass-Through Rate

The aforementioned articles on retailer discounting policies do not consider the effects of manufacturer trade discounts. Here, we discuss both empirical studies and normative models of the retailer's pass-through of manufacturer's promotions.

In empirical studies, Chevalier and Curhan (1976), Walters (1989), and Besanko *et al.* (2005) all find substantial variations in pass-through rates. They observed values less than 100%, as expected, but also rather surprising values of greater than 100%. There is empirical evidence that many factors positively affect retail pass-through. Most often cited are high market share, high revenue or profit contribution, high price elasticity, and private label status. Factors that negatively affect retailer pass-through are large package size and frequent wholesale deals. See Besanko *et al.* (2005), Pauwels (2007), Ailawadi and Harlam (2009), Nijs *et al.* (2010), and references in these articles for further details. Many of the considerations mentioned above are parameters or decisions in our model, and we will see many of the same effects entirely due to rational decision-making on the parts of the various parties.

Blattberg and Levin (1987) develop a predictive model that explicitly includes the effects of retail forward-buying and inventory held by both the retailer and consumers (which we also consider). They use the model to evaluate sales response and profitability of trade promotions for 10 items in six markets, and conclude that most trade promotions are not profitable. An empirical study by Walters and MacKenzie (1988) indicates that "loss-leader" promotions may improve retailer profits by increasing store traffic, but not through sales of promoted items.

Some researchers have studied the determinants of the retailer's pass-through rate using analytical models and suggest that the pass-through rate depends on characteristics of the consumers' purchasing behavior, such as consumers' willingness-to-pay and propensity to switch brands or stores, and the performance of the product, such as its profit margin and demand at the regular price. Tyagi (1999) offers differences in responsiveness of a firm's marginal revenue to a change in its price as an explanation for differences in pass-through rates. A profit-maximizing retailer equates marginal revenue with marginal cost, so when he receives a trade discount, he adjusts his retail price to match the marginal revenue with the reduced marginal cost. If the retailer's marginal revenue is very responsive (or not) to a change in retail price, the retailer must reduce its price by less (more) than the reduction in his marginal cost.

Kumar *et al.* (2001) suggest that the retailer offers a lower pass-through rate when many customers are willing to pay full price and have a high cost of searching for deals elsewhere. Besanko *et al.* (2005) and Moorthy (2005) examine both own-brand pass-through (i.e., retailer's pass-through of a trade discount on the same brand) and cross-brand pass-through (i.e., reduction in the retail price of competing brand(s)) and find significant own-brand pass-through. Their research generally indicates that brands with larger profit margins have higher pass-through rates and are more likely to have a positive pass-through. The question of cross-brand pass-through has generated considerable controversy. We refer interested readers to McAlister (2007) and Dubé and Gupta (2008) and references therein.

Our focus is on a single storable, consumable product, so our literature review on pass-through shares this focus. For a broader survey of recent articles on retailer pass-through, including settings with competing products and durable goods, see Sudhir and Gupta (2009).

2.6 *Other Related Articles*

Our research also falls under the very broad umbrellas of manufacturer trade promotions and retail promotions. In this chapter, we do not address the manufacturer's problem of determining his trade discount strategy, but our results have implications for this decision. The vast majority of articles on manufacturer trade promotions consider competition, multiple products, or other types of promotion or advertising (see, for example, Little, 1975; Lal, 1990; Neslin *et al.*, 1995; Lal *et al.*, 1996; Lal and Villas-Boas, 1996). We refer readers to Poddar and Donthu (2011) and Narasimhan (2009) for recent research surveys on trade promotions.

As we mentioned earlier, our research falls within the broad area of retail promotions. See van Heerde and Neslin (2008) for a tutorial-style survey of the research on sales promotion models, Blattberg *et al.* (1995) for a broad discussion of the effects of sales promotions, and Raju (1995) for a survey of theoretical (normative) models of sales promotions.

Finally, our research falls within the even broader area of pricing in marketing channels. Seminal work on game theoretic models involving manufacturer and retailer pricing was done by Lee and Staelin (1997). For a recent survey on these topics, see Sudhir and Datta (2009).

To the best of our knowledge, there is no research that considers (negative) brand equity effects when analyzing the retailer's optimal pass-through of trade discounts in situations where the retailer makes ordering (and thus also stockpiling) decisions, and where consumers also stockpile in response to temporary retail discounts. In our model, total demand is sensitive to the pattern of retail discounts, and unlike many models in the literature, we account for the reduction in the retailer's inventory holding costs that accrue from temporary retail discounts.

3 Problem Statement and Formulation

We model a retail channel consisting of a single manufacturer, a single retailer, and heterogeneous consumers. In our model, the retailer makes decisions about temporary retail discounts as well as a procurement plan (i.e., when and how much to order). Grocery chains and other similar retailers typically make these decisions on a periodic (e.g., weekly) basis, so we use a discrete time framework in which the basic time unit is chosen consistently with the periodicity of the discounting and procurement decisions. We assume that the basic time unit is determined by institutional arrangements arising from historical, competitive, and/or practical considerations, and therefore will not be influenced by modest changes in the retailer's discounting decisions. The retailer's pass-through rate is implicit in his discounting decisions. We elaborate on the retailer's problem later.

The manufacturer offers a constant regular wholesale price, w, but offers a per unit discount of Δ^M every T periods. We assume that w and T are given, but our analysis applies to any desired values of w and T. We initially assume that Δ^M is given, but we later examine how its value affects the retailer's decisions and the consequent pass-through rate. If one is interested in how the manufacturer's profit changes with Δ^M, it is straightforward to compute the manufacturer's profit for any given Δ^M, taking into account the optimal responses of the retailer (and consumers) that we derive in our analysis.

The total number of potential customers is Γ, and each customer consumes one unit of the product per period if he has a unit available. Customers are heterogeneous with respect to their reservation prices. The distribution of the customers' reservation prices in the absence of retail discounts is denoted by $F(\cdot)$, which we assume is continuous and differentiable; the density is $f(\cdot)$. We assume that if the retailer offers discounts, the entire distribution of reservation prices shifts to the left (downward) by an increment that depends upon the retailer's discounting pattern. The new distribution function of the customers' reservation prices is denoted by $\tilde{F}(\cdot)$, which we refer to as the *adjusted reservation price distribution*; $\tilde{f}(\cdot)$ is the p.d.f. We explain how the customers' reservation prices are affected by the retailer's discounts in Section 3.1.

In our model, all customers have the same holding cost, h per unit per period (incurred on average inventory). Each customer consumes one unit of the product per unit time if he has access to a unit whose *gross cost* (i.e., the purchase cost plus the cost of holding inventory from purchase to consumption) does not exceed his reservation price. If a customer does not have access to such a unit, he foregoes consumption. When the retailer offers a discount, customers may stockpile. So, at various points in time, customers may be depleting their stockpile, they may purchase one unit per period for immediate consumption, or they may not be consuming at all (if the gross cost is too high). We assume that the presence of customer stockpiles (where applicable) do not change the basic consumption rate. We also assume that customers shop frequently enough to take advantage of all discounts if they so choose. Many consumers purchase groceries frequently (e.g., weekly) and most retailers hold prices for nonperishable goods constant for a week (although they may differ from week to week), so our assumption allows us to capture the forward-buying behavior of customers reasonably accurately.

The retailer pays a fixed transportation cost K for each replenishment, and incurs an inventory holding cost of h_r per unit per period (incurred on average inventory). We assume that the regular price, p, is fixed. The retailer chooses the timing and magnitude (or synonymously, depth) of retail discounts and his procurement policy to optimize his profit (revenue less the sum of variable unit costs, transportation, and inventory holding costs) per unit time, taking into account the customers' response. We assume the retailer's discounting and replenishment pattern repeats after T periods, the periodicity of the manufacturer's discount. Within the T periods are two types of replenishment cycles. One type of cycle, which we call a *high* cycle, has a duration denoted by T^H and starts when the manufacturer offers a discount and the retailer places an order at the discounted price. The other type of cycle, which we call a *low* cycle, is a regular replenishment cycle with a duration denoted by T^L in which no discount is offered by the manufacturer, but the retailer may choose to offer a discount. There may be one or more low cycles following each high cycle, so we have $T = T^H + NT^L$ for some integer $N \geq 0$.

We assume that the retailer offers a single discount (perhaps zero) at the beginning of each replenishment cycle (upon receipt of a batch from the manufacturer). The discounts are $\Delta^H \geq 0$ in high cycles and $\Delta_i^L \geq 0$ in the ith succeeding low cycle, $\forall i \in \{1, \ldots, N\}$. It can be shown that if the retailer offers a discount only once during a replenishment cycle, it is optimal to offer it at the beginning of the cycle because customers then stockpile immediately, which leads to the greatest reduction in the retailer's inventory holding costs. By offering a discount, the retailer not only clears inventory more quickly, but he also attracts customers who would not purchase at the regular price, but he sacrifices some profit because customers' reservation prices decline. This is the retailer's fundamental tradeoff.

We analyze the problem as a Stackelberg game, with the retailer as the leader and customers as followers. In the next subsection, we analyze the customers' problem of when and how much to buy for a given discounting strategy chosen by the retailer.

3.1 *Customer's Problem*

Given the fixed regular price p, the retailer's decisions regarding cycle lengths T^H and T^L, and discount magnitudes Δ^H and $\Delta_i^L, i \in \{1 \cdots N\}$, as well as his own parameters, the customer seeks to maximize his net utility (utility from consumption less purchase costs and inventory holding costs), where the utility is equal to his reservation price. As mentioned earlier, Krishna and Johar (1996) suggest that the average of the prices offered by the retailer (across all periods) is a good estimate of the customer's reservation price. This can be translated into an effect on reservation prices as follows: each customer's reservation price declines from his original reservation price by $m \equiv \frac{\Delta^H + \sum_{i=1}^N \Delta_i^L}{T}$, which is the average depth of discount offered over the T-period cycle. (We also refer to m as the *loss of brand equity* due to retailer discounting.) Other researchers have tested other functional forms of the impact of discounts on reservation prices. Many of these expressions are quite complicated, so we elected to use a simple model that captures the first-order effects of discounts on reservation prices. Our key reason for using a continuous distribution of reservation prices is that we are aiming to analyze and optimize the retailer's optimal pass-through in the presence of (continuous) effects of discounts on reservation prices, and this would be difficult to accomplish using discrete reservation prices. Letting R denote the random variable for the adjusted reservation price and r the observed value, the distribution of R is $\tilde{F}(r) = F(r + m)$, and the density is $\tilde{f}(r) = \tilde{F}'(r)$.

Customers are strategic and may stockpile when the retailer offers a discount. A customer whose reservation price, r, is higher than the regular price, p, whom we refer to as a *regular* customer, stockpiles to satisfy his consumption for a duration Δ^C / h, where Δ^C is the discount offered in the current cycle. The duration Δ^C / h is the threshold at which he is indifferent between a unit purchased at the beginning of the replenishment cycle and held until it is consumed, and a unit purchased at the regular price for immediate consumption.

However, if Δ / h exceeds the duration of the current cycle, consumers may stockpile to satisfy demand only up to the end of the cycle if the retailer offers another discount at the beginning of the next cycle. Let T^C, Δ^C, and Δ^N represent the duration of the current cycle, the discount in the current cycle, and the discount in the next cycle, respectively. Then consumers do not stockpile for consumption in the next cycle if $\Delta^C - \Delta^N < hT^C$ (i.e., if the incremental discount offered in the current cycle is not large enough to offset the incremental holding cost due to an early purchase). Although there are instances in which consumers would be willing to stockpile to satisfy demand for longer than T^C, empirical research (e.g., Meyer and Assuncao, 1990) indicates that consumers stockpile less than their economic tradeoffs would dictate. Possible reasons include storage or cash flow limitations. As such, we assume that discounts satisfy $\Delta^C - \Delta^N < hT^C$ and leave other cases for future research. (Preliminary analysis indicates that these cases are complicated and do not offer transparent insights.)

Similarly, customers whose reservation price is below the regular price but above the discount price, whom we refer to as *discount* customers, will stockpile to satisfy their consumption for a duration of $[\Delta^C - (p - r)] / h$, which is always less than T^C if $\Delta^C - \Delta^N < hT^C$. Unlike the regular customers, after their stockpiles are depleted, the discount customers forego consumption until the next time the discount price is below their respective reservation prices.

3.2 *Retailer's Problem*

The manufacturer offers a trade discount every T periods, and within each such T-period cycle, the retailer has a high cycle in which the retailer receives a trade discount and N low cycles in which he does not. (One can think of "high" and "low" as the magnitude of the retailer's likely order quantities.) Let Π^H and Π_i^L represent the *total profit* in the high cycle and the ith low cycle, respectively. The retailer's objective is to maximize his profit per unit time:

$$\Pi = \left(\overset{H}{\Pi} + \sum_{i=1}^{N} \overset{L}{\Pi}_{i} \right) \Big/ T.$$

Recall that the retailer needs to choose Δ^H, Δ_i^L, T^H, T^L, and N. The values of T^H, T^L, and N are integral, but we treat the Δs as continuous variables.

We now derive the components of the retailer's objective function. We focus on the retailer's total profit in a high cycle first; the profit in low cycles is derived similarly.

We assume that $\Delta^H \leq hT^H$ and that $\Delta^L \leq hT^L$ for all low cycles which ensure that customers will not stockpile beyond the current cycle. (Larger discounts can be considered by increasing T^H or T^L, as appropriate.) If the retailer offers a discount $\Delta^H \leq hT^H$ at the beginning of a high cycle, then each *regular* customer stockpiles to satisfy consumption for a duration $\frac{\Delta^H}{h}$. Similarly, each *discount* customer stockpiles to satisfy consumption for a duration $[\Delta^H - (p - r)]/h$. Hence, the total quantity purchased at a discount at the beginning of a high cycle, denoted by d_1^H, is:

$$d_1^H = \Gamma \left[(1 - \tilde{F}(p)) \frac{\Delta^H}{h} + \int_{p-\Delta^H}^{p} \frac{\Delta^H - (p - r)}{h} \tilde{f}(r) dr \right]. \quad (1)$$

The first term is the number of customers with a reservation price higher than p multiplied by the quantity that each customer purchases at a discount of Δ^H. The second term is the total quantity stockpiled by customers whose reservation price is between $p - \Delta^H$ and p; it accounts for the fact that each such customer stockpiles a quantity that depends upon his reservation price.

Regular customers start to purchase just-in-time when their stockpiles are depleted. Therefore, the demand during the remainder of a high cycle, denoted by d_2^H, can be expressed as:

$$d_2^H = \Gamma \tilde{F}(p) \left(T^H - \frac{\Delta^H}{h} \right)^{+}. \quad (2)$$

The retailer's profit in a high cycle is the revenue from quantities purchased at a discount by both types of customers at the beginning of the cycle and from purchases by regular customers during the remainder of the cycle (if any), less variable unit costs, inventory holding costs, and the transportation cost per order. Thus, the retailer's total profit is:

$$\Pi^H(\Delta^H, \Delta^L_i, T^H, T^L, N) = (p - w - \Delta^H + \Delta^m)d^H_1$$

$$+ (p - w + \Delta^m)d^H_2 - hrT^Hd^H_2/2 - K, \quad (3)$$

where d^H_1 and d^H_2 are defined in (1) and (2), respectively. Total profit in the ith low cycle, Π^L_i, can be derived similarly. The total quantity purchased at a discount of Δ^L_i at the beginning of the ith low cycle is:

$$d^L_{1i} = \left[\frac{\Delta^L_i}{h}(1 - \tilde{F}(p)) + \int_{p-\Delta^L_i}^{p} \frac{\Delta^L_i - (p - r)}{h} \tilde{f}(r)dr \right] \Gamma. \quad (4)$$

The total demand during the remainder of the ith low cycle is:

$$d^L_{2i} = \left(T^L - \frac{\Delta^L_i}{h} \right)^+ \tilde{F}(p)\Gamma. \quad (5)$$

Therefore, the total profit in the ith low cycle is:

$$\Pi^L(\Delta^H, \Delta^L_i, T^H, T^L, N) = (p - w - \Delta^L_i)d^L_{1i} + (p - w)d^L_{2i}$$

$$- hrT^Ld^L_{2i}/2 - K, \quad (6)$$

where d^L_{1i} is defined in (4) and d^L_{2i} is defined in (5).

The special case where there are no regular customers is slightly different because the retailer holds no inventory. We omit details here, but they are available from the authors.

We next show how to solve the retailer's problem for fixed T^H, T^L, and N assuming (for analytic tractability) that the distribution of customers' reservation prices is uniform. With this, it is straightforward to enumerate combinations of T^H, T^L, and N satisfying $T^H + NT^L = T$, to solve the retailer's discounting and procurement problem for each, and to find the combination that leads to the best objective value. By enumerating different values of T^H, in particular, we are able to explore the interplay between the manufacturer's depth of trade discount and the retailer's propensity to stockpile, and their combined effect on the retailer's optimal discounting policy. We defer discussion of the T^H, T^L, and N values to Section 5. We discuss the general case with regular customers, and omit details on the simpler case with no regular customers.

4 Retailer's Problem for Uniform Reservation Prices

To gain some insight into the qualitative structure of the retailer's optimal strategy, we analyze the problem under the assumption that the customers' reservation prices follow a Uniform distribution on $[0, R]$. Note that the main effect of the "shape" of the distribution of reservation prices is on the partitioning of customers among three categories: (i) those whose reservation prices exceed the regular price; (ii) those whose reservation prices are between the discount price and the regular price; and (iii) those whose reservation price is below the discount price (and who will never buy). For different reservation price distributions, the relative sizes of these groups will differ, but the qualitative effects of the retailer's decisions remain the same irrespective of the distribution of reservation prices. Under the distributional assumption stated above, the retailer's profit functions in high and low cycles, respectively, can be rewritten as:

$$\Pi^H(\Delta^H, \Delta_i^L, T^H, T^L, N) = a^H(\Delta^H)^3 + b^H(\Delta^H)^2 + c^H\Delta^H + \gamma^H,$$

$$(7)$$

$$\Pi^L(\Delta^H, \Delta_i^L, T^H, T^L, N) = a^L(\Delta_i^L)^3 + b^L(\Delta_i^L)^2 + c^H\Delta_i^L + \gamma^L,$$

$$(8)$$

where $a^H = a^L = -0.5\frac{\Gamma}{h\overline{R}}$, $b^H = [0.5(p - w + \Delta^M) - (\overline{R} - p - m)^+]\frac{\Gamma}{h\overline{R}}$, $c^H = 0.5h_r T^H(\overline{R} - p - m)^+\frac{\Gamma}{h\overline{R}}$, $\gamma^H = (p - w + \Delta^M - 0.5h_r T^H)hT^H(\overline{R} - p - m)^+\frac{\Gamma}{h\overline{R}} - K$, $b^L = [0.5(p - w) - (\overline{R} - p - m)^+]\frac{\Gamma}{h\overline{R}}$, $c^L = 0.5h_r T^L(\overline{R} - p - m)^+$, and $\gamma^L = (p - w - 0.5h_r T^L)hT^L(\overline{R} - p - m)^+\frac{\Gamma}{h\overline{R}} - K$.

In the remainder of this section, we provide relevant structural results and a sketch of the solution procedure, deferring details to the appendices.

4.1 *Optimizing the* Δ *Values*

The optimization problem is:

$$\max_{\Delta^H, \Delta^L_1, \ldots, \Delta^L_N} \prod = \prod^H (\Delta^H) + \sum_{i=1}^{N} \prod^L (\Delta^L_i)$$

$$\text{subject to } 0 \leq \Delta^H \leq hT^H$$

$$0 \leq \Delta^L_i \leq hT^L, \ i = 1, \ldots, N.$$

The constraints ensure that customers do not stockpile more than they will consume before the retailer's next replenishment, which is consistent with our earlier assumptions.

Finding the optimal solution is complicated by the fact that each discount affects brand equity, and hence affects the profit in all cycles. Consequently, the retailer's objective is not always jointly concave in the Δ values. To deal with this complication, we solve the problem using a nested optimization approach. In the "inner" optimization, we optimize Δ^H and the Δ^L_is for a fixed (negative) brand equity effect, m (as a parameter). To do so, we first obtain results that allow us to jointly optimize the Δ^L_i values. These results allow us to collapse the Δ^L_i decisions into a single decision variable. With this, the problem of jointly optimizing Δ^H and the Δ^L_is for a fixed m reduces to a single-variable optimization problem. Then, in the "outer" optimization, we optimize m, utilizing expressions for the optimal Δ^H and Δ^L_is as functions of m. The shape of the objective as a function of m is fairly well behaved (in the worst case, a cubic function), but the solution depends upon the signs and relative values of the coefficients.

In what follows, we assume $N \geq 1$; the special case of $N = 0$ (i.e., no low cycles) is simpler and we omit details. We provide an overview of the key structural results that form the foundation for solution procedure(s), relegating the finer details and proofs to the Appendices.

4.1.1 *Inner Optimization Problem*

In the inner optimization problem, the sum of the discounts is fixed. The average discount per period is m, so the total discount across all periods in a cycle is mT. Therefore, for any fixed m, the problem can be written as:

$$\max_{\Delta^H,\Delta_1^L,\ldots,\Delta_N^L} \Pi = \prod^H(\Delta^H) + \sum_{i=1}^{N}\prod^L(\Delta_i^L)$$

$$\text{subject to } \Delta^H + \sum_{i=1}^{N}\Delta_i^L = mT$$

$$0 \leq \Delta^H \leq hT^H$$

$$0 \leq \Delta_i^L \leq hT^L, \ i = 1,\ldots,N.$$

Both Π^H and Π^L are cubic functions (of Δ^H and Δ^L, respectively) and differ only in their coefficients. Given that $c^H \geq 0$ and $c^L \geq 0$, Π^H and Π^L can take one of two possible functional forms: (i) convex increasing then concave (and unimodal) and (ii) strictly concave. Examples of the functional forms of Π^H are shown in Fig. 1, and the forms of Π^L are exactly the same. Although these two functional forms are unimodal, we cannot guarantee that the objective is jointly unimodal in the discounts. We can, however, obtain a partial characterization of the solution for the low cycles, as stated in Proposition 1 below.

Proposition 1. *Let $(\Delta^{H*}, \Delta_1^{L*},\ldots,\Delta_N^{L*})$ be the optimal solution to the retailer's problem in which there is a high cycle followed by N low cycles.*

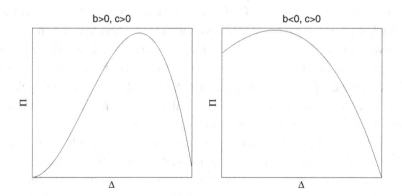

Fig. 1 Examples of Profit Functions for a Replenishment Cycle

For any low cycles i and j such that the discounts Δ_i^{L*} *and* Δ_j^{L*} *are positive,*
$\Delta_i^{L*} = \Delta_j^{L*}(= \Delta^{L*})$.

Proof. See Appendix A.

The intuition underlying the result is as follows. For some combinations of parameter values, Π^L may be convex for small Δ^L. Because we wish to maximize the objective in the N-dimensional space of Δ_i^L values, boundary solutions (i.e., with one or more Δ_i^L values equal to zero) may be optimal. On the other hand, when Π^L is concave increasing, equal positive values of Δ_i^L are optimal. For any fixed number, n, of positive Δ_i^Ls that are equal to each other, optimizing the Δ_i^L values reduces to a single variable problem. Note also that $\Delta^H = mT - \sum_{i=1}^{N} \Delta_i^L$, so the problem of jointly optimizing all of the Δ values for a given n remains a single variable problem, but we need to consider the cases of $n = 0, \ldots, N$ positive Δ_i^L values.

Intuitively, the convexity of Π^L (as function of Δ^L) below a threshold can be explained by the fact that the number of units sold at a discount is convex increasing (roughly quadratic) as the discount increases. Not only do customers who were already purchasing choose to buy more, but customers who did not purchase at smaller discounts now choose to purchase. The retailer thus sells more units at a discount when offering one large discount than when offering two smaller discounts whose sum is equal to the single large discount. Therefore, holding the loss of brand equity constant, if the volume increase outweighs the reduction in the unit profit margin, the retailer may be better off offering a mix of large and zero discounts instead of equalizing discounts across low cycles. Therefore, when Π_i^L has a convex region, the discounts in the low cycles are not necessarily equal to each other despite the fact that we have the same economic parameters in all low cycles. On the other hand, in the absence of the brand equity effect, the retailer faces independent and identical decisions in each low cycle and therefore offers the same discount in all low cycles.

To summarize, for a fixed m, we can reduce the problem of finding Δ^H and the Δ_i^L values to a unidimensional problem by utilizing the fact that all positive discounts in low cycles are equal. If $b^L < 0$, then Π^L is initially convex and then concave, and we need to solve problems with

$n = 1, \ldots, N$ positive discounts and choose the best one. If $b^L \geq 0$, then Π^L is concave, hence we only need to solve the inner problem with $n^* = N$ positive discounts.

For a fixed n, we show in Appendix A that the retailer's objective as a function of the (positive) discount in the applicable low cycles has one of four forms: (i) convex increasing; (ii) convex decreasing and then increasing; (iii) initially concave then convex; (iv) concave decreasing then convex. Which form is pertinent depends upon whether certain coefficients, which can be computed from the problem data, are positive or negative.

4.1.2 *Outer Optimization Problem: Optimizing* **m**

Here, we analyze the outer problem, optimizing m for a fixed n, and provide an overview of properties of the objective function that enable us to identify the optimal solution. Details appear in Appendix B. The relevant functions are cubic or quadratic functions, so the optimal solution is either a stationary point or a boundary solution with Δ^L at its lower or upper limit. The characteristics of these functions (e.g., whether the cubic functions are initially concave then convex or the reverse, and whether the quadratic functions are convex or concave) depend on the coefficients which, in turn, depend upon the problem parameters.

We refer to the coefficients as $\alpha_1, \alpha_2, \alpha_3$, and α_4 and the objective function has the form $\alpha_1 m^3 + \alpha_2 m^2 + \alpha_3 m + \alpha_4$. The expressions for the coefficients can be found in Appendix B. Under the strategy ($\Delta^H = mT$, $\Delta^L = 0$), α_1 is a constant and the other coefficients are linear functions of Δ^M. Under the strategy ($\Delta^{L*} > 0$, $\Delta^H = mT - n\Delta^{L*}$), α_1 is again a constant, α_2 is a linear function of Δ^M, and α_3 and α_4 are both equal to zero. The "shapes" of the functions depend upon the signs (negative, zero, or positive) of the coefficients. Typically, α_1, the coefficient on the cubic term, is negative, and it primarily captures the effect of discounting on overall revenue. If $\alpha_2 > 0$ at a given value of Δ^M, then, roughly speaking, the retailer gains more from selling to discount customers than he loses due to the reduced margin on units sold to regular customers. If $\alpha_3 > 0$ at a given value of Δ^M, then the retailer's savings in inventory

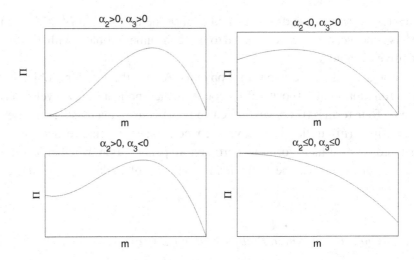

Fig. 2 Retailer's Objective as a Function of m

costs from discounting is greater than the reduction in profit due to the reduction in the number of regular customers owing to the (negative) brand equity effect. If α_2 is positive and α_3 is negative (or the reverse), then the retailer faces competing forces when optimizing his discounts. If both α_2 and α_3 are negative, then the retailer has little incentive to offer discounts at the given value of Δ^M. In most cases, the stationary point can be expressed in closed form, but sometimes a unidimensional numerical search is required. Four typical shapes of the objective function are shown in Fig. 2.

Combining the facts that the coefficients change with Δ^M and that the retailer's profit functions are quadratic or cubic functions of m, we can infer that the optimal value of m may not change smoothly as Δ^M changes. In particular, it is possible for the optimal retailer discount to be zero for small values of Δ^M, eventually becoming positive at some threshold, and then increasing in a convex, concave, or even a discontinuous fashion as Δ^M increases further, due to the the manner in which Δ^M affects α_2 and α_3. So the analytical results indicate there may be threshold effects, and that the pass-through percentage may be increasing, decreasing, or even fluctuating as a function of Δ^M. We observe all of these phenomena in our numerical study.

The model in this section includes the negative effects of discounting on brand equity. We next present analysis for the case in which retail discounting does not affect brand equity.

4.2 Model without a Brand Equity Effect

The retailer's objective has the same general form here as that in the model with a brand equity effect except that the distribution of the customers' reservation prices is the unadjusted distribution, $f(\cdot)$, instead of the adjusted distribution, $\tilde{f}(\cdot)$. The parameters of the objective functions in (7) and (8) become: $a^H = a^L = -0.5\frac{\Gamma}{h\overline{R}}$, $b^H = \left[0.5(p - w + \Delta^M) - (\overline{R} - p)\right]\frac{\Gamma}{h\overline{R}}$, $c^H = 0.5h_r T^H(\overline{R} - p)\frac{\Gamma}{h\overline{R}}$, $\gamma^H = (p - w + \Delta^M - 0.5h_r T^H)hT^H(\overline{R} - p)\frac{\Gamma}{h\overline{R}} - K$, $b^L = \left[0.5(p - w) - (\overline{R} - p)\right]\frac{\Gamma}{h\overline{R}}$, $c^L = 0.5h_r T^L(\overline{R} - p)$, and $\gamma^L = (p - w - 0.5h_r T^L)hT^L(\overline{R} - p)\frac{\Gamma}{h\overline{R}} - K$.

When there is no brand equity effect, the discounts in the high and low cycles have no interactions, so the retailer can maximize Π^H and Π^L independently. Π^H and Π^L are unimodal in Δ^H and Δ^L, respectively, over the relevant range, and both have a local maximum defined by the corresponding stationary point. The optimal discount in a high cycle is $\Delta^{H*} = \frac{-b^H - \sqrt{b^{H^2} - 4a^H c^H}}{2a^H}$ and the optimal discount in a low cycle is $\Delta^{L*} = \frac{-b^L - \sqrt{b^{L^2} - 4a^L c^L}}{2a^L}$.

Observe that b^H is linearly increasing in Δ^M, a^H is a negative constant, and c^H is a positive constant. So from the expression for Δ^{H*}, we can see that the retailer's discount in a high cycle is strictly increasing in Δ^M.

5 Numerical Study

In this section, we report on optimal solutions for problems covering a wide range of parameter combinations. We focus on how various problem parameters, especially the manufacturer's discount, affect the retailer's pass-through and on situations with a brand equity effect. The relationships are much simpler in the absence of a brand equity effect.

The problem parameters are: $\Gamma = 1,000$; $\overline{R} = 3$ and 6; $p = 0.25\overline{R}$, $0.5\overline{R}$, $0.75\overline{R}$, and $0.95\overline{R}$; $w = 0.4p$, $0.6p$, $0.8p$, and $0.9p$; $T = 4, 12$, and 24; $h_r = 0.3w/52$, $w/52$, and $4w/52$; $h = 0.02p$, $0.05p$, $0.3p$, and

$0.5p$; and $K = 100$. These parameter combinations yield a total of 1, 152 instances.

The choices of $\overline{R}$ are arbitrary, as they are simply scale parameters, but we chose the other parameters for the following reasons:

- The three values of p represent situations with 75%, 50%, 25%, and 5% regular customers, respectively, which covers a wide range of willingness-to-pay scenarios vis-a-vis the regular price.
- The four ratios of w to p capture the typical range of retail margins for consumable goods.
- The three values of the customer's holding cost rate (h) represent situations in which the customer will stockpile one unit (one week's usage) for discounts of 2%, 5%, 30%, and 50%, respectively. At the low end of this spectrum, the customer is quite prone to stockpiling whereas at the high end, the customer is reluctant to stockpile.
- The four values of the retailer's holding cost rate (h_r) reflect annual holding cost rates of 30% (typical for nonperishable foods), 100% (appropriate for frozen food), and 400% (appropriate if products have short life cycles or retailer shelf space is extremely limited).
- The values of T are chosen so that several combinations of T^H, T^L, and N are feasible.
- The value of K is chosen so that the retailer's economic order quantity ranges from one week of supply to 22 weeks of supply. We use only a single K value because the variation in h_r yields a wide range of values for the retailer's economic order quantity.

As mentioned earlier, we find the retailer's optimal cycle lengths, T^{H*} and T^{L*}, and the optimal number of low cycles, N^*, within each T-period trade discount cycle by enumeration. Under the framework of integral cycle lengths, we enumerate T^H in $[1, \ldots, T]$; then we find the set of integer divisors of $T - T^H$ (denoted d^N). We enumerate N in d^N and for each relevant N, the length of each low cycle, T^L, is set equal to $(T - T^H)/N$. We use the results in Proposition 2 (see Appendix C), which shows that the retailer offers the same or higher discount if he chooses a longer ordering interval. This intuitive result reduces the number of alternatives that we need to evaluate.

For each parameter combination, we determine the retailer's optimal response for Δ^M equal to $0.1w, 0.2w, \ldots, 0.9w$. Values at the upper end of this range are not common in practice, but we include them for completeness. In the next subsection, we analyze how the manufacturer's discount affects the retailer's optimal discount and ordering schedule, and in the subsequent subsection, we examine under what parameter combinations the retailer tends to pass a large (or small) proportion of the manufacturer's discount on to consumers.

5.1 How Δ^M Affects the Retailer's Discount and Ordering Schedule

The analytical results in the previous section raised the possibility that the retailer's discount in the high cycles (and therefore also the pass-through rate) may increase, decrease, or fluctuate as Δ^M increases. We categorize the observed relationships into six patterns: (i) increasing; (ii) decreasing; (iii) unimodal with a local minimum; (iv) unimodal with a local maximum; (v) fluctuating; and (vi) no change. Out of 1, 152 instances, the number of instances that fall into patterns (i) through (vi) are 467, 39, 15, 126, 36, and 469, respectively. The proportional split of problem instances among the patterns is largely a consequence of our choice of parameters. Our main concern was to have enough instances so that we could relate the patterns to systematic characteristics of the mix of problem parameters. Below, we discuss these relationships.

In some instances with pattern (i), Δ^{H*} is *strictly* monotonically increasing in Δ^M over the entire range of Δ^M values that we considered. These situations tend to arise when the retailer is already offering a discount even in the absence of a manufacturer discount. If the manufacturer offers a discount, the retailer sometimes chooses to increase his discount. If he does so, the discount tends to increase monotonically with the manufacturer's discount, at least up to some threshold where it is no longer advantageous for the retailer. This pattern arises commonly when the retailer has small regular demand (in which case the reduction in profit on sales to regular customers is small), the consumers have a small holding cost (so small changes in the discount can induce substantial additional stockpiling by discount customers, which represents an increase in demand for the retailer), and the manufacturer discounts infrequently (so the retailer stockpiles large quantities and therefore has a greater incentive to clear inventory by discounting).

In other instances where pattern (i) arises, Δ^{H*} is a discontinuous function of Δ^M: it remains zero until Δ^M reaches a threshold, and then jumps from zero to a positive value at the threshold, and may or may not increase further beyond the threshold. The threshold effect is due to the fact that for some parameter combinations, the retailer's objective is a cubic function of the discount, and Δ^M affects the shape of the cubic function. Up to some threshold value of Δ^M the optimum is zero, but when Δ^M reaches the threshold, the α coefficients in the retailer's objective function change enough to alter the shape of the function so that the optimum shifts to a positive value. These instances tend to arise when the retailer has small regular demand and the manufacturer discounts frequently, so the retailer does not bear much expense in holding inventory and therefore has little incentive to offer discounts. The retailer offers a zero discount unless Δ^M is large enough to make it worthwhile to switch to a strategy that focuses on greater penetration among the discount customers. When the retailer makes this switch, the high trade discount provides him an adequate margin despite the deep discounts offered to his customers.

In pattern (ii), Δ^{H*} is nonincreasing in Δ^M and strictly decreasing for at least one Δ^M in the range of values that we consider. In the problem instances that give rise to this pattern, the manufacturer offers a trade discount frequently and the the retailer typically has a large regular demand and moderate holding costs. When the manufacturer offers a small trade discount, the retailer must trade off the benefits of inventory reduction (by inducing customer stockpiling) with the loss of revenue from reduced brand equity. The retailer's moderate holding costs combined with frequent trade discounts give him a fairly small incentive to clear inventory. On the other hand, the reduction in profit on sales to the large portion of customers who would have been willing to pay full price can be substantial. The retailer may choose to offer a small discount but is not inclined to discount very deeply. When the manufacturer offers a large trade discount, the discount subsidizes the retailer's cost of holding inventory (which is still modest due to the retailer's moderate holding cost and the frequent trade discounts). The retailer chooses to stockpile and then sell these items at (close to) the regular price. Hence, the retailer decreases his discount as Δ^M increases.

In pattern (iii), the retailer's discount first decreases in Δ^M (for the same reasons noted for pattern (ii)) and then increases. The primary difference between problem instances that result in pattern (iii) versus pattern (ii) is that the retailer has smaller regular demand in the former, so for sufficiently large values of Δ^M, the retailer is willing to forego some of the profit margin on sales to regular customers in exchange for the opportunity to sell to the much larger number of customers who are willing to purchase only at a relatively deep discount.

In pattern (iv), the retailer's discount initially increases and then decreases as the manufacturer's discount increases. In the problem instances that generate this pattern, the manufacturer discounts infrequently. As Δ^M increases, the retailer increases his stockpiling and simultaneously increases his discount to transfer part or all of his stockpile to customers. For a sufficiently high Δ^M, the retailer opts to purchase only when the manufacturer offers a discount. For Δ^M above this threshold, the incremental trade discount provides a subsidy for the retailer's cost of holding inventory, so the retailer's need to discount declines. If the subsidy is sufficiently high, the retailer prefers to reduce his discount to recapture sales at the full price. This occurs because a reduction in his discount increases the proportion of regular customers, who purchase to satisfy consumption throughout the entire cycle, whereas discount customers purchase to satisfy consumption for only a portion of the cycle. Furthermore, due to the high trade discount, full-price sales provide the retailer a substantial net margin. Thus, for sufficiently high Δ^M, the retailer uses a different discounting strategy than when Δ^M is small, and this causes the retail discounts to first increase and then decrease as the trade discount increases.

The fluctuations in retailer's discount in pattern (v) as Δ^M increases are due to the requirement that the retailer's cycle lengths be integral. In the instances leading to pattern (v), the retailer has a large regular demand and high holding costs. Because the retailer must hold inventory for the regular customers (who purchase just-in-time during the latter part of the cycle) and his high holding costs make it costly to do so, the retailer couples increases in stockpiling with increases in the discount. However, due to integrality of cycle lengths, as Δ^M increases, T^{H*} does not strictly increase. For values of Δ^M at which T^{H*} increases, the retailer's pass-through increases as well; for values of Δ^M at which T^{H*} is unchanged, the retailer's discount decreases for the same reason as noted for pattern (ii). As such, we attribute these fluctuations to "rounding error": if the retailer could choose nonintegral cycle lengths, the discounts would likely change more smoothly.

Among instances leading to pattern (vi), Δ^{H*} is constant at zero as Δ^M increases over its range in 398 out of 469 instances and is constant at a positive value as Δ^M increases in 71 out of 469 instances. Situations with $\Delta^* = 0$ tend to arise when customers have a large holding cost, the retailer has low holding cost and moderate to large regular demand, and manufacturer discounts frequently. Under these conditions, the retailer needs to hold inventory for the regular customers, but it is relatively inexpensive for him to do so because he has a low holding cost rate and does not need to stockpile large quantities because the manufacturer discounts frequently. Because customers have a high holding cost, significant discounts would be needed to induce the relatively small number of discount customers to purchase very much. None of these factors weighs in favor of the retailer offering discounts.

Two different combinations of factors lead to situations in which the retailer offers a positive discount but does not increase it as Δ^M increases. The first combination of factors is a very large proportion of regular customers and a very small customer holding cost. The retailer offers a small discount in all of these instances but can generate considerable sales to discount customers due to their small holding cost. The retailer does not increase his discount as Δ^M increases because he would have to sacrifice considerable profit on sales to regular customers without compensating profit from discount customers. The second combination of factors is a small proportion of regular customers and a large initial profit margin $(p - w)$. In these circumstances, the retailer chooses deep discounts, foregoing the small volume of potential full-price sales, in order to reach a substantial portion of the discount customers who will not otherwise buy. The large initial profit margin allows the retailer to offer deep discounts. The manufacturer's trade discount causes the retailer to purchase only when trade discounts are offered, but because the retailer would offer deep discounts even in the absence of a trade discount, an increase in the trade discount is insufficient incentive for the retailer to offer even deeper discounts. (Beyond a threshold, additional retail discounts only decrease per-unit margin while not increasing unit sales.)

Although the retailer's optimal discount may change in different ways as Δ^M increases, the retailer's ordering schedule changes in a consistent way: the retailer chooses larger values of T^H, and in concert, stockpiles more. The number of low cycles decreases correspondingly, but the lengths of the low cycles remain constant in the vast majority of problem instances and nearly constant (i.e., a mix of two consecutive integer values) in the rest of the instances. Recall that T^H and T^L need to be integers in our model. So, the differences that we observe can be viewed as "rounding error" due to the integrality constraints; the retailer probably would have chosen equal nonintegral values of T^L if he could do so.

We now turn to a discussion of a more commonly-reported metric, the pass-through rate.

5.2 *Retailer's Pass-Through Rate*

The retailer's pass-through rate is traditionally defined as the ratio of the retailer's discount to the manufacturer's discount. Figure 3 shows the cumulative percentage of problem instances with 0, 25%, 50%, 75%, 100%, 200%, 300%, 400%, and over 400% pass-through rates for $\Delta^M = 0.1w, 0.3w, 0.5w, 0.7w$, and $0.9w$. As shown in the figure, for all Δ^M values, roughly 40% of instances have a zero pass-through rate and the majority have pass-through rates below 25%. Thus, broadly speaking, pass-through rates are quite low, but interestingly, a meaningful portion (up to 20%) of instances have pass-through rates above 100% when Δ^M is small. The range and mix of pass-through rates arising in our numerical study (based on our analytical model) is consistent with what researchers have reported in empirical studies.

In a small portion of problem instances, the pass-through rate is as high as 300% or 400%. In these instances, the retailer's profit margin is high in the absence of a trade discount, but the fraction of customers who are willing to pay the regular price is low. So the retailer can "afford" to implement a high pass-through rate because he can maintain a relatively large net margin while simultaneously reaching customers who are unwilling to pay an amount close to the regular price. We observe analogous situations in

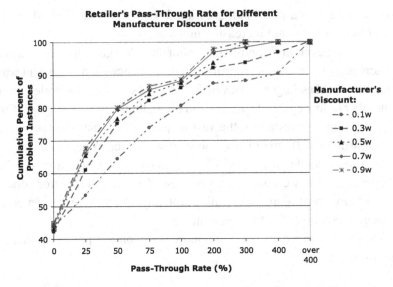

Fig. 3 Distribution of Retailer's Pass-Through Rates for Various Trade Discount Levels

practice for products with frequent "buy one get one free" offers: retail margins are quite high at the regular price and not many customers are willing to pay the full price, so manufacturers invest a lot of money to induce retailers to offer deeply-discounted promotional prices.

In our model framework, the retailer may offer a discount even in the absence of a trade discount. Thus far in this section, we have reported on the traditional pass-through rate metric, but a more accurate metric would be the ratio of the *incremental* discount that the retailer offers due to the trade discount to the trade discount. Figure 4 shows the cumulative percentage of problem instances with −5%, 0%, 10% 15%, 20%, 25%, 30%, 40%, 50%, and 100% incremental pass-through rates.

At all discount levels that we consider, the incremental pass-through rate is zero or negative in about 50% of the problem instances, and problem instances with incremental pass-through rates of more than 10% are rare. For example, when the trade discount is 50% of the wholesale price, the retailer passes through 20% or more of the discount in only about 1% of problem instances. Although the overall incremental pass-through rates are quite low overall, interestingly, they are higher for large trade discounts than they are for small trade discounts; the opposite relationship applies to the

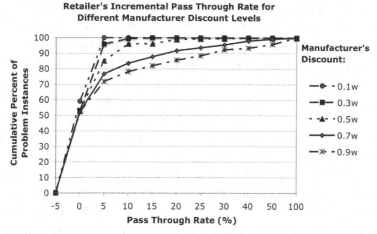

Fig. 4 Distribution of Retailer's Incremental Pass-Through Rates for Various Trade Discount Levels

traditional pass-through rate. These results suggest that manufacturers face extremely difficult tradeoffs: they can keep trade discounts low (or zero) and get minimal reaction from the retailer, or offer very large trade discounts to get a meaningful incremental reaction. These results also raise the question of appropriate pass-through metrics to ensure alignment with the manufacturer's goals.

As expected, both the traditional and the incremental pass-through rates generally decline as the trade discount increases, modulo the effects of the constraints that T^H and T^L be integral, as mentioned in the last subsection. This is true even in cases where Δ^{H*} increases as Δ^M increases, because the former almost always increases more slowly than the latter, and it increases much more slowly or declines for sufficiently large values of Δ^M.

6 Conclusions

In this chapter, we investigate the retailer's optimal pass-through of manufacturer trade discounts. We study a scenario with three types of parties: a manufacturer, a retailer, and customers. The manufacturer offers a constant regular wholesale price but offers periodic trade discounts to the retailer in the hope of achieving higher market penetration and possibly earning a higher profit. The retailer offers a constant regular price and decides the timing and depth of discounts, which may coincide with trade discounts but may also be offered at other times. The retailer chooses his ordering and discounting patterns to maximize his profit per unit time, and stockpiles when the manufacturer offers a discount if the benefit of stockpiling outweighs the cost of holding inventory. Customers, who are heterogeneous with respect to their reservation prices, stockpile when the retailer offers a discount. They wish to consume the product at a constant rate but purchase only if their gross cost — the actual purchase price plus the cost of holding the item until it is consumed — does not exceed their reservation price. It is well known that retail discounts erode brand equity and therefore also reservation prices; we include this effect in our model.

To the best of our knowledge, our study is the first to incorporate the effects of retailer and consumer stockpiling, along with the (negative) effects on brand equity of retail discounts, in a retailer's decision model for choosing discount and ordering patterns when a manufacturer offers periodic trade discounts. We fully characterize the retailer's optimal discount policy for a given ordering schedule, and we use this to determine a jointly optimal discount and ordering plan, assuming that orders can be placed at discrete points in time (e.g., weekly). Our analytical results and numerical study provide several important managerial insights, including:

- The consideration of brand equity effects (due to retailer discounting) may lead to threshold effects: the manufacturer may need to offer a discount above a threshold before there is any reaction on the part of the retailer. We show that the threshold effect is due to the brand equity effect; it does not arise when only stockpiling is considered.
- Our results indicate that the retailer's discount may not be monotonic in the trade discount. Thus, different depths of the manufacturer's trade discount may lead to distinctly different pricing and consumer targeting strategies by the retailer.
- The retailer has a greater incentive to offer a higher (absolute) pass-though when the fraction of customers who are willing to pay full price is small, the retailer has high to moderate holding costs, customers have low to moderate holding costs, and the manufacturer discounts infrequently. Generally speaking, a combination of favorable factors is needed for the retailer to choose a high pass-through rate. It is important

for manufacturers to consider the complex interactions among factors that affect retailer's discounting choice when designing a trade discount plan.

- Although pass-through rates measured by the traditional metric (retailer's discount divided by the manufacturer's discount) tend to be modest, the incremental pass-through rates (retailer's additional discount beyond his normal discount divided by the manufacturer's discount) are even smaller — commonly zero or negative — and rarely are they greater than 10% in our numerical study. Interestingly, (traditional) pass-through rates tend to be higher for small manufacturer discounts (10% or 20% of the wholesale price) but incremental pass-through rates are higher when manufacturer discounts are high. These results raise the question how to choose pass-through metrics to provide incentives that are aligned with the manufacturer's goals.

We close this section with a comparison of results from our analytical model and numerical study with empirical findings in the literature. Although virtually all empirical studies have been conducted in competitive settings with multiple products and multiple retailers, overall, our analytical and numerical results are very consistent with what the empirical studies indicate. First, several studies (Chintagunta, 2002; Besanko *et al.*, 2005; and Nijs, 2010) report negative pass-through rates (i.e., retailers raising the regular price when the manufacturer offers a trade discount). In a study focused on other aspects of retail pricing, Chintagunta (2002) observed a negative correlation between wholesale and retail prices for one of five products that he studied at one retail chain. The product happened to have the highest price, highest retail margin, and smallest volume in its category. He conjectured that retailers could be raising prices during manufacturer promotions to maximize profits from loyal customers. Besanko *et al.* (2005) and Nijs (2010) also found negative pass-through in some instances, but did not provide details on characteristics of the pertinent products nor explanations for the negative pass-through rates. Our numerical study includes problem instances with relatively few customers who are willing to pay the full price. In these circumstances, the retailer's optimal policy is to offer a large discount when the trade discount is small because it is more profitable to target the large number of customers who are only willing to purchase a discount. On the other hand, when the manufacturer's trade discount is large, the retailer uses a completely different strategy and offers zero or a small discount, targeting the customers who are willing to pay the full price. In our model, the regular price is fixed and we assume that discounts are nonnegative, so negative absolute pass-through rates do not arise. But problem instances in which retailer switches strategies as described above have similar characteristics to the situation in which Chintagunta (2002) conjectured that a negative pass-through was occurring.

Results from empirical studies also indicate that pass-through rates are high when demand is elastic (Nijs *et al.*, 2010; Meza and Sudhir, 2006; Walters, 1989), and that the retailer offers a higher pass-through in response to trade deals when the manufacturer discounts infrequently (Walters, 1989; Nijs *et al.*, 2010). Our analytical results are consistent with both of these findings. The impact of demand elasticity is not surprising, but our analytical model explains why the frequency of trade discounts matters when both the retailer and customers stockpile: if trade discounts are infrequent, the retailer stockpiles more, but in turn needs to offer a deeper discount to reduce his inventory holding costs. Also, Nijs *et al.* (2010) found the retail pass-through to be higher for products with larger package sizes. Our results also suggest that retailers tend to offer a high pass-through when the product has a high holding cost; thus pass-through rates for bulky products are higher than for small products with the same unit cost.

These observations indicate that our analytical model, although simple, helps to explain phenomena observed in practice, including negative pass-through rates for which few compelling explanations have been offered in the literature. Further research is needed to study these issues in more realistic contexts with multiple products, competition between retailers and between manufacturers, other types of promotions, and other factors.

Bibliography

Achabal, D. D., McIntyre, S. and Smith, S. A. (1990). Maximizing profits from periodic department store promotions, *Journal of Retailing* **66**, 4, pp. 383–407.
Aggarwal, P. and Vaidyanathan, R. (2003). Use it or lose it: Purchase acceleartion effects of time-limited promotions, *Journal of Consumer Behavior* **2**, 4, pp. 393–403.
Ailawadi, K. L., Gennik, K., Lutzky, C. and Neslin, S. A. (2007). Decomposition of the sales impact of promotion-induced stockpiling, *Journal of Marketing Research* **44**, 3, pp. 450–468.

Ailawadi, K. L. and Harlam, B. A. (2009). Findings — retailer promotion pass-through: A measure, its magnitude, and its determinants, *Marketing Science* **28**, 4, pp. 782–791.

Ailawadi, K. L. and Neslin, S. A. (1998). The effect of promotion on consumption: Buying more and consuming it faster, *Journal of Marketing Research* **35**, 3, pp. 390–398.

Arslan, H. and Kachani, S. (2010). Dynamic pricing under consumer reference price effects, in *Wiley Encyclopedia of Operations Research and Management Science*, J. J. Cochran (ed.) Wiley, New York.

Assuncao, J. L. and Meyer, R. J. (1993). The rational effect of price promotions sales and consumption, *Management Science* **39**, 5, pp. 517–535.

Beasley, F. M. (1998). An examination of stockpiling behavior in response to price deals, *Academy of Marketing Studies Journal* **2**, 1, pp. 23–34.

Bell, D. R. and Bucklin, R. E. (1999). The role of internal reference points in the category purchase decision, *Journal of Consumer Research* **26**, 2, pp. 128–143.

Bell, D. R., Chiang, J. and Padmanabhan, V. (1999). The decomposition of promotional response: An empirical generalization, *Marketing Science* **18**, 4, pp. 504–526.

Bell, D. R., Iyer, G. and Padmanabhan, V. (2002). Price competition under stockpiling and flexible consumption, *Journal of Marketing Research* **39**, 3, pp. 292–303.

Bell, D. R. and Lattin, J. M. (2000). Looking for loss aversion in scanner panel data: The confounding effect of price response heterogeneity, *Marketing Science* **19**, 2, pp. 185–200.

Berling, P. and Martinez-de-Albeniz, V. (2011). Optimal inventory policies when purchase price and demand are stochastic, *Operations Research* **59**, 1, pp. 109–124.

Besanko, D., Dubé, J.-P. and Gupta, S. (2005). Own-brand and cross-brand retail pass-through, *Marketing Science* **24**, 1, pp. 123–137.

Blattberg, R. C., Briesch, R. and Fox, E. J. (1995). How promotions work, *Marketing Science* **14**, 3, pp. G122–G132.

Blattberg, R. C., Eppen, G. D. and Lieberman, J. (1981). Theoretical and empirical evaluation of price deals for consumer nondurables, *Journal of Marketing* **45**, 1, pp. 116–129.

Blattberg, R. C. and Levin, A. (1987). Modeling the effectiveness and profitability of trade promotions, *Marketing Science* **6**, 2, pp. 124–146.

Briesch, R. A., Krishnamurthi, L., Mazumdar, T. and Raj, S. (1997). A comparative analysis of reference price models, *Journal of Consumer Research* **24**, 2, pp. 202–214.

Bucovetsky, S. (1983). Price disperson and stockpiling by consumers, *Review of Economic Studies* **50**, 3, pp. 443–465.

Chandon, P. and Wansink, B. (2002). When are stockpiled products consumed faster? A convenience salience framework of postpurchase consumption incidence and quantity, *Journal of Marketing Research* **39**, 3, pp. 321–335.

Chaouch, B. A. (2007). Inventory control and periodic price discounting campaigns, *Naval Research Logistics* **54**, 1, pp. 94–108.

Chevalier, M. and Curhan, R. (1976). Retail promotions as a function of trade promotions: A descriptive analysis, *Sloan Management Review* **18**, 1, pp. 19–32.

Currin, I. S. and Schneider, L. G. (1991). A taxonomy of consumer purchase strategies in a promotion intensive environment, *Marketing Science* **10**, 2, pp. 91–110.

Dekimpe, M. G. and Hanssens, D. M. (1999). Sustained spending and persistent response: A new look at long-term marketing profitability, *Journal of Marketing Research* **36**, 4, pp. 397–412.

Dubé, J.-P. and Gupta, S. (2008). Cross-brand pass-through in supermarket pricing, *Marketing Science* **27**, 3, pp. 324–333.

Ellickson, P. B. and Misra, S. (2008). Supermarket pricing strategies, *Marketing Research* **27**, 5, pp. 811–828.

Fibich, G., Gavious, A. and Lowengart, O. (2003). Explicit solutions of optimization models and differential games with nonsmooth (asymmetric) reference-price effects, *Operations Research* **51**, 5, pp. 811–828.

Fibich, G., Gavious, A. and Lowengart, O. (2005). The dynamics of price elasticity of demand in the presence of reference price effects, *Journal of the Academy of Marketing Science* **33**, 1, pp. 66–78.

Gabarino, E. and Slonim, R. (2003). Interrelationships and distinct effects of internal reference prices on perceived expensiveness and demand, *Psychology and Marketing* **20**, 3, pp. 227–248.

Gavirneni, S. (2004). Periodic review inventory control with fluctuating purchase costs, *Operations Research Letters* **32**, 4, pp. 374–379.

Geng, Q., Wu, C. and Li, K. (2010). Price and promotion frequency in the presence of reference price effects in supply chains, *California Journal of Operations Management* **8**, 1, pp. 74–82.

Greenleaf, E. A. (1995). The impact of reference price effects on the profitability of price promotions, *Marketing Science* **14**, 1, pp. 82–104.

Gupta, S. (1988). Impact of sales promotions on when, what, and how much to buy, *Journal of Marketing Research* **25**, 4, pp. 342–355.

Gurnani, H. (1996). Optimal ordering policies in inventory systems with random demand and random deal offerings, *European Journal of Operational Research* **95**, 2, pp. 299–312.

Hendel, I. and Nevo, A. (2003). The post-promotion dip puzzle: What do the data have to say? *Quantitative Marketing and Economics* **8**, 4, pp. 409–424.

Ho, T.-H., Tang, C. S. and Bell, D. R. (1998). Rational shopping behavior and the option value of variable pricing, *Management Science* **44**, 12, pp. S145–S160.

Huchzermeier, A., Iyer, A. and Freiheit, J. (2002). The supply chain impact of *smart* customers in a promotional environment, *Manufacturing and Service Operations Management* **4**, 3, pp. 228–240.

Jedidi, K. and Jagpal, S. (2009). Willingness to pay: Measurement and managerial implications, in V. R. Rao (ed.), *Handbook of Pricing Research in Marketing*, Edward Elgar, Cheltenham, United Kingdom.

Jeuland, A. P. and Narasimhan, C. (1985). Dealing — temporary price cuts — by seller as a buyer discrimination mechanism, *Journal of Business* **58**, 3, pp. 295–308.

Kopalle, P. K., Rao, A. G. and Assuncao, J. L. (1996). Asymmetric reference price effects and dynamic pricing policies, *Marketing Science* **15**, 1, pp. 60–85.

Krishna, A. (1994). Impact of dealing patterns on purchase behavior, *Marketing Science* **13**, 4, pp. 351–373.

Krishna, A. and Johar, G. V. (1996). Consumer perceptions of deals: Biasing effects of varying deal prices, *Journal of Experimental Psychology: Applied* **2**, 2, pp. 187–206.

Krishnamurthi, L., Mazumdar, T. and Raj, S. (1992). Asymmetric response to price in consumer brand choice and purchase quantity decisions, *Journal of Consumer Research* **19**, 3, pp. 387–400.

Kumar, N., Rajiv, S. and Jeuland, A. (2001). Effectiveness of trade promotions: Analyzing the determinants of retail pass-through, *Marketing Science* **20**, 4, pp. 382–404.

Kumar, V. and Pereira, A. (1995). Explaining the variation in short-term sales response to retail price promotions, *Journal of the Academy of Marketing Science* **23**, 3, pp. 155–169.

Kurata, H. and Liu, J. J. (2007). Optimal promotion planning — depth and frequency — for a two-stage supply chain under Markov-switching demand, *European Journal of Operational Research* **177**, 2, pp. 1026–1043.

Lal, R. (1990). Manufacturer trade deals and retail price promotions, *Journal of Marketing Research* **27**, 4, pp. 428–444.

Lal, R., Little, J. D. and Villas-Boas, J. M. (1996). A theory of forward buying, merchandising and trade deals, *Marketing Science* **15**, 1, pp. 21–37.

Lal, R. and Villas-Boas, J. M. (1998). Price promotions and trade deals with multiproduct retailers, *Management Science* **44**, 7, pp. 935–949.

Lattin, J. M. and Bucklin, R. E. (1989). Reference effects of price and promotion on brand choice behavior, *Journal of Marketing Research* **26**, 3, pp. 299–310.

Lee, E. and Staelin, R. (1997). Vertical strategic interaction: Implications for channel pricing strategy, *Marketing Science* **16**, 3, pp. 185–207.

Lowengart, O. (2002). Reference price conceptualizations: An integrative framework of analysis, *Journal of Marketing Management* **18**, 1–2, pp. 145–171.

Mazumdar, T., Raj, S. and Sinha, I. (2005). Reference price research: Review and propositions, *Journal of Marketing* **79**, 1, pp. 84–102.

McAlister, L. (2007). Cross-brand pass-through: Fact or artifact? *Marketing Science* **26**, 6, pp. 876–898.

Mela, C. F., Gupta, S. and Jedidi, K. (1998). Assessing long-term promotional influences on market structure, *International Journal of Research in Marketing* **15**, 2, pp. 89–107.

Meyer, R. J. and Assuncao, J. L. (1990). The optimality of consumer stockpiling, *Marketing Science* **9**, 1, pp. 18–41.

Meza, S. and Sudhir, K. (2006). Pass-through timing, *Quantitative Marketing and Economics* **4**, 4, pp. 351–382.

Monroe, K. B. (1973). Buyers' subjective perceptions of price, *Journal of Marketing Research* **10**, 1, pp. 70–80.

Moorthy, S. (2005). A general theory of pass-through in channels with category management and retail competition, *Marketing Science* **24**, 1, pp. 110–122.

Narasimhan, C. (2009). Trade promotions, in V. R. Rao (ed.), *Handbook of Pricing Research in Marketing*, Edward Elgar, Cheltenham, United Kingdom.

Neslin, S. A., Powell, S. G. and Stone, L. S. (1995). The effects of retailer and consumer response on optimal manufacturer advertising and trade promotion stragegies, *Management Science* **41**, 5, pp. 749–766.

Nijs, V., Misra, K., Anderson, E. T., Hansen, K. and Krishnamurthi, L. (2010). Channel pass-through of trade promotions, *Marketing Science* **29**, 2, pp. 250–267.

Nijs, V., Srinivasan, S. and Pauwels, K. (2007). Retail price drivers and retail profits, *Marketing Science* **26**, 4, pp. 473–487.

Nijs, V. R., Dekimpe, M. G., Steenkamp, J.-B. E. and Hanssens, D. M. (2001). The category-demand effects of price promotions, *Marketing Science* **20**, 1, pp. 1–22.

Pauwels, K. (2007). How retailer and competitor decisions drive the long-term effectiveness of manufacturer promotions for fast moving consumer goods, *Journal of Retailing* **83**, 3, pp. 297–308.

Pauwels, K., Hanssens, D. M. and Siddarth, S. (2002). The long-term effects of price promotions on category incidence, brand choice, and purchase quantity, *Journal of Marketing Research* **39**, 4, pp. 421–439.

Poddar, A. and Donthu, N. (2011). What do we know about trade promotions? Contributions, limitations and further research, *Journal of Promotion Management* **17**, 2, pp. 183–206.

Popescu, I. and Wu, Y. (2007). Dynamic pricing strategies with reference effects, *Operations Research* **55**, 3, pp. 413–429.

Raju, J. S. (1995). Theoretical models of sales promotions: Contributions, limitations and a future research agenda, *European Journal of Operational Research* **85**, 1, pp. 1–17.

Raju, J. S., Srinivasan, V. and Lal, R. (1990). The effects of brand loyalty on competitive price promotional strategies, *Management Science* **36**, 3, pp. 276–304.

Shankar, V. and Bolton, R. N. (2004). An empirical analysis of determinants of retailer pricing strategy, *Marketing Science* **23**, 1, pp. 28–49.

Silver, E. A., Robb, D. J. and Rahnama, M. R. (1993). Random opportunities for reduced cost replenishments, *IIE Transactions* **25**, 2, pp. 111–120.

Sivakumar, K. (1996). Tradeoff between frequency and depth of price promotions: Implications for high- and low-priced brands, *Journal of Marketing Theory and Practice* **4**, pp. 1–8.

Slonim, R. and Gabarino, E. (2009). Similarities and differences between stockpiling and reference effects, *Managerial and Decision Economics* **30**, 6, pp. 351–371.

Su, X. (2010). Intertemporal pricing and consumer stockpiling, *Operations Research* **58**, 4, Part 2, pp. 1133–1147.

Sudhir, K. and Datta, S. (2009). Pricing in marketing channels, in V. R. Rao (ed.), *Handbook of Pricing Research in Marketing*, Edward Elgar, Cheltenham, United Kingdom.

Sun, B., Neslin, S. A. and Srinivasan, K. (2003). Measuring the impact of promotions on brand switching when consumers are forward looking, *Journal of Marketing Research* **40**, 4, pp. 389–405.

Tyagi, R. K. (1999). A characterization of retailer response to manufacturer trade deals, *American Marketing Association* **36**, 4, pp. 510–516.

vanHeerde, H. J., Gupta, S. and Wittink, D. (2003). Is 75% of the sales promotion bump due to brand switching? No, only 33% is, *Journal of Marketing Research* **40**, 4, pp. 481–491.

vanHeerde, H. J. and Neslin, S. A. (2008). Sales promotions, in *Handbook of Marketing Decision Models*, B. Wierenga (ed.), Springer Science, New York.

Walters, R. G. (1989). An empirical investigation into retailer response to manufacturer trade promotions, *Journal of Retailing* **65**, 2, pp. 253–272.

Walters, R. G. and MacKenzie, S. B. (1988). A structural equations analysis of the impact of price promotions on store performance, *Journal of Marketing Research* **25**, 1, pp. 51–63.

Winer, R. S. (1986). A reference price model of brand choice for frequently purchased products, *Journal of Consumer Research* **13**, 2, pp. 250–256.

Appendix A: Optimizing Δ^L for a Given n

Here, we derive the optimal Δs for a fixed n. If there are n low cycles in which the retailer offers a positive discount, then we have $m = \frac{\Delta^H + n\Delta^L}{T}$, where we have omitted the subscript on Δ_i^L because, by Proposition 1, all of the positive Δ^L values are equal. (Recall, however, that some of the Δ_i^L values are zero.) To convert the problem to a single-variable problem, we re-express Δ^H as $mT - n\Delta^L$, and the objective becomes a cubic function of Δ^L. We can infer the functional form from the first derivative of the objective with respect to Δ^L, which is:

$$\frac{\partial \Pi}{\partial \Delta^L} = a(\Delta^L)^2 + b\Delta^L + c,$$

where

$$a = 1.5(n^2 - 1)\frac{n}{h\overline{R}T}, \tag{A.1}$$

$$b = \left[-2(\overline{R} - p - m)^+(n + 1) + (p - w)(n + 1) \right.$$
$$\left. + (\Delta^M - 3mT)n \right]\frac{n}{h\overline{R}T}, \tag{A.2}$$

$$c = \begin{cases} (\overline{R} - p - m)^+\left[2mT - 0.5h_r(T^H - T^L)\right] \\ \quad + mT(1.5mT - (p - w + \Delta^M))\frac{n}{h\overline{R}T}, & m < \overline{R} - p, \\[2mm] (\overline{R} - p - m)^+\left[2mT - (p - w + \Delta^M) + 0.5(\overline{R} - p - m) \right. \\ \quad \left. + (p - w)/n - 0.5(\overline{R} - p - m)/n\right] + mT(1.5mT \\[2mm] \quad - (p - w + \Delta^M))\frac{n}{h\overline{R}T}, & m > \overline{R} - p. \end{cases} \tag{A.3}$$

For a fixed m, the problem is to allocate a total discount, mT, among the high cycle and n low cycles, where the discounts in the n low cycles are equal to one another. The optimal solution depends upon the signs of b and c, which define which of the four possible forms of Π (as shown in Fig. 5) applies. We assume $T^H \geq T^L$ in this section, which is commonly true in practice because retailers tend to stockpile, so high cycles tend to be longer

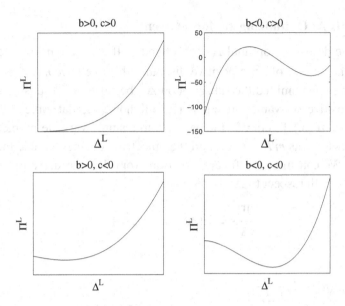

Fig. 5 Π^L For Different Signs of b, c

than low cycles, but we also allow $T^H \leq T^L$ in the numerical study in Section 5.

- $b > 0, c > 0$: If $b > 0$ and $c > 0$, Π is convex increasing in Δ^L. The solution is $\Delta^H = 0$ and $\Delta^L = mT$. We conclude that this solution is suboptimal based on the results in Proposition 2.
- $b < 0, c > 0$: As shown in the upper right plot in Fig. 5, the two local optima are (i) the stationary point $\Delta^L = \frac{-b+\sqrt{b^2-4ac}}{2a}$, if it exists, and (ii) the upper limit of Δ^L (i.e., $\Delta^L = \frac{mT}{n}$, $\Delta^H = 0$). The upper limit is suboptimal based on Proposition 2. If $b^2 - 4ac \geq 0$, the stationary point exists and $\Delta^{L*} = \frac{-b+\sqrt{b^2-4ac}}{2a}$; if $b^2 - 4ac < 0$, the objective is increasing in Δ^L so the solution $\Delta^L = mT/n$ is suboptimal.
- $-\infty < b < \infty, c \leq 0$: When $c \leq 0$, the only difference between the cases with $b \leq 0$ and $b > 0$ is that when $b > 0$, Π^L is convex for small Δ^L. But in both cases, the retailer's profit function is decreasing then increasing and hence the optimal solution is either at the lower limit (i.e., $\Delta^L = 0$), or the upper limit ($\Delta^L = mT/n$). However, by Proposition 2,

the latter solution is suboptimal so the solution is ($\Delta^{H*} = mT$, $\Delta^{L*} = 0$) in this case.

Therefore, the optimal solution to the inner problem is either the boundary solution ($\Delta^{H*} = mT$, $\Delta^{L*} = 0$) or the stationary point ($\Delta^{L*} = \frac{-b+\sqrt{b^2-4ac}}{2a}$, $\Delta^{H*} = mT - n\Delta^{L*}$). We solve the outer problem utilizing these two solutions to the inner problem.

Appendix B: Outer Optimization Problem: Optimizing m

We derive the solution for m^* for the two potentially optimal solutions: (1) $\Delta^{H*} = mT$ and $\Delta^{L*} = 0$ and (2) $\Delta^{L*} = \frac{-b+\sqrt{b^2-4ac}}{2a}$ where a, b and c are defined in (A.1) through (A.3), and $\Delta^{H*} = mT - n\Delta^{L*}$.

Potential Solution 1: $\Delta^H = mT$, $\Delta^L = 0$ with $\alpha_1 < 0$

Substituting for Δ^H and Δ^L in the objective function, the retailer's objective can be rewritten as $\Pi(m) = \alpha_1 m^3 + \alpha_2 m^2 + \alpha_3 m + \alpha_4$ where (Case 1): if $m \leq \overline{R} - p$, then

$$\alpha_1 = 0.5T^2(2 - T)\frac{\Gamma}{h\overline{R}},$$

$$\alpha_2 = \left[(0.5(p - w + \Delta^M) - (\overline{R} - p))T^2 - 0.5h_r T^H T\right]\frac{\Gamma}{h\overline{R}},$$

$$\alpha_3 = \left[0.5h_r(\overline{R} - p)T^H T - (p - w + \Delta^M - 0.5h_r T^H)hT^H\right.$$
$$\left. - n(p - w - 0.5h_r T^L)hT^L\right]\frac{\Gamma}{h\overline{R}},$$

$$\alpha_4 = (\overline{R} - p)\left[(p - w + \Delta^M - 0.5h_r T^H)hT^H\right.$$
$$\left. + n(p - w - 0.5h_r T^L)hT^L\right]\frac{\Gamma}{h\overline{R}} - (n + 1)K.$$

(Case 2): if $m > R - p$, then

$$\alpha_1 = -0.5T(T - 1)^2\frac{\Gamma}{h\overline{R}},$$

$$\alpha_2 = \left[(0.5(p - w + \Delta^M) - (R - p))T^2 + ((\overline{R} - p) - (p - w + \Delta^M))T\right.$$

$$+ 0.5((p - w)(n + 1) + \Delta^M)] \frac{\Gamma}{h\overline{R}},$$

$$\alpha_3 = \left[((\overline{R} - p)(p - w + \Delta^M) - 0.5(\overline{R} - p)^2)T\right.$$

$$\left. - ((p - w)(n + 1) + \Delta^M)(\overline{R} - p)\right] \frac{\Gamma}{h\overline{R}},$$

$$\alpha_4 = 0.5(\overline{R} - p)^2 \left[(p - w)(n + 1) + \Delta^M)\right] \frac{\Gamma}{h\overline{R}} - (n + 1)K.$$

If $m \leq \overline{R} - p$, then α_1 is negative for $T > 2$, and if $m > \overline{R} - p$, then α_1 is negative for $T > 1$. Note that if $T < 2$, then there cannot be a low cycle and the special case with no low cycle applies. Furthermore, if $T = 2$, then the high and low cycles are forced to have the same duration, which is quite restrictive. In the analysis that follows, we initially focus on cases with $T > 2$, and then return to the case of $T = 2$. The analysis depends upon the signs of α_2 and α_3, and the corresponding shape of the retailer's objective is shown in Fig. 2; we divide our analysis accordingly. In all cases, the same analysis applies to both $m \leq \overline{R} - p$ and $m > \overline{R} - p$.
(a) $\alpha_2 \leq 0$, $\alpha_3 \leq 0$: $\Pi(m)$ is decreasing in m for $m \geq 0$, and hence $m^* = 0$.
(b) $\alpha_2 > 0$, $\alpha_3 < 0$: $\Pi(m)$ is decreasing, then increasing, and then decreasing again as m increases from 0. There are two local optima: $m^* = 0$ and the larger of the two stationary points, $m^* = \frac{\alpha_2 + \sqrt{\alpha_2^2 - 3\alpha_1\alpha_3}}{-3\alpha_1}$. This stationary point exists if and only if $\alpha_2^2 + 2T^2(T - 2)\alpha_3 \geq 0$. If $\alpha_2^2 + 2T^2 (T - 2)\alpha_3 < 0$, then $\Pi(m)$ is decreasing in m, so $m^* = 0$ is the optimal solution. Therefore, the optimal solution is $m^* = \min\{\overline{R} - p, \frac{\alpha_2 + \sqrt{\alpha_2^2 - 3\alpha_1\alpha_3}}{-3\alpha_1}\}$ if the stationary solution exists and $m^* = 0$ otherwise.
(c) $-\infty < \alpha_2 < \infty$ and $\alpha_3 > 0$: $\Pi(m)$ is increasing and then decreasing in m for $m \geq 0$, so the unconstrained optimal solution is at the stationary point, $\hat{m} = \frac{\alpha_2 + \sqrt{\alpha_2^2 - 3\alpha_1\alpha_3}}{-3\alpha_1}$. (Note that the stationary point exists because the expression under the square root is positive.) Therefore, in Case 1, $m^* = \min\{\overline{R} - p, \hat{m}\}$ and in Case 2, $m^* = \hat{m}$.

We now provide further economic interpretation of the coefficients in the objective function. Assuming that $\alpha_1 < 0$, the other key parameters that affect characteristics of the solution are α_2 and α_3. If $\alpha_2 > 0$ at a given value of Δ^M, then, roughly speaking, the retailer gains more from selling to discount customers than he loses due to the reduced margin on units sold to regular customers. If $\alpha_3 > 0$ at a given value of Δ^M, then the retailer's savings in inventory costs from discounting is greater than the reduction in profit due to the fact that the (negative) brand equity effect reduces the number of regular customers. If $\alpha_2 > 0$ and $\alpha_3 < 0$ (or the reverse), then the retailer faces competing forces when optimizing his discounts. If both α_2 and α_3 are negative, then the retailer has little incentive to offer discounts at the given value of Δ^M.

Potential Solution 2: $\Delta^{L*} = \frac{-b-\sqrt{b^2-4ac}}{2a}$, $\Delta^H = mT - n\Delta^{L*}$

Substituting for Δ^{L*} and Δ^H in $\Pi(\Delta^L)$ gives the objective expressed as a function of m: $\Pi = \frac{a}{3}\Delta^{L*3} + \frac{b}{2}\Delta^{L*2} + c\Delta^{L*} + \theta$, where $\Delta^{L*} = \frac{-b-\sqrt{b^2-4ac}}{2a}$, $\theta = a^H(mT)^3 + b^H(mT)^2 + c^H(mT) + \gamma^H + nr^L$; a, b, c are functions of m and are defined in (A.1)–(A.3); and $a^H, b^H, c^H, \gamma^H, \gamma^L$ are also functions of m and are defined in Section 4. However, the optimal m cannot be expressed analytically. We provide optimality conditions below; numerical methods can be used to find the optimal m.

The first order condition $\frac{\partial\Pi(\Delta^L)}{\partial\Delta^L} = 0$ can be written as:

$$a\Delta^L(m)\frac{\partial\Delta^L(m)}{\partial m} + 0.5\Delta^L(m)^2[2(n+1) - 3nT] + b\Delta^L\frac{\partial\Delta^L(m)}{\partial m}$$

$$+ [-2mT - 0.5h_r(T^H - T^L) + 2T(R - p - m)]\Delta^L(m)$$

$$+ c\frac{\partial\Delta^L(m)}{\partial m} = 0, \tag{B.1}$$

where

$$\Delta^L(m) = \frac{-b - \sqrt{b^2 - 4ac}}{2a}$$

$$\frac{\partial\Delta^L(m)}{\partial m} = -\frac{1}{2a}\{2(n+1) - 3nT - 2b[2(n+1) - 3nT]$$

$$- 4a\{-2mT - 0.5(T^H - T^L) + 2T(R - p - m)$$

$$+ T[1.5mT - (p - w + \Delta^M) + 1.5mT^2]\}\}/[2\sqrt{b^2 - 4ac}].$$

The optimal value of m is either at the stationary point mentioned above (i.e., the solution to (B.1)) or at the boundary value, 0.

Finally, we turn to the special case of $\alpha_1 = 0$ (which implies that $T = 2$) under the assumption that $m \leq \overline{R} - p$. If $\alpha_1 = 0$ and $m < \overline{R} - p$, the solution procedure for $\alpha_1 < 0$ can be used. The retailer's objective function is $\Pi(m) = \alpha_1 m^3 + \alpha_2 m^2 + \alpha_3 m + \alpha_4$ and expressions for the αs are those listed under Potential Solution 1 at the beginning of this appendix. Because $\alpha_1 = 0$, Π is quadratic in this case, so the solution depends on the signs of α_2 and α_3 and is either at a stationary point or at the boundary of 0. Below, we summarize how the optimal solutions depend on the α values:

- $\alpha_2 > 0, \alpha_3 > 0$: Π is concave increasing for $m \geq 0$, and the optimal solution is $m^* = \overline{R} - p$.
- $\alpha_2 > 0, \alpha_3 < 0$: Π is concave decreasing and then increasing, hence m^* is either 0 or $\overline{R} - p$.
- $\alpha_2 < 0, \alpha_3 > 0$: Π is concave increasing and then decreasing, and m^* is at the stationary point: $\frac{-\alpha_3 - \sqrt{\alpha_3{}^2 - 4\alpha_2\alpha_3}}{2\alpha_2}$.
- $\alpha_2 < 0, \alpha_3 < 0$: Π is concave decreasing for $m \geq 0$, hence $m^* = 0$.

The economic interpretations of α_2 and α_3 are the same as those given earlier, so if both are positive, large discounts are attractive, and if both are negative, discounts are undesirable for the retailer. When these coefficients have different signs, there may be a tradeoff, in which case an intermediate value may be optimal.

Appendix C: Proof of Proposition 2

Proposition 2 relates decisions in the high and low cycles.

Proposition 2. *Let $(\Delta^{H*}, \Delta_1^{L*}, \ldots, \Delta_n^{L*})$ be the optimal solution to the retailer's problem. If $T^H \geq T^L$ and $\Delta^M \geq 0$, then $\Delta^{H*} \geq \Delta_i^{L*}, \forall i = 1, \ldots, N$, that is, the retailer's discount in the high cycle is greater than or equal to the discount in low cycles.*

Proof. Let $(\Delta^{H*}, \Delta_1^{L*}, \ldots, \Delta_N^{L*})$ denote the optimal discounts offered by the retailer, and T^{H*} and T^{L*} denote the optimal durations of the high and low cycles, respectively. We assume $T^{H*} \geq T^{L*}$. We show that if the discount offered in the low cycle, Δ_i^{L*}, is greater than the discount offered in the high cycle, Δ^{H*}, then the retailer can improve his profit by switching the values, and this contradicts the optimality of $(\Delta^{H*}, \Delta_1^{L*}, \ldots, \Delta_N^{L*})$.

Suppose that $\Delta^{H*} < \Delta_i^{L*}$ for some $i \in 1, \ldots, N$. Then we have:

$$\Upsilon \triangleq \Pi(\Delta^{H*}, \Delta_1^{L*}, \ldots, \Delta_N^{L*}) - \Pi(\Delta_i^{L*}, \Delta_1^{L*}, \ldots, \Delta^{H*}, \ldots \Delta_N^{L*})$$

$$= \Pi^H(\Delta^{H*}) + \Pi^L(\Delta_i^{L*}) - \Pi^H(\Delta_i^{L*}) - \Pi^L(\Delta^{H*}).$$

If $m \leq \overline{R} - p$, then $\Upsilon = 0.5\Delta^M((\Delta^{H*})^2 - (\Delta_i^{L*})^2) + 0.5h_r(R - p - m)[T^H(\Delta^{H*} - \Delta_i^{L*}) + T^L(\Delta_i^{L*} - \Delta^{H*})])$ and if $m \leq \overline{R} - p$, then $\Upsilon = 0.5\Delta^M((\Delta^{H*})^2 - (\Delta_i^{L*})^2) + \Delta^M(\Delta^{H*} - \Delta_i^{L*})$. Hence,

$$\Pi(\Delta^{H*}, \Delta_1^{L*}, \ldots, \Delta_N^{L*}) - \Pi(\Delta_i^{L*}, \Delta_1^{L*}, \ldots, \Delta^{H*}, \ldots \Delta_N^{L*}) < 0$$

because $\Delta^{H*} < \Delta_i^{L*}$ and $T^{H*} \geq T^{L*}$. This contradicts the optimality of $(\Delta^{H*}, \Delta_1^{L*}, \ldots, \Delta_N^{L*})$. Hence, we must have $\Delta^{H*} \geq \Delta_i^{L*}$ for all $i \in \{1, \ldots, N\}$ if $T^{H*} \geq T^{L*}$. $\qquad\qquad\square$

Chapter 5

Appropriate Inventory Policies
When Service Affects Future Demands

Lawrence W. Robinson

Johnson Graduate School of Management
Cornell University Ithaca, New York, United States

A major problem in using penalty costs to derive an inventory stocking policy is the accurate assessment of the lost goodwill of a dissatisfied customer. In this chapter, the lost goodwill is explicitly manifested as a drop in future demand, so that the optimal ordering policy balances current holding costs against foregone future profits. Two special cases are examined for which a stationary stocking policy is optimal. These two cases provide bounds for the optimal stocking policy for a very general class of problems where the demand variability changes with the mean.

1 Introduction

The periodic review inventory model was first developed by Arrow *et al.* (1951) and Bellman *et al.* (1955) over 60 years ago. In their model, the inventory level of some item is reviewed at regular intervals. Additional inventory is then ordered, after which random demand for the item occurs. Their objective is to find the ordering policy that minimizes the expected net present value of all present and future costs.

One such cost is that of ordering additional units. Another is the holding cost levied against ending inventory, representing both physical storage costs as well as the opportunity cost of the capital invested.

The third cost typically is a penalty cost (also referred to as a shortage or stockout cost), incurred whenever demand exceeds inventory on hand.

If this excess demand is lost (i.e., if the customers are unwilling to wait), then the penalty cost includes the opportunity cost of the foregone profit. The penalty cost often includes an additional "lost goodwill" component that reflects the consequences of poor service. While this component is sometimes real, more often it is implicitly set by managers in order to yield a service level that they feel is appropriate. As Bursk (1966) points out, customer goodwill can be thought of as a capital asset that is maintained through advertising. The arbitrary nature and vagueness of the penalty cost in general, and the lost goodwill component in particular, has long been of concern. For example, Hadley and Whitin (1963) state that "the usual procedure, if stockout costs are specified at all, is for someone to make a guess at what they are."

The lost goodwill of a customer receiving poor service is likely to be manifested by his or her switching to another firm, reducing demand in the future. But except for Hanssmann (1959) and a trickle of research stemming from Schwartz's dissertation (1965), this approach to modeling consumer's reaction to poor (as well as good) service has been overlooked.

This chapter introduces a periodic review model in which demand changes over time in response to the service received. Of course, revenues will increase as the average demand goes up. But the variability of demand will typically increase as well, and with it, the costs of controlling inventory. The optimal ordering policy will balance the changes in future demand, and their effects on profits and control costs, against current holding costs. The outline of this chapter is as follows. Sections 1 and 2 contain brief reviews of the relevant literature. Section 3 defines the notation used and develops the assumptions underlying the model. Section 4 introduces the general model, and transforms the costs so that the effects of service are attributed to the relevant period. Section 5 shows that the optimal policy will always be to order at least enough to clear current backlogs; the general ordering policy is also discussed. Section 6 examines two special cases for which stationary (transformed) policies are optimal. Section 7 demonstrates how these special cases can provide bounds on the appropriate inventory ordering policies for a much broader class of problems. Finally, Section 8 presents some conclusions and outlines directions of future research.

2 Literature Review: Inventory Theory

Standard inventory models take as a given the existence of known, precise cost parameters. Gardner (1980), taking issue with this underlying premise, maintained that these cost parameters are no more real than the gods of Olympus. Of the various cost parameters, he concluded that "shortage costs present perhaps the most ambiguous measurement problems."

A number of authors have tried to attack this ambiguity. Chang and Niland (1967) used decision trees to delineate the possible consequences of a stockout (e.g., lost sale, temporary cancellation of business, etc.) and their conditional probabilities of occurring, which they used to calculate an expected penalty cost. Oral *et al.* (1972) and Oral (1981), reacting to the tremendous amount of time this procedure required, asked managers to define these costs and probabilities for a stratified sample of their items. They then regressed the shortage cost on the gross unit profit to estimate penalty costs for the remaining items. Walter and Grabner (1975) used customer questionnaires to determine the consequences of stockouts in Ohio liquor stores.

Badinelli (1986) took a different route in calculating penalty functions. After repeatedly asking decision makers to specify their marginal exchange rate between on-hand inventory and backorders, he used the (relatively more exact) holding cost to estimate the shortage cost function through regression.

Brooking (1987) listed various kinds of manufacturing costs and assigned them as holding, ordering, or shortage costs. He made no attempt to include opportunity costs or to estimate goodwill losses.

Hanssmann (1959) was perhaps the first to model a relationship between inventory stocking policies and demand. He balanced higher holding costs against increased sales in response to reduced backlogging and the delivery delays. He assumed that demand was normally distributed; its mean depended on the service received, and its coefficient of variation was constant.

Schwartz (1965, 1966, 1970) expanded the framework for handling lost customer goodwill by developing a model where stockouts affect future demand. He followed the general framework of a continuous review (Q,r) model, although he allowed for some stochastic elements and did not include a fixed order cost. Upon experiencing a stockout, customers reduced their purchases for a while before "forgiving" the firm and returning as regulars. Schwartz examined the steady state results of using a given ordering policy, which is appropriate in a deterministic environment. The steady state demand rate depends on the long run "disappointment factor," the fraction of demand that is not filled from stock.

Hill (1976) extended Schwartz's work to include a fixed ordering cost. He demonstrated that the optimal policy is to either backlog items indefinitely or to never stock out. This result is essentially the same as the deterministic (Q, r) model with a per-unit penalty cost that is independent of the length of the shortage.

The first section of Caine and Plaut (1976) used variable redefinition to arrive at Hill's concurrent result. The second section is more relevant, since it also examined a stochastic periodic review model. As in Schwartz's model, only steady state results were examined, with the demand distribution being determined by the long run expected disappointment factor rather than by the actual service received. Their cost model examined only a single period and placed no value on either ending inventory or backlogged demand. Demands were assumed to be exponentially distributed, with the mean defined by a specific functional form of the disappointment factor.

Finally, Lee and Tapiero (1986) examined a somewhat related model where demand changed over time in response to product quality rather than customer service. In their model, the firm did not hold inventory.

The model presented sharpens the specification of the penalty costs by modeling lost customer goodwill as a drop in the future demand. It differs from previous models in a number of important ways. The underlying model structure is that of a nonstationary stochastic periodic review inventory model operating under an infinite planning horizon. Each period's state is defined by that period's expected demand (parameterizing the underlying demand distribution) as well as the more standard initial inventory level. The model environment is dynamic rather than steady state; both the expectation and the variability of demand will change over time in response to the actual (rather than expected) number of satisfied and dissatisfied customers. Finally, market share can be recaptured through good service rather than by dissatisfied customers ultimately forgiving the firm and returning.

3 Literature Review: Logistics

Two propositions must be demonstrated in order for the concept of the cost of lost goodwill to be valid. First, customers must care about the service they receive — in particular, about product availability. And second, they must react to the service received by changing their purchasing patterns.

Within the marketing profession, logisticians have studied the connection between sales and customer service; Hutchison and Stolle (1968) and Christopher and Wills (1974) provide good introductions to some of the issues involved in customer service. The Council of Logistics Management sponsored two studies of customer service practices by La Londe and Zinszer (1976) and La Londe *et al.* (1988). These two books contain excellent reviews of the logistics literature, and provide a good overall picture of industry attitudes towards customer service. In particular, they cite substantial agreement that "most firms do not specifically measure the cost implications (and) sales impacts of changes in customer service." On a similar note, Stephenson and Willett (1968) conclude that "if one is to properly manage service functions (in terms of total profit), it is necessary to be able to make some estimate of sales that result from changes and competition variations in service given."

A number of authors have examined the importance of customer service in general, and product availability in particular, relative to the typical marketing variables (e.g., price, product, and promotion). Sterling and Lambert (1987) and Lambert and Harrington (1989) surveyed the office systems and plastics industries, respectively, and concluded "in both industries customer service and product quality variables comprised over 75 percent of the variables evaluated as most important by customers." The six customer service variables identified as most important are:

- meeting promised delivery dates
- accuracy in filling orders
- advance notice of shipping delays
- action on complaints

- information exchange
- length of promised lead time.

Although these factors reflect the concerns of an industrial purchasing agent rather than those of a consumer, they demonstrate the importance of customer service in influencing purchases. In two extensive consumer-oriented studies conducted by TARP (1979, 1985), the most common consumer complaint was, "Store did not have product advertised for sale."

Perreault and Russ (1976a) conducted an experiment on purchasing managers that showed that considerations of stockout probabilities were second in importance only to price. Perreault and Russ (1976b) also surveyed 216 purchasing agents, who reported customer satisfaction to be most closely correlated with average delivery time, delivery time variability, rush service, and order status information.

Perreault and Russ (1974) noted that the effect of service on revenues (as opposed to costs) was typically ignored, and emphasized that product availability is of greatest concern. Gilmour (1977) also found that product availability (which he defined as delivery within a generally accepted lead time) was of primary importance to everyone except the government.

Similarly, Willett and Stephenson's (1969) survey of 500 retailers showed that "approximately 71 percent of the variance in customers' ratings of order cycle lengths was accounted for by the variation in service times received. Thus, the predisposition of the retailers toward individual suppliers is substantially related to the length of order cycles provided."

Other authors who describe surveying customers in order to determine the most important attributes of service include Hutchison and Stolle (1968), Sanford and Farrell (1982), Lambert and Zemke (1982), and Shycon and Ritz (1981).

Having demonstrated the importance of customer service in general, the next step is to model customer reactions to changes in service. Most studies have examined the reactions of purchasing agents rather than consumers.

One exception is A.C. Neilsen (1968a, 1968b) who surveyed grocery store customers about their reaction to stockouts (e.g., substituting another item, shopping elsewhere, postponing the purchase). Not surprisingly, their reaction varied dramatically from product to product. For example, when faced with a stockout, most customers would shop elsewhere for their brand of cigarette, but not for canned peaches. As Walters (1974) notes, these reactions will have different consequences for the retailers and the wholesalers.

In another consumer study, Richins (1983) examined the prevalence of negative word-of-mouth among dissatisfied customers.

The logistics research involving industrial purchasing has focused on the relationship between sales and, for example, delivery time and variability. The analytical and empirical models that have been developed reflect this focus on industrial concerns.

Some of the first analytical customer response functions were developed by Mossman and Morton (1965) and Stephenson and Willett (1968). They modeled demand as a nonlinear function of the delivery time, relative to some competitive benchmark. Schary and Becker (1973) adapt the advertising model of Vidale and Wolfe (1957) to model the change in demand as a function of the total logistics expenditures, the current demand, and an upper bound on demand.

Some authors have derived response functions empirically. Ozment and Chard (1986) used a power function to regress sales on current prices and promotional expenditures and customer service. Although they found that sales clearly depended on order cycle time and backorder time (as well as on price, promotion, and credit adjustments), they found no evidence to support a relationship between sales and either order cycle variability or fill rate.

Schary and Becker (1978) studied a beer distributor strike in Seattle, concluding that although "the temporal effects are strongest in the short-run, they persist with measurable effect over a long period of time." But since the distributors' strike affected all retail outlets, the primary response of the proposed model — shopping elsewhere — was not available.

Ballou (1971, 1973) and Gilmour (1979) tried, with mixed results, to model the change in demand by various nonlinear functions of delivery time. Morey (1980) applied a nonlinear regression for sales productivity (dollars per employee hour) at U.S. Navy commissaries. Nuttall (1965) examined the relationship between sales and availability for confectioneries, although he modeled availability as market penetration (the percentage of retail stores that stock the candy), and did not examine the effect of availability on sales within a single store.

Walters (1974), Walter and La Lande (1975), Shycon (1973), Zinszer (1980), and Shycon and Sprague (1975) all describe modifications of Chang and Niland's (1967) approach of calculating expected penalty costs.

A number of consultants from Shycon Associates have examined the problem of constructing an appropriate customer response function in depth; they include Sanford (1982), Krenn and Shycon (1983), Sanford and Farrell (1982), Shycon (1973), Shycon and Ritz (1981), and Ritz (1982). Since their methodologies and results are only cursorily described, their conclusions are not demonstrably well founded.

4 Notation and Assumptions

At the beginning of each period t, the inventory level x_t of an item is monitored and an order is placed to bring it up to some level y_t; the order is assumed to arrive instantly. The ordering cost is assumed to be linear with a per-unit cost of c (\$/unit).

After the order is received, the demand ξ_t is realized. Demand is assumed to be continuous and nonnegative with a known c.d.f. of $\Phi(\xi_t|\mu_t)$, where μ_t denotes the mean demand for period t. The demand distribution is assumed to be characterized uniquely by its mean; while demands may be nonstationary, this characterization is itself stationary. Further, for any μ_t, we assume that there exists some scaling factor $\sigma(\mu_t)$ such that

$$\Phi(\xi_t|\mu_t) = \Psi\left(\frac{\xi_t - \mu_t}{\sigma(\mu_t)}\right) \ \forall\, \xi_t,\ \mu_t \tag{1}$$

for some stationary c.d.f. $\Psi(\cdot)$. The scaling factor $\sigma(\cdot)$ is assumed to be nonnegative, nondecreasing, and concave. The assumption that demand is nonnegative implies that

$$\Psi\left(\frac{-\mu_t}{\sigma(\mu_t)}\right) = 0 \ \forall\, \mu_t.$$

In particular, this implies that $\sigma(0) = 0$. Conditional on their means, demands are assumed to be independent across time. Of course, next period's demand will depend on its mean, which in turn may depend on the demand in the current period.

Whenever demand exceeds the supply on hand, some customers will be dissatisfied; they may elect to wait until stock arrives, or they may choose to leave the system. Let $\beta (0 \leq \beta \leq 1)$ denote the proportion of the dissatisfied customers who decide to wait for inventory to arrive. For the sake of convenience, we assume that the fraction of previously backlogged demand who elect to wait an additional period is also β.

As Schary and Becker (1972) point out, the physical presence of stock can itself stimulate demand via impulse buying, recalling a subconscious purchase plan, or reducing uncertainty about the product. In this case, β reflects the differences in demand as well as the willingness of customers to wait.

Exactly what constitutes a satisfied or dissatisfied customer under backlogging ($\beta > 0$) may be unclear. It is assumed here that fulfilling previously backlogged demand will not transform a dissatisfied customer into a satisfied one. Let s_t denote the number of satisfied customers in period t,

$$s_t \doteq \min\{(y_t)^+, \xi_t\} = \xi_t - ((y_t)^+ - \xi_t)^-, \tag{2}$$

where $(z)^+ = \max\{z, 0\}$ and $(z)^- \doteq (-z)^+$, so that $z = (z)^+ - (z)^-$.

Let d_t denote the number of dissatisfied customers in period t,

$$d_t \doteq \xi_t - s_t = ((y_t)^+ - \xi_t)^-. \tag{3}$$

In addition to foregone profit and lost customer goodwill, there may be additional costs associated with stockouts. For example, Heskett (1971) stated that order processing costs were often at least three times as high for backorders. Let $\hat{\pi}(\$/\text{unit})$ measure these additional costs, incurred by the current dissatisfied demand d_t. (Since the optimal policy will be shown to fulfill all backorders (*i.e.*, to set $y_t \geq 0$), this form of penalty cost can just as easily include time-dependent costs.)

Future cash streams are discounted back by a constant factor $\alpha (0 < \alpha < 1)$, so that \$1 next period is equivalent to \$$\alpha$ this period.

We still need to specify how future demand (specifically, next period's mean μ_{t+1}) changes in response to the service received this period. This change in expected demand may result from any number of possible customer reactions, including changes in the purchasing frequency, the possibility of switching suppliers, "word of mouth" effects, etc. In this chapter, we assume that next period's mean μ_{t+1} depends on the current mean μ_t and the number of satisfied and dissatisfied customers s_t and d_t. In other words, we assume that the amount of overstock does not influence future demand. Similarly, the dissatisfaction from backlogging demand is limited to the period in which the shortage occurs, and does not worsen with the length of the shortage.

The mean may also change over time in response to market changes, independent of customer satisfaction. Virtually all firms will already have a forecast of the expected market changes for each of their items. While these forecasts are important strategically, they can also be used for the more mundane task of inventory management. This chapter assumes that there is an affine relationship between μ_{t+1} and μ_t, s_t, and d_t:

$$\mu_{t+1} \doteq a + b\mu_t + r_s s_t - r_d d_t, \qquad (4)$$

where a and b reflect the underlying market trend, and r_s and r_d are the response rates for satisfied and dissatisfied customers, respectively. Note that the underlying size and growth (or shrinkage) in the market, as captured by a and b, are assumed to be constant over the infinite horizon of this model. (A more realistic alternative might have the demand level off as the industry matures. This added realism comes at the expense of considerable computational tractability, as the nonstationary ordering policy that would then be optimal effectively prevents the problem from being decoupled over time.) For many mature products, the growth in the market should be relatively stable. Of course, $a = 0$ and $b = 1$ reflects the situation where customer (dis)satisfaction is the only determinant of market change.

The nonnegative dimensionless parameters r_s and r_d indicate how quickly the mean changes in response to service received and are, along with the backlogging proportion β, crucial to specifying a good inventory control policy. The linear response to customer (dis)satisfaction was also used in the TARP (1985) study, although they used a five-year horizon on brand loyalty. This linearity should be valid in a competitive situation, where the potential market remains substantially higher than the actual customer base for any individual retailer. In oligopolistic settings, the more involved epidemic-based growth models (see Olinick, 1978, for an overview) would need to be used.

Although it may not always be easy to obtain accurate values for r_s and r_d, the task is certainly less formidable than that of finding the cost of lost goodwill or the appropriate fill rate. The surveys and experiments described earlier in the review of the logistics literature can be used to calculate the customer response function. Similarly, the methodologies used by Chang and Niland (1967) and Oral *et al.* (1972) to specify the penalty costs can easily be modified to instead specify these response rates.

When all demand is always satisfied, the maximum growth rate (excepting the additive term a) will be $b + r_s$. Requiring

$$1 \leq b + r_s < \alpha^{-1} \tag{5}$$

implies that it is possible (if perhaps not cost effective) to maintain the current demand level. It also implies that the market cannot grow faster than the profits are being discounted.

The amount of previously backlogged demand that is sold in period t will be $(x_t)^- - (y_t)^-$. The amount of inventory physically on hand at the end of period t will be $(y_t)^+ - s_t$; each such unit will be assessed a physical holding charge of $\hat{h}$ (\$/unit/period). Since $(y_t)^- + d_t$ customers are not satisfied, the initial inventory level (on hand inventory minus backorders) next period will be

$$x_{t+1} = (y_t)^+ - s_t - \beta\left[(y_t)^- + d_t\right]. \tag{6}$$

In order to avoid situations where the optimal policy is, in some sense, trivial or nonsensical, restrictions are placed on the relationships among the cost parameters. In order to avoid examining situations where it is optimal to stock an infinite amount, we require that

$$\hat{h} + (1 - \alpha)c > 0.$$

Let r (\$/unit) denote the per-unit sales price. In order to ensure that it is sometimes beneficial to order, we require that the item has a positive profit margin; i.e., that

$$r - c > 0.$$

5 Formulation of the General Model

In keeping with the traditional inventory literature, this problem is formulated as a cost minimization model, with sales revenue included as a negative cost. The costs incurred each period include the ordering costs, the physical holding charge levied against ending on-hand inventory, and the physical penalty costs incurred by dissatisfied demand. Define $f_t(x_t|\mu_t)$ to be the net present value of present and future costs from period t on, conditional on the mean μ_t and dependent on the initial inventory level x_t

$$f_0(x_0|\mu_0) \doteq \min_{y_t \geq x_t} \left\{ E_{\xi_t} \left[\sum_{t=0}^{\infty} \alpha^t \left[c(y_t - x_t) + \hat{h}\left[(y_t)^+ - s_t\right] \right. \right. \right.$$

$$\left. \left. \left. + \hat{\pi} d_t - r\left[s_t + (x_t)^- - (y_t)^-\right] \right] \right] \right\} \tag{7}$$

in accordance with definitions (2), (3), (4), and (6).

Equation (7) can be considerably simplified. Since demand is nonnegative,

$$\left((y_t)^+ - \xi_t\right)^+ = (y_t - \xi_t)^+$$

and

$$\left((y_t)^+ - \xi_t\right)^- + (y_t)^- = (y_t - \xi_t)^- ;$$

these allow (6) to be rewritten as

$$x_{t+1} = (y_t)^+ - \left[\xi_t - \left((y_t)^+ - \xi_t\right)^-\right] - \beta\left[(y_t)^- + \left((y_t)^+ - \xi_t\right)^-\right]$$

$$= (y_t - \xi_t)^+ - \beta(y_t - \xi_t)^- , \tag{8}$$

so that

$$\sum_{t=0}^{\infty} \alpha^t x_t = x_0 + \sum_{t=0}^{\infty} \alpha^t \alpha \left[(y_t - \xi_t)^+ - \beta(y_t - \xi_t)^-\right] \tag{9}$$

and

$$\sum_{t=0}^{\infty} \alpha^t (x_t)^- = (x_0)^- + \sum_{t=0}^{\infty} \alpha^t \alpha \beta (y_t - \xi_t)^-. \tag{10}$$

Further, note that y_t can be trivially rewritten as

$$y_t = (y_t - \xi_t)^+ - (y_t - \xi_t)^- + \xi_t, \tag{11}$$

and that

$$(y_t)^+ - s_t = (y_t - \xi_t)^+, \tag{12}$$

$$s_t - (y_t)^- = \xi_t - (y_t - \xi_t)^-, \tag{13}$$

$$d_t = (y_t - \xi_t)^- - (y_t)^-. \tag{14}$$

Substituting (9)–(14) into (7) yields

$$
\begin{aligned}
f_0 (x_0 | \mu_0) = & - (r - c) (x_0)^- - c (x_0)^+ \\
& + \min \left\{ E_{\xi_t} \left[\sum_{t=0}^{\infty} \alpha^t \left[-(r - c) \xi_t - \hat{\pi} (y_t)^- \right. \right.\right. \\
& \left. + \left[\hat{h} + (1 - \alpha) c \right] (y_t - \xi_t)^+ \right. \\
& \left. \left. \left. + \left[\hat{\pi} + (1 - \alpha \beta) (r - c) \right] (y_t - \xi_t)^- \right] \right] \right\},
\end{aligned}
\tag{15}
$$

with definitions (4) and (8).

Lemma 1. *The expected cost $f_0(x_0 | \mu_0)$ is finite (bounded above and below).*

Proof. See Appendix.

Since $f_0(x_0 | \mu_0)$ is finite, we can interchange the expectation and summation operators to pull the first term inside of the summation of (15) outside of the minimization. Replacing $E(\xi_t)$ with μ_t and recursively using

(4) to substitute in for μ_t eventually leads to

$$\sum_{t=0}^{\infty} \mu_t = \mu_0 + \sum_{t=1}^{\infty} \alpha^t (b + r_s) \mu_0$$

$$+ \sum_{t=1}^{\infty} \alpha^t \sum_{\tau=0}^{t-1} (b + r_s)^{t-1-\tau} \left[a + r_s(s_\tau - \mu_\tau) - r_d d_\tau \right]$$

$$= \frac{\mu_0}{1 - \alpha (b + r_s)}$$

$$+ \sum_{t=1}^{\infty} \sum_{\tau=0}^{t-1} [\alpha (b + r_s)]^t (b + r_s)^{-(\tau+1)} \left[a + r_s (s_\tau - \mu_\tau) - r_d d_\tau \right]$$

$$= \left(\frac{\alpha}{1 - \alpha (b + r_s)} \right) \left(\frac{\mu_0}{\alpha} + \sum_{\tau=0}^{\infty} \alpha^\tau \left[a + r_s (s_\tau - \mu_\tau) - r_d d_\tau \right] \right).$$

Extracting the a term and replacing τ with t throughout gives

$$\sum_{t=0}^{\infty} \mu_t = \left(\frac{\alpha}{1 - \alpha (b + r_s)} \right)$$

$$\times \left(\frac{\mu_0}{\alpha} + \frac{a}{1 - \alpha} + \sum_{t=0}^{\infty} \alpha^t \left[r_s (s_t - \mu_t) - r_d d_t \right] \right).$$

Substituting this back into (15) yields

$$f_0 (x_0 | \mu_0) = -c (x_0)^+ - (r - c) (x_0)^-$$

$$- (r - c) \left(\frac{\alpha}{1 - \alpha (b + r_s)} \right) \left(\frac{\mu_0}{\alpha} + \frac{a}{1 - \alpha} \right)$$

$$+ F_0(x_0 | \mu_0),$$

where the first two terms of $f_0(x_0|\mu_0)$ contain costs that depend only on the initial conditions (x_0 and μ_0). $F_0(x_0|\mu_0)$ contains the remaining terms that do depend on our decisions,

$$F_0(x_0|\mu_0) = \min_{y_t \geq x_t} \left\{ E_{\xi_t} \left[\sum_{t=0}^{\infty} \alpha^t \left[h(y_t - \xi_t)^+ + \pi(y_t - \xi_t)^- \right. \right. \right.$$
$$\left. \left. \left. - [\pi - (1 - \alpha\beta)(r - c)](y_t)^- \right] \right] \right\},$$
(16)

subject to definitions (4) and (7), where

$$h \doteq \hat{h} + (1 - \alpha)c \tag{17}$$

and

$$\pi \doteq \hat{\pi} + (r - c)\left[1 - \alpha\beta + \frac{\alpha(r_s + r_d)}{1 - \alpha(b + r_s)} \right]. \tag{18}$$

The holding cost consists of the physical storage cost and the opportunity cost of the capital invested in the unused inventory. The penalty cost includes additional administrative expenses, the delayed (and perhaps lost) profit from the sale, and the lost potential profit resulting from the mean growing at less than the maximum rate.

$F_0(x_0|\mu_0)$ can also be recursively defined as the following infinite horizon dynamic program:

$$F_t(x_t|\mu_t) \doteq \min_{y_t \geq x_t} \{ G_t(y_t|\mu_t) \} \tag{19}$$

where for $y_t \geq 0$,

$$G_t(y_t|\mu_t) \doteq h \int_0^{y_t} (y_t - \xi_t)d\Phi(\xi_t|\mu_t) + \pi \int_{y_t}^{\infty} (\xi_t - y_t)d\Phi(\xi_t|\mu_t)$$
$$+ \alpha \int_0^{y_t} F_{t+1}(y_t - \xi_t|a + b\mu_t + r_s\xi_t)d\Phi(\xi_t|\mu_t)$$
$$+ \alpha \int_{y_t}^{\infty} F_{t+1}(\beta(y_t - \xi_t)|$$
$$a + b\mu_t + r_s y_t - r_d(\xi_t - y_t))d\Phi(\xi_t|\mu_t)$$
(20)

and for $y_t \leq 0$

$$G_t(y_t|\mu_t) = \pi\mu_t - (1 - \alpha\beta)(r - c)y_t$$

$$+ \alpha \int_0^\infty F_{t+1}(\beta(y_t - \xi_t)|a + b\mu_t - r_d\xi_t)d\Phi(\xi_t|\mu_t). \tag{21}$$

6 The Optimal Policy

Any ordering policy will assign to every initial inventory x_t some order-up-to point $y_t(x_t|\mu_t)$. Let $y_t^*(x_t|\mu_t)$ denote the optimal order-up-to point that minimizes $G_t(y_t|\mu_t)$ over the range $[x_t, \infty)$.

Lemma 2. *The optimal policy is to satisfy all backlogs.*

Proof. See Appendix.

One consequence of Lemma 2 is that under the optimal ordering policy, the final term in (16) will always be zero. And since the only effect of eliminating the final term of (16) is to increase the reported costs for a class of ordering policies ($y_t \leq 0$) that is already known to be suboptimal, the $(y_t)^-$ term can be eliminated with no consequence, yielding the familiar cost function

$$F_0(x_0|\mu_0) = \min\left\{E_{\xi_t}\left[\sum_{t=0}^\infty \alpha^t\left[h(y_t - \xi_t)^+ + \pi(y_t - \xi_t)^-\right]\right]\right\}, \tag{22}$$

subject to (4) and (7).

7 Two Special Cases

The optimal ordering policy will not in general be stationary, but will vary with μ. This effectively prevents the periods from being decoupled, so that finding the optimal ordering policy becomes computationally intractable. This section introduces two special cases for which a stationary (transformed) policy is optimal. Unlike the results of the previous sections, these special cases will depend on the specific form of $\Phi(\xi_t|\mu_t)$ given in (1).

Defining the obvious transformations of y_t and ξ_t

$$z_t \doteq \frac{y_t - \mu_t}{\sigma(\mu_t)}$$

$$\zeta_t \doteq \frac{\xi_t - \mu_t}{\sigma(\mu_t)}$$

allows (22) to be rewritten as

$$F_0\left(x_0 | \mu_0\right) = \min\left\{\sum_{t=0}^{\infty} \alpha^t \sigma\left(\mu_t\right) L\left(z_t\right)\right\} \tag{23}$$

s.t.

$$\mu_0 + \sigma(\mu_0)z_0 \geq x_0 \tag{24}$$

$$\left.\begin{array}{l} \mu_{t+1} + \sigma\left(\mu_{t+1}\right) z_{t+1} \geq \\ \quad \sigma\left(\mu_t\right)\left[(z_t - \zeta_t)^+ - \beta\left(z_t - \zeta_t\right)^-\right] \\ \mu_{t+1} = a + (b + r_s)\,\mu_t \\ \quad + \sigma\left(\mu_t\right)\left[r_s\zeta_t - (r_s + r_d)\left(z_t - \zeta_t\right)^-\right] \end{array}\right\} \quad \begin{array}{l} t = 0, 1, \ldots \end{array} \tag{25}\tag{26}$$

where $L(z)$ is independent of μ_t,

$$L(z) = h \int_{-\infty}^{z} (z - \zeta)d\Psi(\zeta) + \pi \int_{z}^{\infty} (\zeta - z)d\Psi(\zeta).$$

In transforming the dynamic programming formulation (19)–(20), a few additional modifications are introduced. First, the constraints on nonnegative order quantities (24)–(25) are temporarily relaxed; sufficient conditions under which they will automatically be satisfied by the stationary policy will be given in Lemmas 3 and 4. This means that there is no need to keep track of the starting inventory levels x_t. Second, the time subscripts are dropped in this infinite horizon model, so that (19)–(20) become

$$F(\mu) = \min_{z}\left\{G\left(z | \mu\right)\right\}$$

$$G(z|\mu) = \sigma(\mu)L(z) + \alpha \int_{-\infty}^{\infty} F\left(\mu_{\text{new}}\right)d\Psi\left(\zeta\right),$$

where μ_{new} is the equivalent of μ_{t+1},

$$\mu_{\text{new}} = a + (b + r_s)\,\mu + \sigma\,(\mu)\left[r_s\zeta - (r_s + r_d)\,(z - \zeta)^-\right].$$

Scaling the cost functions by dividing through by $\sigma(\mu)$,

$$\hat{F}(\mu) \doteq \frac{F(\mu)}{\sigma(\mu)}$$

$$\hat{G}(z|\mu) \doteq \frac{G(z|\mu)}{\sigma(\mu)}$$

yields

$$\hat{F}(\mu) = \min_z \left\{ \hat{G}(z|\mu) \right\}$$

$$\hat{G}(z|\mu) = L(z) + \alpha \int_{-\theta}^{\infty} \left[\frac{\sigma(\mu_{\text{new}})}{\sigma(\mu)}\right] \hat{F}(\mu_{\text{new}}) d\Psi(\zeta).$$

The two special cases will be members of the class of $\sigma(\cdot)$ that has the property that the ratio $\sigma(\mu_{\text{new}})/\sigma(\mu)$ is independent of μ. If this property happens to hold, then neither the current period costs $L(z)$ nor the multiplier of future cost $\sigma(\mu_{\text{new}})/\sigma(\mu)$ will depend on μ. Thus, $\hat{F}(\mu)$ and $\hat{G}(z|\mu)$ are constant across μ, and can be simplified to

$$\hat{F} = \min_z \left\{ \hat{G}(z) \right\}$$

$$\hat{G}(z) = L(z) + \alpha K(z)\hat{F},$$

where

$$K(z) \doteq \int_{-\infty}^{\infty} \left[\frac{\sigma(\mu_{\text{new}})}{\sigma(\mu)}\right] d\Psi(\zeta).$$

Note that the optimal z^* satisfies

$$\hat{F} = \hat{G}(z^*) = L(z^*) + \alpha\hat{F}K(z^*),$$

and so z^* will solve

$$\hat{F} = \min_z \left\{ \frac{L(z)}{1 - \alpha K(z)} \right\}. \tag{27}$$

The next step is to find functional forms of $\sigma(\cdot)$ that have the desired property that $\sigma(\mu_{\text{new}})/\sigma(\mu)$ is independent of μ. The obvious case is the constant function $\sigma(\mu) = \sigma_0 \forall \mu$. Although this case is certainly inconsistent with the previous assumption of nonnegative demand for small values of μ, for a fairly high mean subject to only moderate changes, the probability of demand going negative may well be negligible.

For $\sigma(\mu) = \sigma_0$, $K(z) = 1$, and the myopic policy of minimizing each period's cost in isolation will be optimal, with

$$z^* = \Psi^{-1}\left(\frac{\pi}{\pi + h}\right).$$

The proof of the following Lemma, showing that this stationary myopic policy is feasible, depends on the admittedly inconsistent assumption of nonnegative demand.

Lemma 3. *When $\sigma(\mu) = \sigma_0$, any reasonable (i.e., backlog-clearing) stationary policy $y_t^*(\mu_t) = \mu_t + \sigma_0 z^*$ will be feasible as long as $y_0(\mu_0) \geq x_0$.*

Proof. (Dependent on the assumption of nonnegative demand)

A stationary policy will be feasible as long as an order is placed every period; i.e., as long as $y_{t+1}^*(\mu_{t+1}) \geq x_{t+1} \forall \xi_t$. Note that when there is a shortage ($x_{t+1} \leq 0$), then this lemma follows immediately from Lemma 2 for all potentially optimal cases. When there is not a shortage in period t, then an order will be placed in period $t + 1$ if

$$\mu_{t+1} + \sigma_0 z^* \geq \sigma_0(z^* - \zeta_t) \forall \zeta_t.$$

Since ζ_t and ζ_{t+1} are identically distributed, this is equivalent to

$$\mu_{t+1} + \sigma_0 \zeta_{t+1} \geq 0 \; \forall \; \zeta_{t+1}.$$

The left-hand side of this inequality is equal to ξ_{t+1}, which is nonnegative by assumption, showing that an order will be placed every period. Thus, to the extent that this nonnegativity assumption holds, the stationary myopic policy will be optimal, with

$$F_t\left(x_t|\,\mu_t\right) = \sigma_0 \hat{F} = \frac{\sigma_0}{1-\alpha} L\left(z^*\right).$$

The second special case is the specific affine form,

$$\sigma(\mu) = c_v \left(\frac{a}{b + r_s - 1} + \mu\right),$$

for some constant parameter c_v. In this case,

$$\frac{\sigma\left(\mu_{\text{new}}\right)}{\sigma\left(\mu\right)} = b + r_s + c_v \left[r_s\zeta - (r_s + r_d)\left(z - \zeta\right)^-\right],$$

which is independent of μ. $K(z)$ becomes

$$K\left(z\right) = b + r_s - c_v\left(r_s + r_d\right) \int_z^\infty \left(\zeta - z\right) d\Psi\left(\zeta\right). \qquad (28)$$

If $a = 0$, this special case simplifies to $\sigma(\mu) = c_v\mu$, with a constant coefficient of variation. Differentiating (27), setting the result equal to zero, and multiplying through by $\left[1 - \alpha K(z)\right]^2$ yields the necessary condition for optimality,

$$\Delta\left(z\right) \doteq L'\left(z\right)\left[1 - \alpha K(z)\right] + \alpha L(z) K'\left(z\right)$$

$$= \left[1 - \alpha(b + r_s)\right]\left[(h + \pi)\Psi(z) - \pi\right]$$

$$+ \alpha h c_v(r_s + r_d) \int_z^\infty \zeta d\Psi\left(\zeta\right) = 0. \qquad (29)$$

Since

$$\lim_{z \to -\infty} \Delta\left(z\right) = -\left[1 - \alpha\left(b + r_s\right)\right]\pi < 0$$

and

$$\lim_{z \to \infty} \Delta\left(z\right) = \left[1 - \alpha\left(b + r_s\right)\right]h > 0,$$

at least one solution to (29) exists. And since

$$\Delta'\left(z\right) = \left[\left[1 - \alpha(b + r_s)\right](h + \pi) - \alpha h c_v(r_s + r_d)z\right]\psi(z)$$

changes sign only once (from positive to negative), the solution will be unique.

Lemma 4. *When the underlying market is not contracting (i.e., when $a \geq 0$ and $b \geq 1$), then any reasonable (i.e., backlog-clearing) stationary policy $y_t^*(\mu_t) = \mu_t + \sigma(\mu_t)z^*$ will be feasible provided that $y_0^*(\mu_0) \geq x_0$.*

Proof. (Dependent on the assumption of nonnegative demand)

A stationary policy will be feasible as long as an order is placed every period; i.e., as long as $y_{t+1}^*(\mu_{t+1}) \geq x_{t+1} \forall \xi_t$. Of course, if there was a shortage ($x_{t+1} \leq 0$), this follows immediately from Lemma 2. If there was not a shortage, then this will be true if

$$\mu_{t+1} + \sigma(\mu_{t+1})z^* \geq \sigma(\mu_t)(z^* - \zeta_t)$$

or

$$\mu_{t+1} + \sigma(\mu_{t+1})\zeta_t \geq \left[(\sigma(\mu_t) - \sigma(\mu_{t+1})\right](z^* - \zeta_t) \forall \zeta_t \leq z^*. \quad (30)$$

Now since ξ_{t+1} is assumed to be nonnegative,

$$\mu_{t+1} + \sigma(\mu_{t+1})\zeta_{t+1} \geq 0 \ \forall \ \zeta_{t+1}. \quad (31)$$

In particular, (31) holds for $\zeta_{t+1} = \zeta_t$, showing that the left-hand side of (30) is nonnegative. And since $\sigma(\cdot)$ is constructed to be nondecreasing, the right-hand side will be nonpositive if

$$\mu_{t+1} \geq \mu_t \ \forall \ \zeta_t \leq z^*$$

or

$$a + (b - 1)\mu_t + r_s(\mu_t + \sigma(\mu_t)\zeta_t) \geq 0 \ \forall \ \zeta_t \leq z^*,$$

which follows from the assumptions of noncontracting market and nonnegative mean μ_t and demand ξ_t.

8 Using These Special Cases as Bounds

Although these special cases of $\sigma(\cdot)$ are of interest in themselves, they can also be used to provide upper and lower bounds for the broad class of problems for which the scaling functions $\sigma(\cdot)$ are nonnegative, concave, and nondecreasing.

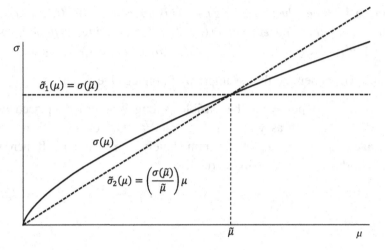

Fig. 1 $\sigma(\mu)$ and Its Approximations

Consider the case where $\sigma(\cdot)$ is of this general form, and the mean for the current period is $\tilde{\mu}$. What would be the consequence of approximating $\sigma(\mu)$ by

$$\tilde{\sigma}_1\left(\mu\mid\tilde{\mu}\right) \doteq \sigma\left(\tilde{\mu}\right) \tag{32}$$

and following the policy that is optimal for this approximation (i.e., the first special case)? Since $\sigma(\cdot)$ is nondecreasing, it is clear that $\tilde{\sigma}_1(\mu\mid\tilde{\mu})\leq\sigma(\mu) \ \forall \ \mu \geq \tilde{\mu}$ and $\tilde{\sigma}_1(\mu\mid\tilde{\mu})\geq\sigma(\mu) \ \forall \ \mu \leq \tilde{\mu}$, as shown in Fig. 1. And since period costs are proportional to $\sigma(\cdot)$, the appropriate policy under this $\tilde{\sigma}_1(\mu\mid\tilde{\mu})$ approximation errs by underestimating period costs for $\mu > \tilde{\mu}$ and overestimating them for $\mu < \tilde{\mu}$. These misestimations imply that this policy overprotects against decreases in the mean. This bias towards satisfying demand can be accomplished only through overstocking inventory. Thus, the stationary policy of the first special case, with $\tilde{\sigma}_1(\mu\mid\tilde{\mu}) = \sigma(\tilde{\mu})$, provides an upper bound on $z^*(\mu)$.

Similarly, consider the consequences of approximating $\sigma(\mu)$ by the affine form,

$$\tilde{\sigma}_2\left(\mu\mid\tilde{\mu}\right) \doteq \left[\frac{a + (b + r_s - 1)\mu}{a + (b + r_s - 1)\tilde{\mu}}\right]\sigma\left(\tilde{\mu}\right). \tag{33}$$

Note that when $a = 0$, this reduces to the case where the coefficient of variation is constant

$$\tilde{\sigma}_2(\mu|\tilde{\mu}) = \left(\frac{\sigma(\tilde{\mu})}{\tilde{\mu}}\right)\mu. \tag{34}$$

Note that $\tilde{\sigma}_2(\mu|\tilde{\mu}) \geq \sigma(\mu)\forall\mu \geq \tilde{\mu}$ from the assumption that $\sigma(\cdot)$ is concave; see Fig. 1. The converse assertion, that $\tilde{\sigma}_2(\mu|\tilde{\mu}) \leq \sigma(\mu)\forall\mu \leq \tilde{\mu}$, will be true only if

$$\tilde{\sigma}_2(0|\tilde{\mu}) \leq \sigma(0) \ \forall \ \tilde{\mu}.$$

And since $\sigma(0) = 0$, this will hold only if

$$-(b + r_s - 1)\tilde{\mu} \leq a \leq 0.$$

So if this inequality holds, then using the approximation $\tilde{\sigma}_2(\mu|\tilde{\mu})$ in the second special case yields a policy that misestimates costs in the opposite direction as did the first special case, and so will provide a lower bound on $z^*(\mu)$.

Although the optimal stocking policy $z^*(\mu)$ is generally nonstationary and computationally intractable, under some very general conditions on the form of $\sigma(\cdot)$, it will have easily computable upper and lower bounds. Of course, the value of these bounds (which are based on approximating $\sigma(\cdot)$ by the two special cases in which the optimal policy is stationary) depends on their tightness, which depends in turn on the particular values of the parameters.

Consider the following numerical example. Using

$$c = 1 \quad \hat{h} = 0 \quad \alpha = .99 \quad a = 0 \quad r_s = .001$$
$$r = 1.1 \quad \hat{\pi} = 0 \quad \beta = 1 \quad b = 1 \quad r_d = .005$$

with

$$\sigma(\mu) = \mu^{2/3}. \tag{35}$$

The choice of the exponent 2/3 corresponds to the situation where demand is somewhat, but not completely, correlated across customers. We use (17) and (18) to calculate $h = 0.01$ and $\pi = 0.0669$, and consider the scaled demand ζ_t under both the normal and uniform distributions

$$\zeta_t \sim N(0, 1) \quad \text{and} \quad \zeta_t \sim U(\pm\sqrt{3}), \tag{36}$$

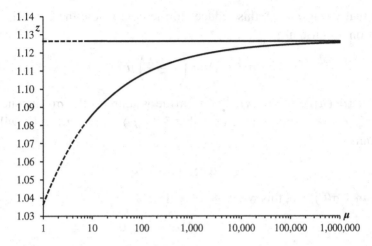

Fig. 2 Bounds on the Optimal Order-Up-To Values (Normal Distribution)

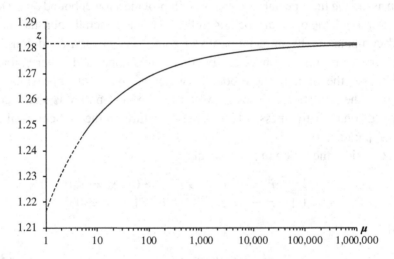

Fig. 3 Bounds on the Optimal Order-Up-To Values (Uniform Distribution)

yielding the upper and lower bounds on $z^*(\mu)$ graphed in Figs. 2 and 3, respectively. For the smallest values of μ, assumptions (35) and (36) will be inconsistent. For the normal distribution, we require

$$\mu - 2\sigma \geq 0, \quad \text{or} \quad \mu \geq 8,$$

while for the uniform distribution we require

$$\mu - \sqrt{3}\sigma \geq 0, \quad \text{or} \quad \mu \geq 3^{1.5} = 5.196;$$

values of μ that are not consistent are represented by dashed lines in Figs. 2 and 3.

For this particular example, the bounds were quite tight throughout, resulting in a lower bound almost linear in $c_v(\mu) = \sigma(\mu)/\mu = \mu^{-1/3}$, with

$$1.12642 - 0.08976 \cdot c_v(\mu)^{1.04317} \leq z^*(\mu) \leq 1.12642$$

and

$$1.28174 - 0.06577 \cdot c_v(\mu)^{1.08442} \leq z^*(\mu) \leq 1.28174$$

for the normal and uniform cases, respectively. The goodness-of-fit for these two regressions was surprisingly high, with adjusted R^2 of 99.998% and 99.969%, respectively.

9   Conclusions and Future Research

The problem with using penalty costs to find the optimal order-up-to points is in accurately assessing the lost goodwill of a dissatisfied customer. The difficulty of quantifying this lost goodwill results in managers guessing at an appropriate value more often than using a more involved procedure, such as those suggested by Chang and Niland (1967) and Badinelli (1986).

In this chapter, we propose that the most likely manifestation of lost customer goodwill will be a drop in future demand. By developing a reasonable model of these changing demands, the goodwill costs can be evaluated as the net present value of the expected profits foregone due to the drop in demand.

The additional data requirements of this model are quite small, since most of the parameters would need to be specified in the traditional inventory models. The effect of goodwill changes from satisfied and dissatisfied customers is handled by only two additional parameters, r_s and r_d.

Although changing variability leads to an optimal ordering policy which depends on the mean (even after transformation) and is computationally intractable, the optimal stocking policy is bounded above and below by policies that can be easily calculated.

One obvious direction of future research is to search for further forms of $\sigma(\cdot)$ for which $\sigma(\mu_{\text{new}})/\sigma(\mu)$ is independent of μ. Another is to generalize the functional relationship between μ_{t+1} and μ_t, perhaps by means of a more complicated epidemic-based relationship, or through the use of known natural upper and lower bounds on the mean. The difficulty in modeling these more complicated nonlinear relationships is in retaining the ability to extract the effect of the mean on the period costs, and retaining costs that are stationary over time.

Another direction of future research is to more thoroughly investigate the tightness of the bounds provided in these special cases. It would be valuable to learn the circumstances for which they are especially tight or loose.

In addition, the very close linear relationship between the lower bound provided by the second special case and the coefficient of variation $c_v(\mu)$ implies that approximations to the lower bound (e.g., a Taylor series expansion) might be quite close.

Finally, the standard extensions in the inventory literature (e.g., nonlinear cost functions, positive lead times between placing and receiving an order, etc.) could also be applied to this problem. Other extensions would allow for more general effects of customer (dis)satisfaction; e.g., delayed, gradually realized, and/or transient changes in demand.

Bibliography

Arrow, K. J., Harris, T. and Marschak, J. (1951). Optimal inventory policy, *Econometrica* **19**, pp. 250–272.

Badinelli, R. D. (1986). Optimal safety-stock investment through subjective evaluation of stockout costs, *Decision Sciences* **17**, pp. 312–328.

Ballou, R. H. (1971). Developing definitive statements of the customer service function, *Proceedings of the National Council of Physical Distribution Management*, Vol. 9.

Ballou, R. H. (1973). Planning a sales strategy with distribution service, *The Logistics and Transportation Review* **9**, pp. 323–334.

Bellman, R., Glicksberg, I. and Gross, O. (1955). On the optimal inventory policy, *Management Science* **2**, pp. 84–104.

Brooking, S. A. (1987). Inventory system costs; source data for analysis, *Engineering Costs and Production Economics* **13**, pp. 1–12.

Bursk, E. C. (1966). View your customers as investments, *Harvard Business Review* **44**, 3, pp. 91–94.

Caine, G. J. and Plaut, R. H. (1976). Optimal inventory policy when stockouts alter demand, *Naval Research Logistics Quarterly* **23**, pp. 1–13.

Chang, Y. S. and Niland, P. (1967). A model for measuring stock depletion costs, *Operations Research* **15**, pp. 427–447.

Christopher, M. and Wills, G. (1974). Developing customer service policies, *International Journal of Physical Distribution* **4**, pp. 321–352.

Gardner, E. S. (1980). Inventory theory and the Gods of Olympus, *Interfaces* **10**, pp. 42–45.

Gilmour, P. (1977). Customer service: differentiating by market segment, *International Journal of Physical Distribution* **7**, pp. 141–148.

Gilmour, P. (1979). Development of a demand response function, *Journal of Business Logistics* **1**, 2, pp. 83–102.

Hadley, G. and Whitin, T. M. (1963). *Analysis of Inventory Systems*, Prentice-Hall, Englewood Cliffs, New Jersey.

Hanssmann, F. (1959). Optimal inventory location and control in production and distribution networks, *Operations Research* **7**, pp. 483–498.

Heskett, J. L. (1971). Controlling customer logistics service, *International Journal of Physical Distribution* **1**, pp. 140–145.

Hill, T. W. (1976). A simple perturbed demand inventory model with ordering cost, *Management Science* **23**, pp. 38–42.

Hutchison, W. M. and Stolle, J. F. (1968). How to manage customer service, *Harvard Business Review* **46**, 6, pp. 85–96.

Krenn, J. M. and Shycon, H. M. (1983). Modeling sales response to customer service for more effective distribution, *Proceedings of the National Council of Physical Distribution Management* **21**, pp. 582–601.

LaLonde, B. J. and Zinszer, P. H. (1976). *Customer Service: Meaning and Measurement*, National Council of Physical Distribution Management, Chicago.

LaLonde, B. J., Cooper, M. C. and Noordewier, T. G. (1988). *Customer Service: A Management Perspective*, Council of Logistics Management, Oak Brook, Illinois.

Lambert, D. M. and Harrington, T. C. (1989). Establishing customer service strategies within the marketing mix: more empirical evidence, *Journal of Business Logistics* **10**, 2, pp. 44–60.

Lambert, D. M. and Zemke, D. E. (1982). The customer service component of the marketing mix, *Proceedings of the National Council of Physical Distribution Management* **20**, pp. 1–24.

Lee, H. L. and Tapiero, C. S. (1986). Quality control and the sales process, *Naval Research Logistics Quarterly* **33**, pp. 569–587.

Morey, R. C. (1980). Measuring the impact of service level on retail sales, *Journal of Retailing* **56**, 2, pp. 81–90.

Mossman, F. H. and Morton, N. (1965). *Logistics of Distribution Systems*, Allyn and Bacon, Boston.

Neilsen, A. C. (1968a). The out-of-stock study: A crusade against stockouts, *Progressive Grocer* **47**, 10, pp. 55–71.

Neilsen, A. C. (1968b). Out-of-stock study: Part II — Growing problem of stockouts verified by Nielsen research, *Progressive Grocer* **47**, 11, pp. 49–64.

Nuttall, C. (1965). The relationship between sales and distribution of certain confectionery lines. *Commentary* **7**, pp. 272–285.

Olinick, M. (1978). An Introduction of Mathematical Models in the Social and Life Sciences, Addison-Wesley, Reading, Massachusetts.

Oral, M. (1981). Multi-item inventory management with monetary objective function, *AIIE Transactions* **13**, pp. 41–46.

Oral, M., Salvador, M. S., Reisman, A. and Dean, B. V. (1972). On the evaluation of shortage costs for inventory control of finished goods, *Management Science* **18**, pp. B-344–351.

Ozment, J. and Chard, D. N. (1986). Effects of customer service on sales: An analysis of historical data, *International Journal of Physical Distribution and Materials Management* **16**, 3, pp. 14–28.

Perreault, W. D. and Russ, F. A. (1974). Physical distribution service: a neglected aspect of marketing management, *MSU Business Topics* **22**, 3, pp. 37–45.

Perreault, W. D. and Russ, F. A. (1976a). Quantifying marketing trade-offs in physical distribution policy decisions, *Decision Sciences* **7**, pp. 186–201.

Perreault, W. D. and Russ, F. A. (1976b). Physical distribution service in industrial purchase decisions, *Journal of Marketing* **40**, 2, pp. 3–10.

Richins, M. L. (1983). Negative word-of-mouth by dissatisfied consumers: A pilot study, *Journal of Marketing* **47**, 1, pp. 68–78.

Ritz, C. J. (1982). Analytical methods for measuring the effect of customer service on sales, *Proceedings of the National Council of Physical Distribution Management* **20**, pp. 540–544.

Sanford, R. T. (1982). The cost/benefit approach to designing better customer service strategies, *Proceedings of the National Council of Physical Distribution Management* **20**, pp. 546–562.

Sanford, R. T. and Farrell, J. W. (1982). A study of customer service perceptions, requirements and effects on American industry, *Proceedings of the National Council of Physical Distribution Management* **20**, pp. 234–245.

Schary, P. B. and Becker, B. W. (1972). Distribution and final demand: The influence of availability, *Mississippi Valley Journal of Business and Economics* **8**, 1, pp. 17–26.

Schary, P. B. and Becker, B. W. (1973). The marketing/logistics interface, *International Journal of Physical Distribution* **3**, pp. 245–288.

Schary, P. B. and Becker, B. W. (1978). The impact of stock-out on market share: Temporal effects, *Journal of Business Logistics* **1**, 1, pp. 31–44.

Schwartz, B. L. (1965). Inventory models in which stockouts influence subsequent demand, Technical Report No. 12, Graduate School of Business, Stanford University, Palo Alto, California.

Schwartz, B. L. (1966). A new approach to stockout penalties, *Management Science* **12**, pp. B-538–544.

Schwartz, B. L. (1970). Optimal inventory policies in perturbed demand models, *Management Science* **16**, pp. B-509–518.

Shycon, H. M. (1973). Customer service, measuring its value, *Proceedings of the National Council of Physical Distribution Management* **11**, pp. 420–441.

Shycon, H. M. and Ritz, C. J. (1981). Analytical techniques to evaluate service levels required for sales growth and profitability, *Proceedings of the National Council of Physical Distribution Management* **19**, pp. 452–461.

Shycon, H. N. and Sprague, C. R. (1975). Put a price tag on your customer service levels, *Harvard Business Review* **53**, 4, pp. 71–78.

Stephenson, P. R. and Willett, R. P. (1968). Selling with physical distribution service, *Business Horizons* **11**, 6, pp. 75–85.

Sterling, J. U. and Lambert, D. M. (1987). Establishing customer service strategies within the marketing mix, *Journal of Business Logistics* **8**, 1, pp. 1–30.

TARP. (1979). *Consumer Complaint Handling in America: Summary of Findings and Recommendations*. U.S. Department of Health, Education, and Welfare, Washington, D.C.

TARP. (1985). Consumer complaint handling in America: An update study, Part I, U.S. Department of Health, Education, and Welfare, Washington, D.C.

Vidale, M. L. and Wolfe, H. B. (1957). An operations-research study of sales response to advertising, *Operations Research* **5**, pp. 370–381.

Walter, C. K. and Grabner, J. R. (1975). Stockout cost models: Empirical tests in a retail situation, _Journal of Marketing_ **39**, pp. 56–68.

Walter, C. K. and LaLonde, B. J. (1975). Development and tests of two stockout cost models, _International Journal of Physical Distribution_ **5**, pp. 121–132.

Walters, D. (1974). The cost of a stock-out, _International Journal of Physical Distribution_ **5**, pp. 36–48.

Willett, R. P. and Stephenson, P. R. (1969). Determinants of buyer response to physical distribution service, _Journal of Marketing Research_ **6**, pp. 279–283.

Zinszer, P. H. (1980). Customer service: Handling limited product availability, _Proceedings of the National Council of Physical Distribution Management_ **18**, pp. 257–263.

Appendix

This appendix contains proofs of two lemmas. The first proves that the expected cost $f_0(x_0|\mu_0)$ is finite; i.e., that it is bounded above and below. The second demonstrates that the optimal ordering policy is nonnegative.

Lemma A.1 *The expected cost $f_0(x_0|\mu_0)$ is bounded below.*

Proof. A lower bound on $f_0(x_0|\mu_0)$ can be constructed by relaxing constraints (13) and allowing the order-up-to point to be determined after demand has been observed. Clearly, the optimal policy will set $y_t = \xi_t$, yielding a lower bound on (15) of

$$
f_0(x_0|\mu_0) \geq -(r-c)(x_0)^- - c(x_0)^+ - (r-c) \sum_{t=0}^{\infty} \alpha^t \mu_t,
$$

with

$$
\mu_{t+1} = a + (b + r_s)\,\mu_t \quad t = 0, 1, \ldots
$$

Repeating the development that led to (11) yields

$$
f_0(x_0|\mu_0) \geq -(r-c)(x_0)^- - c(x_0)^+ - (r-c) \left[\frac{\mu_0 + \frac{\alpha a}{1-\alpha}}{1 - \alpha(b + r_s)} \right],
$$

and since $1 - \alpha(b + r_s) > 0$ from requirement (5), $f_0(x_0|\mu_0)$ will have a finite lower bound.

Any feasible ordering policy will provide an upper bound on the costs. Consider a "make to order" policy of ordering only enough to satisfy previously backlogged demand; i.e., setting $y_t = 0 \ \forall t$. While the presence of the initial inventory $(x_0)^+$ would make this policy infeasible, it is clear that the most costly use of this inventory would be to hold it unused forever. Thus, (15) becomes

$$
f_0(x_0|\mu_0) \leq -(r-c)(x_0)^- + \left(\frac{\hat{h}}{1-\alpha} + c \right)(x_0)^+
$$

$$
+ \left[\hat{\pi} - \alpha\beta(r-c) \right] \sum_{t=0}^{\infty} \alpha^t \mu_t,
$$

with

$$\mu_{t+1} = a + (b - r_d)\mu_t.$$

Again, repeating the development that led to (11) yields

$$f_0(x_0|\mu_0) \leq -(r - c)(x_0)^- + \left(\frac{\hat{h}}{1 - \alpha} + c\right)(x_0)^+$$

$$+ [\hat{\pi} - \alpha\beta(r - c)]\left[\frac{\mu_0 + \frac{\alpha a}{1-\alpha}}{1 - \alpha(b - r_d)}\right],$$

showing $f_0(x_0|\mu_0)$ to be bounded above and completing the proof.

Lemma A.2 *The optimal policy is to satisfy all backlogs.*

Proof. It is sufficient to show that the global minimum $y_t^*(\mu_t)$ is nonnegative, which will be true if $\frac{\partial}{\partial y_t}G_t(y_t|\mu_t) \leq 0$ for all $y_t \leq 0$. Consider the following restricted model. Starting in some future period τ, all backlogs will be required to be satisfied as soon as they occur; this is equivalent to adding the constraints

$$y_t \geq 0 \quad t = \tau, \tau + 1, \ldots$$

to the formulation. Define $\tilde{F}_t(x_t|\mu_t)$ and $\tilde{G}_t(y_t|\mu_t)$ to correspond to $F_t(x_t|\mu_t)$ and $G_t(y_t|\mu_t)$, under these additional constraints. Clearly,

$$\tilde{F}_t(x_t|\mu_t) \geq F_t(x_t|\mu_t), \tag{A.1}$$

$$\tilde{G}_t(y_t|\mu_t) \geq G_t(y_t|\mu_t). \tag{A.2}$$

Since the costs are finite from Lemma A.1, (A.1) and (A.2) will hold as equalities as $\tau \to \infty$.

Define $\tilde{y}_t^*(\mu_t)$ to be the point which minimizes $\tilde{G}_t(y_t|\mu_t)$ without regard to the initial inventory x_t. This may differ from the global minimum for $t \geq \tau$, since $\tilde{y}_t^*(\mu_t)$ is constrained to be nonnegative for those t.

For $t \geq \tau$, $\tilde{y}_t^*(\mu_t)$ will be nonnegative by construction. We can use backwards induction to extend this result to $t < \tau$ as well. Assume that the result holds for periods $t+1$ on. Note that for $y_t < 0$, $x_{t+1} = \beta(y_t - \xi_t) < 0$, and so $x_{t+1} \leq \tilde{y}^*_{t+1}(\mu_{t+1})$ by the inductive assumption. Thus, for $y_t \leq 0$,

$$F_{t+1}(x_{t+1}|\mu_{t+1}) = G_{t+1}(y^*_{t+1}(\mu_{t+1})|\mu_{t+1}),$$

and so from (21),

$$\frac{\partial}{\partial y_t}\tilde{G}_t(y_t|\mu_t) = -(1-\alpha\beta)(r-c) < 0,$$

demonstrating that $y^*_t(\mu_t)$ is nonnegative as well.

Finally, since (A.2) holds as an equality as $t \to \infty$, any policy that minimizes the former must also minimize the latter in the limit. Thus, the global minimum for $G_t(y_t|\mu_t)$ will be nonnegative for the original problem as well.

Chapter 6

Practical Inventory Planning Strategies for E-Commerce

Juan Li* and John Muckstadt[†]

*Scalable Data Analytics Lab, PARC, a Xerox company, Webster, NY 14580
[†] School of Operations Research and Information Engineering,
Cornell University, Ithaca, NY 14853

1 Introduction

When designing their multi-warehouse distribution systems, online retailers must ensure the system provides timely response to customer's orders while minimizing total inventory, warehousing, and transportation costs. This order fulfillment system must contain enough geographically distributed warehouse capacity to hold inventories required to meet uncertain and time varying demand for millions of items. Multiple warehouses are needed so that orders can be filled cost effectively from warehouses that are relatively close to the customer's delivery address. These "last mile delivery costs" are substantial, and must be controlled as the scale of online retailers increases. Take Amazon.com for example. The cost to ship 608 million items (Bensinger and Stevens, 2014) was $6.6 billion (Amazon.com Annual Report, 2014), a major portion of which was last mile delivery costs.

Recently, we worked with a major online retailer to reduce inventory and distribution costs in its fulfillment system. For online retailers, it is a common practice to provide both slow and fast shipping service to customers. As a result, while some orders need to be satisfied immediately, some orders have a difference between a customer's order date and the customer's desired fulfillment date. Recognizing this difference changes the way inventories are managed and orders are fulfilled. By allowing for flexibility as to when it could fulfill an order, the retailer's inventories, warehouse space requirements, and last mile delivery costs were reduced substantially. Overall, these costs were reported to us to have been reduced by a few hundred million dollars per year.

When working with a large-scale, complex, multi-echelon order fulfillment system, the main challenge is to develop a model that can be solved in a reasonable time frame with realistic computing power. We tackle this challenge by first constructing a model and a computationally tractable method for planning procurements and allocating stocks among warehouses without workload smoothing. Our model is based on taking advantage of the difference between the time a customer places an order and when it must be fulfilled. Then we demonstrate the effect of workload smoothing and flexible delivery dates on the total system inventories, and describe a model for adjusting inventory requirements accordingly. This effect is important to understand since online retailers have been encouraging customers to request immediate fulfillment of their orders through enrolling in annual membership with one-time payment. Amazon Prime, for example, allows customers to place as many two-day shipping orders as desired.

2 Background

We now discuss some of the key attributes that exist in the online retailer's operating environment. As a consequence of the system's redesign, the online retailer currently operates a multi-echelon fulfillment system structured as follows. Each item is managed through a single warehouse, called the *primary warehouse* for the item. Each warehouse serves as a primary warehouse for a collection of items. The choice of the primary warehouse for an item depends largely on the supplier's location. Balancing warehouse workloads and recognizing facility capacities also affects the number of items managed by each warehouse. Items normally ordered together by a customer also have a common primary warehouse. Once a primary warehouse is selected for an item, that warehouse procures and receives inventory from an external supplier. Suppliers ship items only to the item's designated primary warehouse. The primary warehouse then distributes inventory to the other warehouses, which we call *regional warehouses*, on an as needed basis. We refer to this system as the primary warehouse system (PWS). Every warehouse in the PWS serves as a primary warehouse for hundreds of thousands of items and a regional warehouse for an even larger number of items.

Each primary warehouse is conceptually thought of as two entities, although there is only one physical entity. One entity performs procurement, warehousing, and allocation tasks. The other entity is responsible for satisfying demand that arises in the geographical region in which the warehouse is located. We call this second entity, which is a virtual warehouse, the *co-located warehouse*. Since this virtual co-located warehouse is physically located in the same facility as the primary warehouse, shipping to it is assumed to occur instantaneously.

Within the PWS, orders are planned to be satisfied from the regional warehouse closest to the customer's delivery address to minimize last mile delivery costs, which are a substantial component of the retailer's operating cost. Recall that when customers place orders, they also choose a delivery option which indicates when they want to receive the shipment. The options include delivery to the customer in one or two days following the order's placement or delivery to the customer a week or more following the placement of the order. In the former case, a premium delivery charge normally is incurred by the customer. In the other case, shipping may be free or at a low cost to the customer. We categorize orders by the length of time by which the goods must be shipped. We call this time the *response lead time*. Suppose a customer places an order that will be fulfilled from a particular regional warehouse. If the response lead time specified by the customer is less than the sum of the shipping lead time from the primary warehouse to that regional warehouse and the time to ship to the customer from that warehouse, we call this a *short-response lead time demand*. Otherwise, we call it a *long-response lead time demand*.

In principle, the only reason to stock inventory for an item at a regional warehouse is to satisfy short-response lead time demand arising in the nearby region. The inventory to fulfill long-response lead time demand occurring anywhere in the system is stocked at the primary warehouse. When a long-response lead time demand occurs, the primary warehouse sends the inventory to the regional warehouse that is responsible for satisfying the customer's order. The inventory is then cross-docked at the regional warehouse and sent directly to the customer. The primary warehouse must also carry inventory so that it can replenish each regional warehouse's inventory, which is needed to satisfy the regional warehouse's short-response lead time demand. We note that for the online retailer we worked with, short-response lead time demand usually accounted for between 13% to 20% of the total demand for an item, and the percentage varied by item and sometimes by the time of the year. Since such a large percentage of the demand is long-response lead time demand, the majority of this demand is fulfilled by first shipping inventory from the primary warehouse's on-hand stock to the appropriate regional warehouse, cross-docking the material at the regional warehouse and shipping it to the customer from that regional warehouse. These transshipments from the primary to the regional warehouses are normally executed in full truck loads. This is possible because there are so many items ordered by thousands of customers that require transshipping. These long haul, full truck load shipments followed by "last mile" shipping from a regional warehouse are far less expensive to make than shipping directly to the customer from a primary warehouse. Furthermore, since all long-response lead time demand is satisfied from a single source, a pooling effect is present, i.e., system safety stocks are lowered. The company also lowered cycle stocks due to changes in procurement policies. In aggregate, the retailer reduced cycle and safety stocks and lowered transportation costs. Previous to the implementation of what the online retailer called the "delayed allocation policy," order fill rates at the closest regional warehouse were below 50%. This resulted in shipping portions of orders to a customer from other than the desired regional warehouses. Since transportation costs are a concave function of volume/weight and the shipping distance, transportation costs were substantially higher than under the delayed allocation policy. The benefits of the delayed allocation policy are directly related to the percentage of total demand that can be pooled. But, the percentage of short-response lead time demand has been increasing recently, thereby increasing inventories and inventory related costs. As mentioned, a key question is the following: how does the total inventory requirement change as this percentage increases?

There are two distinct but interrelated decisions related to setting stock levels and fulfilling customer orders. First, procurement decisions are made on an item basis. These decisions take into account fixed ordering costs, quantity discounts, holding and shortage costs, workload smoothing, the multi-echelon nature of the PWS, and, of course, the uncertainty and timing aspects of the demand process throughout a planning horizon. Second, fulfillment decisions are made on an order-by-order basis. Once a customer order is received, a decision needs to be made about how best to fulfill it. The model developed in this chapter is focused on the planning problem. The inventory levels or targets set in the planning process guide procurement decisions for individual items over time. The way existing inventories should be best allocated for either replenishment or cross-docking from warehouses to fulfill a customer's order in a timely and cost effective manner is presented by Li and Muckstadt (2013).

Even though the actual fulfillment decisions depend on the composition of customer orders, we do not consider it in the planning problem for two reasons. First, in practice, no single customer order accounts for more than a small fraction of 1% of the demand for the items of interest. Second, the procurement lead times are normally weeks to months in length, whereas fulfilling orders must be accomplished in time intervals measured in days. Forecasting customer orders in terms of content and timing weeks or months in advance of their placement has not proven to be possible. Hence, we have separated the decision-making process into two segments, one for planning the target inventory levels and the other for fulfilling orders.

In the remainder of this chapter, we will focus our discussion on the planning model. The organization of the remainder of the chapter is as follows. In Section 3, we briefly discuss literature related to our efforts. In Section 4, we present an exact planning model for setting stock levels for each item at each warehouse. This model is formulated as a dynamic program that cannot be solved directly in real problem settings. We then develop an approximation approach for determining stock levels that is scalable and applicable to the planning activity in the environment that motivated this research. In Section 5, we describe an approach to augment target inventory levels when a workload smoothing constraint is present. In Section 6, we provide concluding remarks.

3 Literature Review

There are four streams of literature related to the problem we are addressing. We will discuss them separately.

Recall we propose to operate the system with the PWS approach where we stock the inventories for long-response lead time items at the primary warehouse and the short-response lead time items at the regional warehouses. This idea is related to material found in Muckstadt *et al.* (2001). Our approach is similar to their "No B/C strategy" in the sense that the long-lead time demand can be viewed as their B/C type items, which are not stocked at the regional warehouses in general. The short-response lead time demand can be viewed as their A type items, which are stocked at all regional warehouses. In this chapter, long-response lead time demand and short-response lead time demand may overlap. Hence, when the primary warehouse is not able to satisfy a long-response lead time demand, the regional warehouse may use its on-hand inventory to satisfy the demand.

We assume the primary warehouse places orders from an external supplier under a fixed schedule. Eppen and Schrage (1981) do as well. The primary focus in their chapter is to demonstrate how risk and inventory requirements are reduced by operating a two-echelon distribution system in a certain manner. In their system, the central warehouse places an order every period under a base stock policy, and no stock is held at the central warehouse. In our system, this is not the case. Jackson (1988) built both an exact cost model and a computationally tractable approximation cost model to find a ship-up-to-S allocation policy for a cyclic system that serves *N* warehouses. In each cycle, the central warehouse allocates inventories to each regional warehouse periodically. Jackson and Muckstadt (1989) extend this idea to a two-echelon, two-period allocation problem.

Our multi-echelon inventory model is based on Clark and Scarf's (1960) echelon inventory position concept. They found that solving a distribution system type of problem is difficult due to the possible "imbalance" of inventories among the regional warehouses. Such systems are "balanced" if there is no desire to redistribute the inventories among the regional warehouses whenever inventories are allocated to regional warehouses. Clark and Scarf found that under their balance assumption the systems can be decomposed into individual location problems which can be optimized separately. However, this balance assumption may not necessarily hold. When it is violated, the optimal allocation strategy could be to allocate negative quantities to a location. Federgruen and Zipkin (1984) obtain a lower bound on a value function by relaxing the imbalance constraints. Kunnumkal and Topaloglu (2008, 2011) associated Lagrangian multipliers with the balance constraints. By introducing the Lagrangian multipliers, the resulting relaxed problem can be solved easily. They discussed several approximation methods that can be used to select a good set of multiplier values. They also show that Fedegruen and Zipkin's approach is equivalent to setting the multiplier values to zero. Hence, their approach permits them to obtain tighter lower bounds on the optimal objective function value than the value achieved using Federgruen and Zipkin's methodology.

In this chapter, shipping capacity from the primary warehouse to a non-co-located regional warehouse is limited. Many papers have studied capacitated systems. Glasserman and Tayur (1994) discussed conditions under which a capacitated system is stable. They found that a multi-echelon inventory system that operates under a base-stock inventory policy is stable if the mean demand per period is smaller than the capacity at every regional warehouse. Muckstadt *et al.* (2001) used a shortfall process approach to develop a cost model. When demand is stationary, we extend the idea to the case when the system does not need to satisfy demand immediately. This approach is usually implemented by finding the transition matrix of the shortfall process and then finding the stationary distribution. When the mean demand is large, Glasserman (1997) and Roundy and Muckstadt (2000) found that the shortfall process can be approximated by a mass exponential function. We will use this idea to approximate the probability distribution of the shortfall process.

As mentioned earlier, the system provides two levels of service, which correspond to the short-response lead time demand and long-response lead time demand. The long-response lead time demand can be thought of as having advanced demand information. The effect of the advanced demand information is examined by Hariharan and Zipkin (1995) in a continuous-review framework. In many papers, one of two assumptions is made. Either the advance demand must be satisfied on a fixed schedule or the system has the flexibility to satisfy the demand within some amount of time. Gallego and Özer, (2002, 2003) and Özer (2003) make the first type of assumption and conclude that state-dependent (s, S) and base-stock policies are optimal for stochastic inventory systems depending on the cost structure. Wang and Toktay (2008) extend this conclusion to the flexible delivery case.

4 The Planning Model

Before we present our model, we first discuss attributes of the demand
process experienced by the online retailer. Although there are millions of
items available for purchase from the online retailer, most items have very
low demand rates. In fact, most items have four or fewer units demanded
annually. These items are sometimes stocked in a single warehouse
operated by the online retailer. However, in most cases, these items are
not stocked by the online retailer at all but rather in some other company's
warehouse. Other items may be ordered only a few times per year; but, many
units may be requested in a single order. Some textbooks are examples of
such items. These items are also normally stocked in a single location. For
the online retailer we worked with, these low demand items account for
over 70% of the items offered in the system.

On the other hand, for the online retailer we studied, under 2% of the
items account for about 30% of the system's total sales, measured in units
and in monetary terms. These very high demand items are stocked at all
warehouses. We will not focus on either the low or very high demand rate
items in this chapter. Rather, we will focus on the roughly 27% of the
items that are relatively high demand rate items and that are stocked in
the multiple-warehouse PWS system operated by the online retailer.

The mean and variance of the demand process varies over time for a
large portion of these higher demand rate items. For many items, most of
their demand occurs from mid-November through the end of December. For
others, spikes in demand occur according to school calendars or perhaps
due to the launch of the item into the market.

We now develop a planning model designed to establish inventory levels
for the relatively high demand rate items that are managed in the PWS
structure. We first construct an exact model that cannot be used to solve
realistic problems due to the size of the state space. We then construct
an approximation model and a computationally tractable solution method.
We begin our model development by stating our assumptions concerning
the fulfillment system's operation and by introducing some nomenclature.
Additional nomenclature is presented as we proceed.

We assume that decisions for each item are made on a periodic basis.
Thus, the model we develop is a periodic review model, a period being a

day in length. Each day at each primary warehouse, two decisions must be made for each item that is managed there. The first is a procurement decision and the second is an allocation decision.

To manage both costs and workloads, for planning purposes, procurement orders for an item are placed according to a schedule. That is, we assume that for each item there is a pre-determined set of times at which orders are placed on a supplier. We call the time between the placing of successive procurement orders a cycle length. Items are ordered by the retailer using a power-of-two type of policy, that is, orders are placed weekly, bi-weekly, monthly, or quarterly. In practice, the exact timing of the placing of orders is done to smooth buyer and warehouse workloads. The frequency of placing orders depends largely on the economics of ordering. Determining the schedule for placing procurement orders for each item is in itself an interesting problem. Since this topic is not the focus of this chapter, we assume in the following sections that the cycle lengths are known and the timing of procurement actions has been established for each item.

The second decision made each day is to determine how much inventory to allocate to each regional warehouse from the primary warehouse. The allocation decisions for an item depend on demand forecasts, costs, inventory availability at the primary warehouse, and the inventory positions at the regional warehouses.

The entire fulfillment system can be analyzed one primary warehouse at a time since there are no constraints that link decisions made for one primary warehouse to another primary warehouse. Thus, our model focuses on a system consisting of one primary warehouse that manages inventories for several hundred thousand items. Li and Muckstadt (2013) directly consider the interdependencies of warehouses when fulfilling customer orders.

Suppose there are N regional warehouses in the PWS including the co-located warehouse. Let us denote the primary warehouse as location 0. Regional warehouses numbered 1 through $N - 1$ correspond to those that are not co-located with the primary warehouse. Regional warehouse N is the one co-located with the primary warehouse. Let I denote the set of items managed in the PWS.

In every period, two types of demands may arise for an item, short-response lead time and long-response lead time demands. We define $D_{it}^{n,\alpha}$ and $D_{it}^{n,\beta}$ to be random variables for the short- (α) and long- (β) response lead time demand at regional warehouse i in period t for item n, respectively. We also define $d_{it}^{n,\alpha}$ and $d_{it}^{n,\beta}$ to be the realizations of these random variables, and $d_{it}^n = d_{it}^{n,\alpha} + d_{it}^{n,\beta}$. Also, let $D_{it}^\alpha = \sum_n D_{it}^{n,\alpha}$, $D_{it}^\beta = \sum_n D_{it}^{n,\beta}$, and $D_{it} = D_{it}^\alpha + D_{it}^\beta$.

We assume in Section 5 that the workload associated with shipping from a primary warehouse to a regional warehouse is limited in each period. We let C_{it} represent this capacity for regional warehouse i in period t. We assume that $C_{it} > \mathbf{E}[D_{it}]$ for all i and t. In this section, we assume that C_{it} is infinite, i.e., there is no workload limit at any primary warehouse.

There are two types of lead times that determine whether an order is a short- or long-response lead time demand. The first is the customer specified response lead time, and the second is the internal shipping lead time from the primary warehouse to a regional warehouse. Some customers would like to have their order satisfied immediately. These orders can be satisfied at a low fulfillment cost only from stock located at regional warehouse i, the one closest to the customer. These are the short-response lead time demands. When a customer's expectation for delivery is greater than the internal transportation lead time plus the transportation time from the regional warehouse to the customer, the order can be satisfied at a low fulfillment cost by shipping from stock held in the primary warehouse. These are the long-response lead time demands. In this case, let L_i^β measure the time following the receipt of a customer order by which the shipment must leave the regional warehouse.

Suppose the shipping lead time from the primary warehouse to regional warehouse i is L_i periods and $L_i^\beta \geq L_i$. Let $l_i = L_i^\beta - L_i$, the slack time between the long-response customer time window and the transportation time. We call l_i the grace period. If $l_i = 0$, the primary warehouse must immediately ship the item to the regional warehouse where it will be cross-docked and shipped to the customer. When $l_i = 0$, we call this the immediate response time case. When $l_i > 0$, there is greater flexibility in the timing of shipments to the regional warehouse. This helps smooth workloads, as we discuss later.

Our final assumption pertains to the sequence in which events occur in each period, which we assume occur as follows for each item. First, we observe the echelon inventory positions at all locations. Second, when appropriate, we receive a replenishment order at the primary warehouse corresponding to an order placed a procurement lead time ago. Third, we observe the demands at all regional warehouses. Fourth, when appropriate, the primary warehouse places a replenishment order on an external supplier. Fifth, based on availability and the inventory positions at the regional warehouses, we allocate inventory on-hand at the primary warehouse to the regional warehouses. Sixth, we receive stocks at the regional warehouses that were shipped a lead time ago from a primary warehouse. These stocks can be used to satisfy the current period's short-response lead time demand and the long-response lead time orders that were received from customers a transportation lead time or more ago. Seventh, we backlog the unsatisfied demands at the regional warehouses. At the end of each period, holding costs are charged based on on-hand inventories at all warehouses. Backorder costs are charged only at regional warehouses at each period's end.

4.1 *An Exact Model*

We now construct an exact model for determining stock levels for the fulfillment system based on the assumptions we have made. Suppose the planning horizon over which we are placing procurement orders and making inventory allocation decisions for each item is Γ days in length. The length of Γ usually ranges from a few weeks to a few months. During this horizon, there is a set of periods in which item n is permitted to be procured from the external supplier. Let P_n denote the set of days for item n. Thus q_{0t}^n, the amount ordered from the external supplier for item n in period t, can be positive only if $t \in P_n$. To simplify our discussion, we assume procurement orders can be placed only every τ^n periods for item n, which is the cycle length for item n. In reality, the cycle lengths can and do vary over time. As you will observe, this assumption can be relaxed without impacting the modeling approach we present subsequently.

Let x_{it}^n represent the echelon inventory position for item n at location i, $i \in \{0, \ldots, N\}$, at the beginning of period t before any inventory has arrived to i or has been shipped from it. Let q_{it}^n be the amount allocated from on-hand stock of item n at the primary warehouse to regional warehouse

i, $i \in \{1, \dots, N\}$, in period t. Then at regional warehouse i, $x^n_{i,t+1} = x^n_{it} + q^n_{it} - d^n_{it}$. Let $y^n_{it} = x^n_{it} + q^n_{it}$. Thus, y^n_{it} represents the echelon inventory position for regional warehouse i after the allocation is made to it but before satisfying demand in period t. Furthermore, the echelon net inventory for the PWS at the end of period $t + L^n_0$ for item n is

$$x^n_{0t} + q^n_{0t} - \sum_{k=t}^{t+L^n_0} \sum_{i=1}^{N} d^n_{ik}, \tag{1}$$

when $t \in P_n$, and L^n_0 is the replenishment lead time from a supplier for item n. Also, let $y^n_{0t} = x^n_{0t} + q^n_{0t}$.

There are two types of costs considered in our model, holding and backorder costs. Let h^n_i denote the per unit installation holding cost for item n at location i charged at the end of a period. Let b^n be the backorder cost for a unit of item n at a regional warehouse at the end of a period. Thus, we assume the backorder cost for item n is the same across regional warehouses and time. This assumption ensures the model formulation yields a convex problem.

Next, we formulate the decision problem as a dynamic program. We begin by showing how to calculate the costs associated with holding inventories and incurring backorders at the end of a period.

4.1.1 Costs at a Regional Warehouse

Expected holding and backorder costs are charged in each period at each regional warehouse. An allocation of q^n_{it} units to regional warehouse i in period t results in expected costs being incurred at the end of period $t + L_i$. The net inventory at the end of period $t + L_i$ at regional warehouse i is

$$x^n_{it} + q^n_{it} - \sum_{k=t+1}^{t+L_i} D^{n,\alpha}_{ik} - d^{n,\alpha}_{it} - d^{n,\beta}_{it}$$

$$= y^n_{it} - \sum_{k=t+1}^{t+L_i} D^{n,\alpha}_{ik} - d^{n,\alpha}_{it} - d^{n,\beta}_{it}, \tag{2}$$

when $l_i = 0$. Note we know the demand that occurred in period t prior to making the allocation decision, i.e., we know $d^{n,\alpha}_{it}$ and

$d_{it}^{n,\beta}$. However, the short-response lead time demands in periods $t + 1$ though $t + L_i$ are unknown at that time. The resulting expected holding and backorder costs incurred as a consequence of allocating q_{it}^n units to regional warehouse i in period t for item n, i.e., ordering up to y_{it}^n, are

$$
\mathbf{E}\left[h_i^n \left(y_{it}^n - \sum_{k=t+1}^{t+L_i} D_{ik}^{n,\alpha} - d_{it}^n \right)^+ + b^n \left(\sum_{k=t+1}^{t+L_i} D_{ik}^{n,\alpha} + d_{it}^n - y_{it}^n \right)^+ \right],
$$

(3)

where the expectation is taken over the short-response lead time demand random variables for periods $t + 1$ through $t + L_i$. Since no inventory is held in regional warehouse N, this co-located warehouse will incur only expected backorder costs.

4.1.2 *Holding Costs at the Primary Warehouse*

Since no customer demands are satisfied directly from the primary warehouse inventory, only holding costs are incurred there.

Suppose $t' \in P_n$. The echelon inventory position at the beginning of period $t' + L_0^n$ is

$$
x_{0,t'+L_0^n}^n = y_{0,t'}^n - \sum_{i=1}^{N} \sum_{k=t'}^{t'+L_0^n-1} D_{i,k}^n.
$$

(4)

For $t \in \{t' + L_0^n, \cdots, t' + L_0^n + \tau^n - 1\}$, the net inventory at the primary warehouse at the end of period t is

$$
x_{0,t'+L_0^n}^n - \left\{ \sum_{i=1}^{N} \left[x_{i,t'+L_0^n}^n + \sum_{k=t'+L_0^n}^{t} q_{i,k}^n \right] \right\}
$$

(5)

$$
= y_{0,t'}^n - \sum_{k=t'}^{t'+L_0^n-1} D_k^n - \left\{ \sum_{i=1}^{N} \left[x_{i,t'+L_0^n}^n + \sum_{k=t'+L_0^n}^{t} q_{i,k}^n \right] \right\}.
$$

(6)

Consequently, the expected holding cost incurred at the primary warehouse at the end of period t, $t \in \{t' + L_0^n, \cdots, t' + L_0^n + \tau^n - 1\}$, is

$$
\mathbf{E}\left[h_0^n \left\{ \left(y_{0t'}^n - \sum_{k=t'}^{t'+L_0^n-1} D_k^n \right) \right. \right.
$$

$$
\left. \left. - \sum_{i=1}^{N} \left[x_{i,t'+L_0^n}^n + \sum_{k=t'+L_0^n}^{t} q_{i,k}^n \right] \right\} \right] \tag{7}
$$

$$
= \mathbf{E}\left[h_0^n \left\{ \left(y_{0t'}^n - \sum_{k=t'}^{t} D_k^n \right) - \sum_{i=1}^{N} y_{it}^n \right\} \right]. \tag{8}
$$

4.1.3 *The Objective Function*

The expected cost functions given in Equations (3) and (7) provide the basis for making procurement and allocation decisions. However, we do not use them directly in our decision model. Rather, we define another but equivalent set of functions, which are of the type introduced by Clark and Scarf (1960) in their seminal paper and later used, for example, by Kunnumkal and Topaloglu (2008, 2011).

Let us first focus on each regional warehouse i, $i = 1, \ldots, N-1$, for item n. Define

$$
G_{it}^n(y_{it}^n) = -h_0^n y_{it}^n + \mathbf{E}\left[h_{i,t+L_i}^n \left(y_{it}^n - \sum_{k=t+1}^{t+L_i} D_{ik}^{n,\alpha} - d_{it}^n \right)^+ \right]
$$

$$
+ \mathbf{E}\left[b^n \left(\sum_{k=t+1}^{t+L_i} D_{ik}^{n,\alpha} + d_{it}^n - y_{it}^n \right)^+ \right]. \tag{9}
$$

At the beginning of time period t, we do not know the values of d_{it}^n, but we do know these values when making the allocation decision later in that period. Thus, $G_{it}^n(y_{it})$ reflects the knowledge we have when making the allocation decision in period t.

For regional warehouse N,

$$G_{Nt}^n(y_{Nt}^n) = -h_0^n y_{Nt}^n + [b^n(d_{Nt}^n - y_{Nt}^n)^+], \tag{10}$$

since we know d_{Nt}^n when making the allocation of q_{Nt}^n units.

Let us next turn to the primary warehouse. Let

$$G_{0t}^n(y_{0t}^n) = h_0^n y_{0t'}^n, \quad t \in \{t' + L_0^n, \ldots, t' + L_0^n + \tau^n - 1\}, \tag{11}$$

where $y_{0t'}^n$ is the system echelon inventory position corresponding to the procurement order placed at time t'.

Observe that $G_{0t}^n(y_{0t}^n) + \sum_{i=1}^N G_{it}^n(y_{it}^n)$ yields, except for a constant, the same period t expected costs for item n as would result from using expressions (3) and (7) to compute these costs. Thus, the total expected period t cost function used in our model is

$$\sum_n \left\{ G_{0t}^n(y_{0t}^n) + \sum_{i=1}^N G_{it}^n(y_{it}^n) \right\}. \tag{12}$$

Expressing our cost function in this manner permits us to solve the problem more efficiently as we will observe subsequently and as was observed in (Clark and Scarf, 1960), (Kunnumkal and Topaloglu, 2008, 2011) and by others.

4.1.4 *A Dynamic Programming Formulation of the Planning Problem*

We now construct a dynamic programming recursion that could be employed, at least theoretically, to determine the optimal procurement and allocation decisions over the Γ period planning horizon, when C_{it} is infinite for all i and t.

Let $V_t(\bar{x}_t)$ be the expected minimum cost over periods t through Γ that could be achieved given that the system is in state $\bar{x}_t$ at the beginning of period t, where $\bar{x}_t$ is the vector of the x_{it}^n values at that time.

Three types of constraints exist when making decisions in each period. First, there is a logical constraint that implies that the quantity of an item allocated to each regional warehouse in each period cannot be negative. That is $q_{it}^n \geq 0$. This is the balance constraint. Second, procurement of each item n can take place only in period $t \in P_n$. Third, we cannot ship more than is on hand at the primary warehouse for any item in any period.

Combining the results obtained in the previous section with these constraints, we can now express $V_t(\bar{x}_t)$. Let $\bar{D}_t$ be the vector of random variables for demands arising in period t for all items at all regional warehouses and $\bar{y}_t$ be the vector of order-up-to levels, y_{it}^n. The following dynamic program is an example when $L_0^n = 0$.

$$V_t(\bar{x}_t) = \mathbf{E}_{D_t} \left\{ \min \sum_n \left\{ G_{0t}^n(y_{0t}^n) + \sum_{i=1}^{N} G_{it}^n(y_{it}^n) \right\} + V_{t+1}(\bar{y}_t - \bar{D}_t) : \right.$$

$$\text{(13)}$$

$$\text{s.t.} \sum_{i}^{N} y_{it}^n \le y_{0t}^n, \quad \forall n, \tag{14}$$

$$y_{it}^n \ge x_{it}^n, \quad \forall n, i, \tag{15}$$

$$y_{0t}^n \ge x_{0,t}^n, \quad t \in P_n, \; \forall n, \tag{16}$$

$$\left. y_{0t}^n = x_{0,t}^n, \quad t \notin P_n, \; \forall n. \right\}. \tag{17}$$

Note that we do not depend on the assumption that $L_0^n = 0$ in what follows.

Observe that this problem is separable by item. However, the size of the state space corresponding to this dynamic programming formulation grows exponentially with the number of regional warehouses and possible demand values in a day at each warehouse. Hence, we now discuss an approximation approach for computing recommended stock levels.

4.2 An Approximation Approach

We begin our development of an approximate model and method for obtaining a solution to a single item problem by making some observations and assumptions.

Demand from cycle-to-cycle may be nonstationary. However, we assume the demand in any cycle is large enough so that the system echelon inventory position at the time an order is placed is not greater than the one that is desired. That is, a positive quantity will always be ordered ($q_{0t}^n > 0$, $t \in P_n$). This is virtually always the case in the environment we studied for the type of items we are considering. The experiments discussed in Sections 4.3 and 5.4 support this assumption. By assuming so, we are able to formulate the problem as a sequence of independent problems, one for each cycle. This myopic, cycle-based approach for setting stock levels will yield optimal order-up-to levels throughout the planning horizon.

Another observation pertains to the holding and backorder costs. Since the per period backorder costs are high relative to the holding costs (over 100 to 1 for many items), inventory levels are high enough to ensure that backorders occur only infrequently. Then this observation leads to the following two assumptions. First, we assume that when a procurement order arrives it is possible to make allocations so that all regional warehouses achieve their desired stock level. Second, we assume that the balance assumption will be satisfied without explicitly considering constraints which enforce the balancing of inventories. That is, in our approach we assume q_{it}^n could be negative or equivalently y_{it}^n could be less than x_{it}^n. We make this assumption for two reasons.

First, recall that inventory is held at a regional warehouse to satisfy short-response lead time demand. Recall also that these demands have historically accounted for less than 20% of the total demand each day for an item. Since most of the demand is satisfied from stock held at the primary warehouse, most of the inventory is held there. As the percentage of demand that is short-response lead time demand increases, we test the validity of the balance assumption in Section 4.3.

Second, a cycle is always a week or longer, demand rates for items managed using the PWS are high and relatively stable from period-to-period, and our data indicate that short-response lead time demand tends to have low variance-to-mean (VTM) ratios. Consequently, stock imbalance will likely occur, if at all, only at the end of a cycle. For example, if a cycle is a week in duration, imbalance may occur on the last day of the cycle, but is very unlikely to occur prior to that day.

4.2.1 *An Approximation Model for a Single Item*

Since we assume that decisions made in one cycle do not affect those made in other cycles, we will model a single cycle for some item. We drop the item identifier from our notation in this section since we focus on a single item. We do so since at this point we do not consider workload smoothing that links the decisions made among the items. For ease of exposition, we again assume $l_i = 0$. The effect of $l_i > 0$ on the system's performance will be addressed subsequently.

Suppose the item is ordered at time 0 and its echelon inventory position for the primary warehouse, or system, is raised to y_{00} units. The amount ordered arrives at the beginning of period L_0, at which time the system echelon inventory is $x_{0,L_0} = y_{00} - \sum_{k=0}^{L_0-1} d_k$ units. Thus, $P[x_{0,L_0} = w] = P[\sum_{k=0}^{L_0-1} D_k = y_{00} - w]$.

Let y_{it} represent the order-up-to level for regional warehouse i following the allocation decision made in period t. Consequently, the expected cost incurred at regional warehouse i in period $t + L_i$ is

$$h_i \mathbf{E}\left[y_{it} - d_{it} - \sum_{k=t+1}^{t+L_i} D_{ik}^\alpha \right]^+ + b\mathbf{E}\left[d_{it} + \sum_{k=t+1}^{t+L_i} D_{ik}^\alpha - y_{it} \right]^+, \quad (18)$$

where $t \in \{L_0, \ldots, L_0 + \tau - 1\}$. Remember d_{it} includes the long-response lead time demand that arises in period t, which must be shipped to the customer in period $t + L_i$.

Similarly, the expected holding cost charged at the primary warehouse at the end of period t is $\mathbf{E}[h_0[y_{00} - \sum_i y_{it} - \sum_{k=0}^{t} D_k]]$ since y_{it} can be negative.

Let $G_{0t}(y_{0t}) = h_0 y_{00}$ and

$$G_{it}(y_{it}) = -h_0 y_{it} + h_i \mathbf{E}\left[y_{it} - d_{it} - \sum_{k=t+1}^{t+L_i} D_{ik}^\alpha \right]^+$$

$$+ b\mathbf{E}\left[d_{it} + \sum_{k=t+1}^{t+L_i} D_{ik}^\alpha - y_{it} \right]^+. \quad (19)$$

Then $G_{0t}(y_{0t}) + \sum_{i=1}^{N} G_{it}(y_{it})$ is, within a constant, the expected cost incurred resulting from the allocation decisions made in period t, where the procurement decision made in period 0 and $t \in \{L_0, \ldots, L_0 + \tau - 1\}$.

Let x_{0t} be the system echelon inventory position at the beginning of period t, $t \in \{L_0, \ldots, L_0 + \tau - 1\}$, resulting only from a procurement decision made in period 0. We now construct a scalable dynamic programming recursion that can be used to find the values of y_{it} and ultimately y_{00}. Recall that we have relaxed the balance constraints. The recursion we use has a single dimensional state space and is defined as follows:

$$V_t(x_{0t}) = \mathbf{E}_{D_t} \left[\min \left\{ G_{0t}(y_{0t}) + \sum_{i=1}^{N} G_{it}(y_{it}) + V_{t+1}(x_{0t} - D_t) \right\} \right.$$

$$\left. : \sum_i y_{it} \le x_{0t} \right] \tag{20}$$

$$= G_{0t}(y_{0t}) + E \left[\min \sum_{i=1}^{N} G_{it}(y_{it}) + V_{t+1}(x_{0t} - D_t) \right.$$

$$\left. : \sum_i y_{it} \le x_{0t} \right]. \tag{21}$$

Once $V_{L_0}(x_{0,L_0})$ is computed for a range of values for x_{0,L_0}, we compute the expected value $\sum V_{L_0}(x_{0,L_0}) \cdot P\left[\sum_{k=0}^{L_0-1} D_k = y_{00} - x_{0,L_0}\right]$, which we call $F(y_{00})$. It is easy to show that $F(\cdot)$ is a convex function of y_{00} and hence it is easy to determine the optimal value of y_{00} using a line search. Since we determine the order-up-to levels for each item independently of the other items, the calculations can be executed in a parallel manner.

4.3 *Impact of Short-Response Lead Time Demand*

In this section, we demonstrate through numerical experiments that as the percentage of demand that is short-response lead time demand increases, inventory requirements increase substantially. In addition, our model and algorithm were based on the assumption that stock imbalance among regional warehouses occurs rarely. The numerical experiments presented in this section also validate the assumption that the imbalance constraints can be safely ignored in our model.

4.3.1 *Experimental Design*

To test our imbalance assumption, we simulated the operation of the online retailer's five regional warehouse system. For each item, we simulated 600 cycles of operation where the cycle length ranged from one to five weeks. One primary warehouse was responsible for managing 234, 564 relatively high demand rate items in the experiment. This is approximately the number of such items managed within each of the five primary warehouses.

In the simulation experiment, we assumed that daily demand is negatively binomially distributed for each item. This assumption is based on evaluating the distribution of forecast errors in the real application. We scaled costs and demand rates to protect their true values. After scaling, daily demand rates ranged from 0.5 to 120 units per day, and unit costs ranged from $4 to $120. Also, demand VTM ratios ranged from 1.01 to 4.10. Procurement lead times ranged from one to five weeks in length.

Shipping lead times from the primary warehouse to the regional warehouses numbered one through five were 1, 2, 3, 1, and 0 days, respectively. Holding costs were charged at a rate of 20% of the product cost on an annual basis. Thus, for example, the cost to hold an item costing $50 for a year is $10 or approximately $0.0274 per day.

Recall that backorder costs are high and are most often in excess of 25 times the daily holding cost rates. For lower cost items, these costs are greater than 100 times higher. In our experiments, we conservatively assumed the backorder costs were 25 times greater than the holding costs. Since the backorder costs are normally higher in practice, our computed inventory levels would be lower bounds on their true values. Thus, the results of our simulation experiments will provide an upper bound on the possibility of an imbalance situation occurring.

We began the experiment by grouping items according to their cost, demand rate, VTM ratios, and procurement lead times. We found that items could be placed into 10 unit cost, 10 demand, 4 variance-to-mean ratio, and 5 procurement lead time categories, or $10 \times 10 \times 4 \times 5$ possible categories. Of these 2000 possible categories, 739 categories contained at least one item. The categories containing the most items consisted of about 3% of the items. The category containing the highest total demand had 3.1% of the items in it. We also ranked the category by demand rate. The largest category accounts for about 2.3% of total demand.

For each of the 739 categories, we defined a representative item. To do so, we calculated the average unit cost, cycle length, VTM ratio, procurement lead time, and demand rate over all items in the category. This representative item was simulated to obtain investment and imbalance estimates for all items within that category.

After simulating each of the 739 representative items for 600 cycles, we estimated the system inventory holding cost by multiplying the average annual holding cost for reach representative item by the number of items in the category. The simulation experiments were conducted for each of four scenarios. The percentage of the total demand that was short-response lead time demand varied in each scenario and was set at 10%, 20%, 30%, or 80%.

When we first worked with the online retailer, inventories of all items were managed at each of the five warehouses. That is, each warehouse placed and received procurement orders for each item. To illustrate the effect of adopting the PWS, we also simulated the system's performance when each warehouse manages all items. In this system, all demands for all items that arise in a geographical region are fulfilled by the warehouse in that region. The fulfillment system has longer cycle lengths and larger safety stocks since demand for each item was distributed among the five warehouses. We demonstrate how much the inventory costs were lowered by switching to the PWS architecture.

4.3.2 *Experiment Results*

The first question that we address pertains to our imbalance assumption. That is, does imbalance exist to an extent that invalidates our assumption that we can ignore imbalance constraints in our model's formulation? And how does the extent of demand imbalance change as we increase the percentage of demand that is short-response lead time demand? The data displayed in Table 1 indicate that our assumption pertaining to the imbalance constraint is valid. While insignificant across scenarios, we observe that the percentage of periods experiencing imbalance increases by 60% when the percentage of short-response lead time demand increases from 10% to 80%. We would expect this to occur since a greater portion of system stock is located at the regional warehouses as the percentage of short-response lead time demand

Table 1 Percentage of Periods in which Imbalance
Occurs

% Short-Response Lead Time Demand	% Periods in which Imbalance Occurs
10%	0.015%
20%	0.018%
30%	0.018%
80%	0.024%

Table 2 Annual Holding and Backorder Costs

% Short-Response Lead Time Demand	Average Annual Cost
10%	$86,344,071
20%	$92,121,685
30%	$96,317,015
80%	$110,281,815

increases. Thus, for the reasons discussed earlier, the online retailer can employ our model without being concerned about imbalance becoming an issue.

Let us now ask another important question: how do inventory holding and backorder costs change as the percentage of demand that is short-response lead time demand increases? The data displayed in Table 2 show that these costs are highly sensitive to this percentage. Thus, average cost increases by about 31.5% as the percentage of short-response lead time demand increases from 10% to 80%. Since profit margins are low, typically well less than 1% of sales, the increased costs associated with carrying inventories could result in an operational loss.

Suppose the five warehouses operated independently and had to meet all demands in their region using only their inventories. For one of the warehouses, the expected annual inventory costs would be approximately $392 million. This is over four times greater than the annual cost of operating a primary warehouse when short-response lead time demand is about 20% of the total demand. This reduction in operating costs was another key reason for adopting the PWS architecture.

Recall that the online retailer had about 20% of short-response lead time demand several years ago when we worked with it. In the past few years, they have encouraged customers to place short-response lead time demand by selling memberships. Qualified customers would get short-response lead time shipping with no additional cost for any amount of purchase. From our analysis, this would increase the inventory holding and backorder costs significantly. We have seen that the online retailer made several changes to control this cost. First, they increased the subscription fee of their membership. Second, they are offering discounts when members are willing to take the long-response lead time option. Third, inexpensive items can no longer be ordered alone to qualify for expedited shipping.

5 Setting Stock Levels when the Workload Smoothing Constraint is Present

Previously we assumed that the workload associated with shipping to each regional warehouse in each period did not exceed the available capacity and that inventories were always balanced among the regional warehouses for every item. We now see how to include the workload smoothing capacity constraints into our model. Specifically, our goal in this section is to present a method that can be used to determine how much incremental inventory is needed for each item at a regional warehouse to maintain the desired level of service when these constraints are active.

To simplify our analysis, assume that both the short- and long-response lead time demand processes are stationary and demands are independent from period-to-period for an item at each location and across locations. Furthermore, assume that the capacity at each warehouse is constant throughout the planning horizon, i.e., $C_{it} = C_i$ for all t. We also assume the system is stable, that is,

$$\mathbf{E}\left[\sum_n (D_i^{n,\alpha} + D_i^{n,\beta})\right] < C_i, \quad \text{for all } i, \tag{22}$$

where $D_i^{n,\alpha}$ and $D_i^{n,\beta}$ are random variables for the number of short- and long-response lead time demands that arise daily, respectively, for item n at location i.

Recall that when there is sufficient capacity, regional warehouses only carry inventories to satisfy short-response lead time demand. The inventory to satisfy long-response lead time demand is stored at the primary warehouse. When the capacity is limited, we assume that priority is given to replenishing the regional warehouse's inventory needed to satisfy short-response lead time demand. Thus, the effective capacity available in a period for shipping long-response lead time demand is $\tilde{C}_{it} = \left[C_i - D_{it}^\alpha \right]^+$. Note that we ship D_{it}^α units because we are assuming that a stationary order-up-to policy is employed.

By making this assumption, we can plan the incremental inventory requirements for the short- and long-response lead time demands separately. When short-response lead time demand is a small percentage of the total demand, it is almost always true that

$$P(D_{it}^\alpha \leq C_i) \approx 1. \tag{23}$$

In fact, when the expected daily demand is larger than 1000 units, even under the extreme case, where VTM ratio is 10 and when capacity utilization rate is 99%, with 60% of short-response lead time demand, the probability of short-response lead time demand exceeding the capacity is negligible. Hence, we can safely assume that there is always sufficient capacity to satisfy the replenishment for short-response lead time demand, and there is no need to augment inventory to protect against capacity insufficiency. The incremental inventory is used to satisfy long-response lead time demand that cannot be fulfilled due to limited capacity.

In the planning stage, we will first use the approximation method to determine the inventory level required to satisfy short-response lead time demand using the approach described in Section 4.2. Then we determine the amount of incremental inventory needed to satisfy long-response lead time demand due to capacity limitations.

The extent to which these levels need to be augmented due to the limited amount of capacity depends on two factors. The first is the amount of workload smoothing capacity that exists at a regional warehouse. The second factor is the length of the grace periods. Without loss of generality, we assume that the grace period at each regional warehouse is the same, that is $l_i = l$. Intuitively, by extending the fulfillment date of an order, the system can utilize its capacity more effectively by smoothing the workload.

5.1 *Augmenting Stock Levels using a Shortfall Process Approach*

There are several ways to determine the desired incremental inventory for each item. One way is to employ a Lagrangian relaxation method similar to the one introduced by Kunnumkal and Topaloglu (2008, 2011). This approach requires choosing an algorithm to obtain good multiplier values. Two common algorithms are gradient descent and Monte Carlo simulation. Both approaches are iterative methods to compute the impact of the workload smoothing constraints. We employ a different approach based on the so called shortfall process. The shortfall method we use computes the incremental stock levels directly. Glasserman (1997) and Roundy and Muckstadt (2000) used the shortfall process to compute the target inventory level for the immediate response case when there is only one type of demand. For a complete discussion of the shortfall process, see (Glasserman, 1997) or (Roundy and Muckstadt, 2000). We first summarize the shortfall process and then show how to extend it to a system with both short- and long-response lead time demand with positive grace period.

Let S_{it} denote the "shortfall process random variable" corresponding to regional warehouse i following the allocation decision made to satisfy the long-response lead time demand $D_{it}^{n,\beta}$ at the primary warehouse in period t. Also, define T_i to be the aggregate incremental target inventory position for regional warehouse i, i.e., the sum of the individual item incremental target inventory levels. Then

$$S_{it} = T_i - \sum_n (y_{it}^n - y_{it}^{n*}), \tag{24}$$

where y_{it}^n is the echelon inventory position and y_{it}^{n*} is the optimal target echelon inventory position for short-response lead time demand found in Section 4.2 with no capacity limitation. The shortfall process can be defined recursively as

$$S_{it} = \left[S_{i,t-1} + \sum_n D_{it}^{n,\beta} - \tilde{C}_{it} \right]^+ \tag{25}$$

$$= \left[S_{i,t-1} + \sum_n D_{it}^{n,\beta} - (C_i - \sum_n D_{it}^{n,\alpha}) \right]^+ \tag{26}$$

$$= \left[S_{i,t-1} + \sum_n D_{it}^n - C_i \right]^+. \tag{27}$$

In this recursive definition, D_{it}^n is a random variable. Note, importantly, that S_{it} does not depend on T_i in (25). This formulation is the same as the ones discussed by Roundy and Muckstadt (2000).

For ease of exposition, we drop the subscript i. Given our assumptions, we could calculate the steady state distribution of S_t by first determining the transition matrix for the shortfall process, $P_{kj} = P\{S_t = j | S_{t-1} = k\}$, and then by calculating the stationary distribution of the shortfall process in the usual manner. Unfortunately, this approach is impractical due to the scale of the problem. Hence, we use the ideas put forth by Roundy and Muckstadt (2000) to determine a continuous approximation of the probability distribution corresponding to the shortfall process.

Roundy and Muckstadt (2000) show that for a fixed capacity C, the steady state distribution function for S can be approximated by a mass exponential distribution. That is,

$$\bar{F}_S(s) = \begin{cases} \bar{P}_0 e^{-\gamma s}, & s \geq 0, \\ 1, & \text{otherwise,} \end{cases} \tag{28}$$

where $\bar{F}_S(s)$ is the complementary cumulative distribution function of the random variable S, $\bar{P}_0 = 1 - P[S = 0]$, and γ satisfies $e^{\gamma C} = \mathbf{E}[e^{\gamma D_t}]$ for a fixed capacity C.

Given that D_t is the cumulative demand per period over all items, it is reasonable to approximate its distribution with a normal distribution with mean and variance equal to μ and σ^2, respectively. In this case, Glasserman (1997) shows that for a given value of C, $\gamma = 2(C - E[D_t])/\sigma^2$, where

σ^2 is the variance of the random variable D_t. Then we see that

$$\bar{F}_S(s) = \begin{cases} \bar{P}_0 e^{-2(c-E[D_t])/\sigma^2 s}, & s \geq 0, \\ 1, & \text{otherwise.} \end{cases} \tag{29}$$

Next, we compute the expected demand that will be backordered as a function of the incremental inventory T. We use $\eta(T)$ to denote the expected number of long-response lead time demands that are backordered. In Section 4.2.1, we showed how to obtain an order-up-to value for each item. Corresponding to this stock level for item n is a fill rate, which we denote by f^n. Then the average regional warehouse fill rate is

$$\bar{f} = \sum_n \left\{ \frac{E[D^n]}{\sum_n E[D^n]} \right\} f^n. \tag{30}$$

To find T^*, we seek the value of T that satisfies

$$\eta(T) = E(D)(1 - \bar{f}). \tag{31}$$

That is, we seek to achieve the same customer service level that was planned in the absence of capacity constraints.

In the next section, we will discuss how to compute $\eta(T)$ through the shortfall process.

5.2 Computing Expected Backorders

We have assumed that the short-response lead time demand never exceeds the capacity in any period and the priority of allocation is given to the short-response lead time demand. Hence, the number of units of long-response lead time demand placed by period t backordered at the end of period $t+l$ is

$$\left[S_t - T - \left(lC - \sum_{k=t+1}^{t+l} D_k^\alpha \right) \right]^+, \tag{32}$$

where $\sum_{k=t+1}^{t+l} D_k^\alpha = 0$ when $l = 0$.

Note that the number of long-response lead time demands placed by period $t - 1$ backordered at the end of period $t + l$ is

$$\left[S_{t-1} - T - \left((l+1)C - \sum_{k=t}^{t+l} D_k^\alpha\right)\right]^+. \tag{33}$$

Hence, $\eta(T)$, the expected number of units of long-response lead time demands that arrived in period t and are backordered at the end of period $t + l$ is

$$\mathbf{E}\left[\left[S_t - T - \left(lC - \sum_{k=t+1}^{t+l} D_k^\alpha\right)\right]^+ \\ - \left[S_{t-1} - T - \left((l+1)C - \sum_{k=t}^{t+l} D_k^\alpha\right)\right]^+\right]. \tag{34}$$

In the steady state, $n(T)$ is given by

$$\mathbf{E}\left[\left[S - T - lC + \bar{D}_l^\alpha\right]^+ - \left[S - T - (l+1)C + \bar{D}_{l+1}^\alpha\right]^+\right], \tag{35}$$

where $\bar{D}_t^\alpha$ is the total short-response lead time demand over t time periods.

We have assumed that the daily demand follows a normal distribution with mean and variance μ and σ^2, respectively. Let $\kappa \leq 1$ denote the percentage of the total demand that is short-response lead time demand. In this case, when $l > 0$, $\bar{D}_l^\alpha$ follows a normal distribution with mean and variance of $\kappa l \mu$ and $\kappa l \sigma^2$, respectively.

Let $S_l' = S + \bar{D}_l^\alpha$ when $l > 0$ and $S_0' = S$. Let $\bar{F}_{S_l'}(s)$ denote the complementary cumulative distribution of S_l'. Next we will prove how to compute the value of $\eta(T)$.

Theorem 1.1.

$$\eta(T) = \mathbf{E}\left[S_l' - T - lC\right]^+ - \mathbf{E}\left[S_{l+1}' - T - (l+1)C\right]^+. \tag{36}$$

When $l = 0$,

$$\mathbf{E}\left[S_l' - T\right]^+ = \frac{\bar{P}_0}{\gamma}e^{-\gamma T}. \tag{37}$$

When $l > 0$,

$$E\left[S_l' - T - l \cdot C\right]^+ \tag{38}$$

$$= \sqrt{\kappa l}\sigma\phi\left(\frac{T + lC - \kappa l\mu}{\sqrt{\kappa l}\sigma}\right) - (T + lC - \kappa l\mu)\bar{\Phi}\left(\frac{T + lC - \kappa l\mu}{\sqrt{\kappa l}\sigma}\right) \tag{39}$$

$$+ \frac{\bar{P_0}}{\gamma}e^{-\gamma(T + lC - \kappa lC)}\Phi\left(\frac{T + lC + \kappa l\mu - 2\kappa lC}{\sqrt{\kappa l}\sigma}\right)$$

$$+ \frac{\bar{P_0}}{\gamma}\bar{\Phi}\left(\frac{T + lC - \kappa l\mu}{\sqrt{\kappa l}\sigma}\right). \tag{40}$$

Note that when $l > 0$,

$$E\left[S_l' - T - l \cdot C\right]^+ = \int_{T + lC}^{\infty} \bar{F}(S_l')dS_l'. \tag{41}$$

We start by proving the following lemma.

Lemma 1.1.

$$\bar{F}_{S_l'}(s) \approx 1 - \Phi\left(\frac{s - kl\mu}{\sqrt{\kappa l}\sigma}\right) + \bar{P_0}e^{-\gamma(s - \kappa lC)}\Phi\left(\frac{s + \kappa l\mu - 2\kappa lC}{\sqrt{\kappa l}\sigma}\right), \tag{42}$$

for $l > 0$.

Proof of Lemma 1.1.

$$P(S_l' > s) = P(S + \bar{D}_l^\alpha > s) \tag{43}$$

$$= \int_{-\infty}^{\infty} P(S > s - x)f_{\bar{D}_l^\alpha}(x)dx \tag{44}$$

$$= \int_{-\infty}^{s} \bar{P_0}e^{-\gamma(s - x)}f_{\bar{D}_l^\alpha}(x)dx + \int_{s}^{\infty} f_{\bar{D}_l^\alpha}(x)dx. \tag{45}$$

But

$$\int_{-\infty}^{s} \bar{P}_0 e^{-\gamma(s-x)} f_{\bar{D}_l^\alpha}(x) dx$$

$$= \bar{P}_0 \int_{-\infty}^{s} e^{-\gamma(s-x)} \frac{1}{\sqrt{2\pi}\sigma_l} e^{-\frac{(x-\mu_l)^2}{2\sigma_l^2}} dx \tag{46}$$

$$= \bar{P}_0 e^{-\gamma s} \int_{-\infty}^{s} e^{\gamma(\mu_l + \frac{1}{2}\gamma\sigma_l^2)} \frac{1}{\sqrt{2\pi}\sigma_l} e^{-\frac{(x-(\mu_l+\gamma\sigma_l^2))^2}{2\sigma_l^2}} dx \tag{47}$$

$$= \bar{P}_0 e^{-\gamma(s-\mu_l-\frac{1}{2}\gamma\sigma_l^2)} \Phi\left(\frac{s-(\mu_l+\gamma\sigma_l^2)}{\sigma_l}\right) \tag{48}$$

and

$$\int_{s}^{\infty} f_{\bar{D}_l^\alpha}(x) dx = 1 - \Phi\left(\frac{s-\mu_l}{\sigma_l}\right), \tag{49}$$

where $\mu_l = \kappa l \mu$ and $\sigma_l = \sqrt{\kappa l}\sigma$.

Therefore,

$$P(S_l' > s) = 1 - \Phi\left(\frac{s-\mu_l}{\sigma_l}\right) + \bar{P}_0 e^{-\gamma\left(s-\mu_l-\frac{1}{2}\gamma\sigma_l^2\right)}$$

$$\times \Phi\left(\frac{s-(\mu_l+\gamma\sigma_l^2)}{\sigma_l}\right) \tag{50}$$

$$= 1 - \Phi\left(\frac{s-\kappa l\mu}{\sqrt{\kappa l}\sigma}\right) + \bar{P}_0 e^{-\gamma(s-\kappa lC)} \Phi\left(\frac{s+\kappa l\mu - 2\kappa lC}{\sqrt{\kappa l}\sigma}\right). \tag{51}$$

$\square$

Proof of Theorem 1.1. When $l = 0$, it is easy to see that

$$\mathbf{E}[S_l' - T]^+ = \frac{\bar{P}_0}{\gamma} e^{-\gamma T}. \tag{52}$$

When $l > 0$ from Equation (41) and Lemma 1.1, we get

$$\mathbf{E}\big[S'_l - T - lC\big]^+ \tag{53}$$

$$= \int_{T+lC}^{\infty} \bar{F}(S'_l) dS'_l. \tag{54}$$

$$= \int_{T+lC}^{\infty} \left[1 - \Phi\left(\frac{s - \kappa l \mu}{\sqrt{\kappa l}\sigma} \right) + \bar{P}_0 e^{-\gamma(s - \kappa lC)} \right. $$

$$\left. \times \Phi\left(\frac{s + \kappa l \mu - 2\kappa lC}{\sqrt{\kappa l}\sigma} \right) \right] ds. \tag{55}$$

Let $\bar{\Phi}(\cdot)$ denote the complementary cumulative distribution of a standard normal variable, $a = T + lC$, $\bar{\mu} = \kappa l \mu$, and $\bar{\sigma} = \sqrt{\kappa l}\sigma$. Then

$$\int_{T+lC}^{\infty} \left[1 - \Phi\left(\frac{s - \kappa l \mu}{\sqrt{\kappa l}\sigma} \right) \right] ds = \int_{a}^{\infty} \bar{\Phi}\left(\frac{s - \bar{\mu}}{\bar{\sigma}} \right) ds. \tag{56}$$

Let $y = \frac{s - \bar{\mu}}{\bar{\sigma}}$ and $b = \frac{a - \bar{\mu}}{\bar{\sigma}}$, then

$$\int_{a}^{\infty} \left[1 - \Phi\left(\frac{s - \kappa l \mu}{\sqrt{\kappa l}\sigma} \right) \right] ds \tag{57}$$

$$= \bar{\sigma} \int_{b}^{\infty} \bar{\Phi}(y) dy \tag{58}$$

$$= \bar{\sigma} \big[\phi(b) - b\bar{\Phi}(b) \big] \tag{59}$$

$$= \sqrt{\kappa l}\sigma\phi\left(\frac{T + lC - \kappa l \mu}{\sqrt{\kappa l}\sigma} \right) - (T + lC - \kappa l \mu)\bar{\Phi}\left(\frac{T + lC - \kappa l \mu}{\sqrt{\kappa l}\sigma} \right). \tag{60}$$

Furthermore, let $\mu' = \kappa l \mu - 2\kappa l C$.

$$\int_a^\infty \bar{P}_0 e^{-\gamma(s-\kappa l C)} \Phi\left(\frac{s + \kappa l \mu - 2\kappa l C}{\sqrt{\kappa l}\sigma}\right) \tag{61}$$

$$= \bar{P}_0 e^{\gamma \kappa l C} \int_a^\infty e^{-\gamma s} \Phi\left(\frac{s + \mu'}{\bar{\sigma}}\right) ds \tag{62}$$

$$= \bar{P}_0 e^{\gamma \kappa l C} \left[\frac{1}{\gamma} e^{-\gamma a} \Phi\left(\frac{a + \mu'}{\bar{\sigma}}\right) + \frac{1}{\gamma} \int_a^\infty e^{-\gamma s} \frac{1}{\sqrt{2\pi}\bar{\sigma}} e^{-\frac{(s+\mu')^2}{2\bar{\sigma}^2}} ds\right] \tag{63}$$

$$= \bar{P}_0 e^{\gamma \kappa l C} \left[\frac{1}{\gamma} e^{-\gamma a} \Phi\left(\frac{a + \mu'}{\bar{\sigma}}\right) + \frac{1}{\gamma} e^{-\gamma \kappa l C} \bar{\Phi}\left(\frac{a - \kappa l \mu}{\bar{\sigma}}\right)\right] \tag{64}$$

$$= \frac{\bar{P}_0}{\gamma} e^{-\gamma(T + lC - \kappa l C)} \Phi\left(\frac{T + lC + \kappa l \mu - 2\kappa l C}{\sqrt{\kappa l}\sigma}\right)$$

$$+ \frac{\bar{P}_0}{\gamma} \bar{\Phi}\left(\frac{T + lC - \kappa l \mu}{\sqrt{\kappa l}\sigma}\right). \tag{65}$$

Therefore,

$$\mathbf{E}\left[S_l' - T - lC\right]^+ \tag{66}$$

$$= \sqrt{\kappa l}\sigma \phi\left(\frac{T + lC - \kappa l \mu}{\sqrt{\kappa l}\sigma}\right) - (T + lC - \kappa l \mu)\bar{\Phi}\left(\frac{T + lC - \kappa l \mu}{\sqrt{\kappa l}\sigma}\right)$$

$$+ \frac{\bar{P}_0}{\gamma} e^{-\gamma(T + lC - \kappa l C)} \Phi\left(\frac{T + lC + \kappa l \mu - 2\kappa l C}{\sqrt{\kappa l}\sigma}\right)$$

$$+ \frac{\bar{P}_0}{\gamma} \bar{\Phi}\left(\frac{T + lC - \kappa l \mu}{\sqrt{\kappa l}\sigma}\right). \tag{67}$$

□

Note that T^* can be determined quickly using this approach. Given that there are hundreds of thousands of items managed at each warehouse, computational efficiency is important. Remember the value of T^* is a lower bound on the optimal aggregate incremental amount of inventory required to achieve a desired fill rate when the shipping constraint is active.

5.3 *Allocating the T* Units among Items*

We now discuss how to disaggregate the T^* units needed to compensate for the workload smoothing constraint. That is, we provide a method to find the value of $\tilde{y}^n$, the amount of incremental stock needed for item n at a regional warehouse such that $\sum \tilde{y}^n = T^*$.

There are many ways to determine the values of $\tilde{y}^n$. We do so by minimizing the sum of the total current period's holding plus backorder costs plus the sum of future expected holding costs resulting from the choice of $\tilde{y}^n$. We include the term for the expected future holding costs so that items whose demand processes have high coefficients of variation will not be stocked as heavily as those having lower coefficients of variation. Stated differently, we want to add this capacity-protecting inventory in items whose demands are most predictable and likely to be needed in the near future.

As discussed by Chan (1999), the function

$$Q^n(x) = \sum_{k=2}^{\infty} \mathbf{E}\left[x - D_{[1,k]}^n\right] \qquad (68)$$

measures the expected number of future unit inventory periods that will result from stocking x units of item n in the current period, where $D_{[1,k]}^n$ represents the random variable for the cumulative demand for item n for periods 1 through k.

The optimization problem we propose solving to find the value of y^n is

$$\min \quad \left[\sum_n \{G^n(\tilde{y}^n + y^{n*}) + h^n Q^n(\tilde{y}^n + y^{n*})\}\right] \qquad (69)$$

$$\text{s.t.} \quad \sum_n \tilde{y}^n = T^* \qquad (70)$$

$$\tilde{y}^n \geq 0, \qquad (71)$$

where y^{n*} is the optimal order-up-to value determined by solving a problem whose objective function is given by expression (21) when the demand process is stationary. We assume that the current period's demand

d_{it}^n is replaced by the expected demand $\mathbf{E}[D_{it}^n]$ when setting the value of y^{n*}. This problem can be solved easily using a marginal analysis method.

5.4 Computational Results

In this section, we focus on determining the effect of workload smoothing and the length of the grace period on incremental inventory requirements. To do so, we constructed a test in which the aggregate daily expected demand for a regional warehouse was scaled to 1000 units. We then determined the value of T^* using the methods described in this chapter for various combinations of the VTM ratio and the available capacity per period. We will also demonstrate the impact on the value of T^* of having different percentages of the total demand that are short-response lead time demands.

We determined the value of T^* for four daily capacity levels: 1010, 1050, 1100, and 1200 units. These levels correspond to utilization rates of 99.01%, 95.24%, 90.92%, and 83.33%, respectively. Although in the environment we studied, the planned utilization rate does not normally exceed 90%, we wanted to see how the incremental inventory levels would increase as a consequence of high utilization rates.

Obviously, the VTM ratio will also impact the amount of required incremental inventory. We considered five values for VTM: 1.01, 2, 3, 5, and 10. Data that we examined from the online retailer indicated that the VTM of the distribution of forecast errors for most items ranged from 1.1 to 3. We considered larger values in the experiment to estimate the consequences of increased uncertainty on the inventory requirements. Furthermore, we considered two values for l, $l = 0$, and $l = 1$, and two levels of the percentage of total demand that is short-response lead time demand, 20% and 60%.

The resultant values for T^* are given in Tables 3 and 4 for all combinations of the aforementioned factors. Keep in mind that these values are lower bounds. These results indicate that for practical problem environments, when the capacity utilization rate is around 80%, no incremental inventory is required. However, it is not surprising that when capacity is just above the expected demand and there is substantial uncertainty concerning the aggregate demand process, then inventory levels will increase significantly

Table 3 Desired Incremental Stock Level with 20% of Short-Response Lead Time Demand

Capacity (Utilization)	Grace Period = 0, SLT Pncg = 20%				Grace Period = 1, SLT Pncg = 20%			
	1010 (99.01%)	1050 (95.24%)	1100 (90.91%)	1200 (83.33%)	1010 (99.01%)	1050 (95.24%)	1100 (90.91%)	1200 (83.33%)
VTM = 1.01	1	0	0	0	0	0	0	0
VTM = 2	84	0	0	0	0	0	0	0
VTM = 3	195	0	0	0	0	0	0	0
VTM = 5	461	0	0	0	0	0	0	0
VTM = 10	1210	39	0	0	402	0	0	0

Table 4 Desired Incremental Stock Level with 60% of Short-Response Lead Time Demand

Capacity (Utilization)	Grace Period = 0, SLT Pncg = 60%				Grace Period = 1, SLT Pncg = 60%			
	1010 (99.01%)	1050 (95.24%)	1100 (90.91%)	1200 (83.33%)	1010 (99.01%)	1050 (95.24%)	1100 (90.91%)	1200 (83.33%)
VTM = 1.01	36	0	0	0	0	0	0	0
VTM = 2	151	0	0	0	0	0	0	0
VTM = 3	290	0	0	0	0	0	0	0
VTM = 5	589	0	0	0	185	0	0	0
VTM = 10	1372	107	0	0	968	0	0	0

when $l = 0$. The desired incremental inventory levels will decrease significantly by having a one-day grace period. Also, we observe that when the percentage of total demand that is short-response lead time demand increases, the desired incremental inventory levels also increase. The benefit of having a positive grace period decreases when there is a higher percentage of short-response lead time demand. These observations are important for planners to comprehend when creating a workforce plan.

Recall that the values of T^* that we calculated are lower bounds. Thus, we constructed an experiment to test the impact of limited capacity using these values in cases of interest to the online retailer. While keeping costs and shipping lead times the same as before, assume each regional warehouse has an aggregate daily demand rate of 1000 units. In addition, we assume that the procurement lead time is 30 periods in length and the cycle length is 20 periods. When solving the dynamic program (20)–(21) for each item, we found that the order-up-to inventory position at the primary warehouse equals the expected demand over the planning horizon. This target provides ample inventory due to the magnitude of the demand. In this experiment, we consider a single-item case. Hence, the workload constraint is the limiting constraint. The goal is to test our conjecture that no incremental inventory is needed in practical situations. Specifically, we performed two sets of experiments by letting the capacity utilization be 83.33% and 95.2%, which corresponds to daily capacities of 1200 and 1050 units, respectively. In this case, we assume the short-response lead time demand is 20% of total demand on average. The data displayed in Table 3 suggest that no incremental inventory is needed in both cases. The VTM values were 1.01 and 3. In these cases, $T^* = 0$. We simulated the demands incurred in 2000 periods and allocated the inventories based on the method introduced in Section 4.2.1.

Tables 5 and 6 report the average number of backorders and variance of daily allocations when the utilization rate is 83.33%. The reported percentages use the values of backorders and variance when $l_0 = 0$ as baselines, respectively. It shows the magnitude of the impact on backorders and variance as grace period increases. For example, in Table 5, when VTM ratio is 1.01, the baseline average number of backorders at regional warehouse 1 is 571.40. As grace period increases from 0 to 1, the average

Juan Li and John Muckstadt

Table 5 Total Backorders in 100 Cycles with 83.33% of Utilization Rate

		RW1		RW2		RW3		RW4	
VTM = 1.01	$l_0 = 0$	571.40	(100.0%)	1881.30	(100.0%)	819.10	(100.0%)	564.10	(100.0%)
	$l_0 = 1$	550.15	(96.3%)	1836.10	(97.6%)	767.50	(93.7%)	540.00	(95.7%)
	$l_0 = 2$	550.15	(96.3%)	1836.10	(97.6%)	767.50	(93.7%)	540.00	(95.7%)
VTM = 3	$l_0 = 0$	1351.30	(100.0%)	1540.15	(100.0%)	1664.95	(100.0%)	1344.30	(100.0%)
	$l_0 = 1$	1310.45	(97.0%)	1446.30	(93.9%)	1545.15	(92.8%)	1309.25	(97.4%)
	$l_0 = 2$	1310.45	(97.0%)	1446.30	(93.9%)	1545.15	(92.8%)	1309.25	(97.4%)

Table 6 Variance of Daily Allocation with 83.33% of Utilization Rate

		RW1		RW2		RW3		RW4	
VTM = 1.01	$l_0 = 0$	1007.12	(100.0%)	1017.23	(100.0%)	1023.33	(100.0%)	1011.34	(100.0 %)
	$l_0 = 1$	809.17	(80.3%)	811.02	(79.7%)	814.60	(79.6%)	810.06	(80.1%)
	$l_0 = 2$	838.21	(83.2%)	840.26	(82.6%)	843.40	(82.4%)	839.30	(83%)
VTM = 3	$l_0 = 0$	3036.35	(100.0%)	3018.15	(100.0%)	3048.80	(100.0%)	3019.63	(100.0 %)
	$l_0 = 1$	2435.32	(80.2%)	2415.55	(80.0%)	2423.84	(79.5%)	2423.94	(80.3%)
	$l_0 = 2$	2524.53	(83.1%)	2495.27	(82.7%)	2507.98	(82.3%)	2509.26	(83.1%)

number of backorders decreases to 550.15, which is 96.3% of 571.40. Tables 7 and 8 report the same values when utilization rate is 95.2%.

The results suggest three interesting points. First, in both cases, the data found in Tables 5 and 7 show that the total number of backorders in each regional warehouse is at most 5929 units, which is about 0.30% of the total expected demand. Second, the number of backorders is slightly larger when $l = 0$ in both cases. When $l > 0$ and the workload capacity is sufficient, long-response lead time demands are always satisfied on time using the inventory at the primary warehouse. The backorders result from the variation in short-response lead time demand only. These results support our conclusion that when capacity utilization rates are 90% or lower, inventory levels can be determined without considering the capacity constraints directly in the optimization process. Lastly, the results in Tables 6 and 8 suggest that a grace period of length of one day reduces the variance of daily allocations, that is, having $l \geq 1$ makes smoothing of workloads easy to accomplish.

The above experiment supports our conjecture that under the delayed allocation system, when the short-response lead time items account for only 20% of the total demand, no incremental inventory is needed under the presence of workload smoothing constraints. Thus, the question posed by the online retailer concerning the impact of using the delayed allocation system to manage inventories is answered. When the grace period is two or more days, that is, $l_i \geq 2$, which is the case in the system we studied, then it is possible to smooth the flow of inventory and workloads throughout the system. This observation is made by applying rules for satisfying customer orders that are discussed in detail by Li and Muckstadt (2013).

6 Final Comments

We have described a modeling approach that can be employed to plan inventory, storage space, and workload smoothing requirements for an online retailer's multi-location fulfillment system. We showed that balance and shipping constraints can be safely ignored when planning stock levels for the type of system we studied, i.e., a system in which fill rates are high, utilization rates are no greater than 90% on average, and the grace period is two or more days in length. These conditions exist in the system

Table 7 Total Backorders in 100 Cycles with 95.24% of Utilization Rate

		RW1		RW2		RW3		RW4	
VTM = 1.01	$I_0 = 0$	959.10	(100.0%)	2393.10	(100.0%)	1207.10	(100.0%)	912.90	(100.0%)
	$I_0 = 1$	576.95	(60.2%)	1748.55	(73.1%)	744.70	(61.7%)	546.95	(59.9%)
	$I_0 = 2$	576.95	(60.2%)	1748.55	(73.1%)	744.70	(61.7%)	546.95	(59.9%)
VTM = 3	$I_0 = 0$	5902.75	(100.0%)	5174.80	(100.0%)	5214.95	(100.0%)	5928.75	(100.0%)
	$I_0 = 1$	1128.95	(19.1%)	1295.70	(25.0%)	1625.30	(31.2%)	1163.55	(19.6%)
	$I_0 = 2$	1128.95	(19.1%)	1295.70	(25.0%)	1625.30	(31.2%)	1163.55	(19.6%)

Table 8 Variance of Daily Allocation with 95.24% of Utilization Rate

		RW1		RW2		RW3		RW4	
VTM = 1.01	$l_0 = 0$	913.12	(100.0%)	915.83	(100.0%)	933.47	(100.0%)	914.71	(100.0%)
	$l_0 = 1$	759.30	(83.2%)	757.01	(82.7%)	764.03	(81.8%)	760.37	(83.1%)
	$l_0 = 2$	843.41	(91.4%)	834.71	(91.1%)	840.35	(90.0%)	837.00	(91.5%)
VTM = 3	$l_0 = 0$	2117.70	(100.0%)	2100.42	(100.0%)	2098.31	(100.0%)	2099.01	(100.0%)
	$l_0 = 1$	1841.13	(86.9%)	1823.57	(86.8%)	1811.44	(86.3%)	1827.74	(87.1%)
	$l_0 = 2$	2473.58	(116.8%)	2454.06	(116.8%)	2443.82	(116.5%)	2460.67	(117.2%)

we examined. Thus, the desired order-up-to levels can be determined one cycle at a time for each item using the method we described.

We initially stated that our goal is to create a scalable computational procedure. For a PWS consisting of five regional warehouses, we determined order-up-to levels for approximately 250, 000 items for a 15-month planning horizon. To calculate these levels required approximately 9.8 minutes on a PC with an Intel$^®$ Xeon$^®$ Processor E5520 (2.26GHz). In practice, these calculations can be carried out separately for each primary warehouse and in a parallel manner and executed in well less than a minute.

Thus, the approach we have presented is one that planners can use in practical environments. Throughout this chapter, we have emphasized that our model is designed to be used when planning fulfillment system operations. The planning model focuses on setting inventory levels. Customers, however, place orders which may contain many different item types. Thus, allocation and fulfillment actions must recognize that orders must be satisfied as they arrive. Positive grace periods and workload smoothing considerations among others must be taken into account. All these factors are considered in the analysis and models presented by Li and Muckstadt (2013).

Bibliography

Amazon.com Annual Report (2014). 2013 amazon.com annual report, http://phx.corporate-ir.net/phoenix.zhtml?c=97664&p=irol-reportsAnnual.

Bensinger, G. and Stevens, L. (2014). Amazon, in threat to ups, tries its own deliveries, Website, http://www.wsj.com/articles/SB10001424052702304788404579521522792859890.

Chan, E. (1999). Markov chain models for multi-echelon supply chains, School of Operations Research and Industrial Engineering, Cornell University 14850, dissertation.

Clark, A. and Scarf, H. (1960). Optimal policies for a multi-echelon inventory problem, *Management Science* **6**, pp. 475–490.

Eppen, G. and Schrage, L. (1981). Centralized ordering policies in a multi-warehouse system with lead times and random demand, *Management Science* **30**, pp. 69–84.

Federgruen, A. and Zipkin, P. (1984). Approximations of dynamic, multilocation production and inventory programs, *Management Science* **30**, 1, pp. 69–84.

Gallego, G. and Özer, Ö. (2002). Optimal use of demand information in supply chain management, in *Supply Chain Structures*, J.-S. Song and D. Yao (eds.), Springer, US, pp. 119–160.

Gallego, G. and Özer, Ö. (2003). Optimal replenishment policies for multiechelon inventory problems under advance demand information, *Manufacturing and Service Operations Management* **5**, 2, pp. 157–175.

Glasserman, P. (1997). Bounds and asymptotics for planning critical safety stocks, *Operations Research* **45**, 2, pp. 244–257.

Glasserman, P. and Tayur, S. (1994). The stability of a capacitated, multiechelon production-inventory system under a base-stock policy, *Operations Research* **42**, 5, pp. 913–925.

Hariharan, R. and Zipkin, P. (1995). Customer-order information, leadtimes, and inventories, *Management Science* **41**, pp. 1599–1607.

Jackson, P. (1988). 'stock allocation in a two-echelon distribution system or' what to do until your ship comes in, *Management Science* **34**, pp. 880–895.

Jackson, P. and Muckstadt, J. (1989). Risk pooling in a two-period, two-echelon inventory stocking and allocation problem, *Naval Research Logistics* **31**, 1, pp. 1–26.

Kunnumkal, S. and Topaloglu, H. (2008). A duality-based relaxation and decomposition approach for inventory distribution systems, *Naval Research Logistics Quarterly* **55**, 7, pp. 612–631.

Kunnumkal, S. and Topaloglu, H. (2011). Linear programming based decomposition methods for inventory distribution systems, *European Journal of Operational Research* **211**, 2, pp. 282–297.

Li, J. and Muckstadt, J. (2013). Fulfilling orders in a multi-echelon capacitated on-line retail system: PART TWO, real-time purchasing and fulfillment decision making, School of Operations Research and Information Engineering, Cornell University 14850, Technical Report, No. 1482.

Muckstadt, J., Murray, D. and Rappold, J. (2001). Capacitated production planning and inventory control when demand is unpredictable for most items: The no B/C strategy, School of Operations Research and Industrial Engineering, Cornell University 14850, Technical Report, No. 1306.

Özer, Ö. (2003). Replenishment strategies for distribution systems under advance demand information, *Management Science* **49**, 3, pp. 255–272.

Roundy, R. and Muckstadt, J. (2000). Heuristic computation of periodic-review base stock inventory policies, *Management Science* **46**, 1, pp. 104–109.

Wang, T. and Toktay, B. (2008). Inventory management with advance demand information and flexible delivery, *Management Science* **54**, 4, pp. 716–732.

Chapter 7

On Operations Management MBA Teaching in 21st Century Business Schools

Sridhar Tayur

Tepper School of Business,
Carnegie Mellon University Pittsburgh, Pennsylvania, United States

Twenty-five years of academic research, consulting experience, and teaching in a business school, along with substantial entrepreneurial experience — as founder and CEO of an enterprise software company and a social enterprise, as an investor in private equity and co-investor with venture capitalists, and as a board member in several startups — have provided me ample opportunity to reflect upon the role and the responsibilities of MBA educators in Operations Management (OM) in our current times. This chapter, on the occasion to celebrate one of my favorite MBA teachers, Joe Thomas, has provided me an opportunity to pen some of my thoughts.

Keywords: Business and society; capitalism and inequality; entrepreneurship; gender studies; social enterprises; liberal education; cases and mathematical models; teaching and research.

1 School in the Cloud

This is the title of the TED Prize-winning talk by Sugata Mitra (2013). It discusses how the current learning approach came to being, and then asks, what is the future of learning? While I have some concerns about the talk — I inevitably do when it comes to these sorts of topics especially when neatly packaged into an 18-minute narrative — it does provide a bold vision for the future of learning. He essentially asks: What are the needs of the future? Does the current system achieve those goals? Is the current learning approach obsolete? And, equally provocatively, he asks: What is the role of a teacher? Essentially, he is asking whether the current "service of education" needs to be revamped entirely.

I am asking here a much simpler, far more limited, and vastly more modest set of questions: can we improve how we (OM faculty) teach our MBA students to prepare them better for the future? Can we also educate them to shape the future?

Let me begin with two seemingly different perspectives on the role of education.

2   Universities in the Marketplace

This title pays homage to a very informative book by Derek Bok (2009) by the same name.

Drew Gilpin Faust, President of Harvard University, wrote in a *New York Times* piece (2009):

> Universities are meant to be producers not just of knowledge but also of (often inconvenient) doubt. They are creative and unruly places, homes to a polyphony of voices. But at this moment in our history, universities might well ask if they have in fact done enough to raise the deep and unsettling questions necessary to any society.
>
> As the world indulged in a bubble of false prosperity and excessive materialism, should universities — in their research, teaching and writing — have made greater efforts to expose the patterns of risk and denial? Should universities have presented a firmer counterweight to economic irresponsibility? Have universities become too captive to the immediate and worldly purposes they serve? Has the market model become the fundamental and defining identity of higher education?
>
> As a nation, we need to ask more than this from our universities. Higher learning can offer individuals and societies a depth and breadth of vision absent from the inevitably myopic present. Human beings need meaning, understanding and perspective as well as jobs. The question should not be whether we can afford to believe in such purposes in these times, but whether we can afford not to.

Herbert A Simon (1915–2001), then a professor at Carnegie Mellon University, wrote in his essay "The Business School: a Problem in Organizational Design," as part of the book *Administrative Behavior: A Study of Decision-Making Processes in Administrative Organization* (1976):

The tasks of a business school are to train men for the practice of management (or some special branch of management) as a profession, and to develop new knowledge that may be relevant to improving the operation of business.

The objectives of all professional schools — medicine, law, education, business, architecture, or what not — can be stated in the same general terms: education and training for prospective or present practitioners in the profession and for persons wanting to do teaching and research in the professional school; research to advance knowledge relevant to the practice of the professions.

3 The Two Cultures

I would like to use the title of the influential 1959 Rede Lecture by C.P. Snow to articulate what I see as the state of MBA education today: (1) use of Harvard (or Darden) cases ("Harvard approach") and (2) sophisticated mathematical models and analysis ("Carnegie approach") based on Operations Research or Mathematical Economics. I understand that even Snow later (in 1963) considered his framing to be an exaggerated dichotomy, but I think it will serve my purpose well here.

Let us look at five similarities, or the five shared shortcomings, rather than the many differences.

(S1) First, what is common in both the case method and the mathematical model/analysis approach is the focus on "solving a practical problem likely faced by an MBA." That is, neither approach satisfies Gilpin's elevated need for a larger "meaning of life," but are simply two (usually considered mutually exclusive) methods, to help the student navigate the typical professional challenges of the present or the near future. It is job oriented. Herb Simon will likely be pleased.

(S2) A second similarity is that both these approaches "analyze" — using toy mathematical models such as single product Economic Order Quantity (EOQ), the single machine Economic Lot Scheduling Problem (ELSP), the single product-single stage Newsvendor problem, and so on — rather than "implement" industrial strength decision support systems that create measurable value. At the end of these activities, the students do not learn how to put these concepts into action or actual practice where they might see results or experience the consequences of failure.

(S3) A third similarity is in who is doing the teaching, driven in large part by the process of recruiting and a tenure system of promotion that values rigorous, mathematical, theorem-proving research. While the professors may be of different cultures, few have any first-hand understanding of the managerial challenges (of a senior executive in a line of business) of the specific situation that the students, especially the successful ones, may face in their professional career. In many cases, the teacher has no practical managerial/entrepreneurial/leadership experience in anything at all. That is, the professor has not faced the real consequences of negotiating a multi-million dollar contract, or buying/selling a firm, or laying off people, or shutting down plants in an actual firm.

(S4) The fourth similarity is that each case or model is taught as if these decisions are made in isolation. That is, it is rarely the situation that there are two or three cases on the same company, either taking place at the same time or in some chronological order, where decisions across these cases (or models) cannot be independent. (There are exceptions.)

(S5) The fifth similarity is that an Harvard Business School (HBS) case rarely connects to a sophisticated mathematical model, and vice versa.

In my opinion, their similarities greatly overwhelm their differences! Much of the writings have concentrated on the differences. Some have argued for more of the case method (and attempted to place it in some intellectually respectable basis), while others have insisted that the "rigorous" modeling approach leads to true understanding of the underlying fundamentals and have ridiculed the case approach.

I am advocating something entirely different: (a) combine the best of both methods into an integrated whole that spans multiple decisions over time at an individual firm, and (b) elevate the discussions to include the potential (intended or unintended) consequences of business actions on other stakeholders of society.

I will mention some concrete ideas shortly. Before I do that, I want to touch upon two more topics of contemporary importance: entrepreneurship and women.

4 No Longer Rogues

Jason L. Baptiste, in *The Ultralight Startup* (2012), wrote:

> In the past, "entrepreneur" was, at best, a name given to rogue risk takers who couldn't accept authority and, at worst, a code word for those who were either broke and unemployed or rich and bored. Today that is no longer the case.

Traditionally, business school education has focused on large/mature organizations, and on problem solving. As OM faculty, we concentrate almost entirely on well-understood problems (and models) to tackle high-volume, "canonical" problems. What is needed now is to deal with entrepreneurial ventures and focus on problem finding and/or novel approaches to solving existing problems by mechanisms that are not limited to existing (large) companies or consulting firms.

Indeed, what was said by Sumner Slichter in *Fortune* (1945) is perhaps really true today:

> Jobs do no simply exist. They are created by alert, imaginative and resourceful men who discover or think that they have discovered opportunities to sell something at a profit. These opportunities are exploited by adventurous investors who are willing to risk heavy losses in order to make large gains. A community in which everyone attempted to make a living by getting on someone else's payroll would be a community of the unemployed.

5 Lean In

Yes, I am referring to Sheryl Sandberg's 2013 book that has received both positive reviews as well some negative reactions. It is quite entertaining and a worthwhile read. Essentially, it develops the case that while there are systemic issues in society (including the behavior of men) that block women from becoming leaders (this is not controversial among women), it also places some of the blame on the way women behave and make decisions (this has created annoyance among some women). She wonders why it is the case that while women make up 50% (or more) of the working population at the start of a (business) career, with qualifications equal (if not better) than men (on average), we do not see enough women at the very top of the chain (in corporate America, in politics). For example, she recommends that in situations of a heterosexual, married couple with dual careers, women should "lean in" more at work, and men can (and should) "lean in" more at home. I realize that I am treading on some really dangerous ground here, and it is indeed simpler to avoid this topic. Indeed, as *The Economist* (March 16, 2013) writes in their review of this book:

> Still, "Lean In" is a brave book to write. Gender is still an uncomfortable subject in corporate America. One chief executive told Ms Sandberg that it is more difficult to talk about gender than about one's sex life.

I bring gender up for two reasons.

1. Recently I was a guest speaker at HBS to comment on the students' analysis of a HBS case called "OrganJet and GuardianWings" (Battilana and Weber, 2013). I was representing my social enterprise, a contract hybrid that combines a for-profit with a not-for-profit to provide inclusive access to kidney transplantation in the U.S. There were two sections of 90 students each, with 50–50 split between the genders in both. The discussions in both sections were similar and were quite good.

What was interesting is what happened after the class. Several students spent a couple of hours with me, and then many others sent me emails. Over 80% of the women wanted to know more about OrganJet and GuardianWings, and other such initiatives that are aimed at applying business skills to reduce inequity in society. Over 80% of the men wanted to know how they could be financially successful in "big data" and "analytics", how to be successful at McKinsey, or if I would help them in (for profit) entrepreneurial ventures they are about to undertake! About an equal number of women and men contacted me after class.

2. Studies done at HBS have shown that women entrepreneurs have more difficulty obtaining funding. Even more critically, women venture capitalists (VCs) have had difficulty having male entrepreneurs accept their money!

MBA education of the future should consider the fact that nearly 50% of the class is likely to be women. While some women are more oriented (like many men) towards business success, many women (and men) may find meaning in areas that are not traditionally the focus of business school education, like social enterprises and social entrepreneurship.

6 What Can Be Done Differently in MBA Education?

It is unlikely that every case (or model or set of cases/models) can alleviate all five of the shortcomings that I have brought up above, and also deal with entrepreneurship and women in some beneficial manner. Let me present a few examples to illustrate what I am doing to deal with these issues in my MBA teaching.

1. Consider an HBS case on video games and marketing, "Massive Incorporated" (a startup, co-founded by a female MBA from HBS, and acquired by Microsoft).

The case itself does not wonder if marketing sugary drinks and fatty foods to children or young adults through video games, and making money by doing so, is in itself something one should be concerned about. Rather, the focus is on how to do the advertising well, gain market share, create value for investors, and monetize the entrepreneurial efforts in the most effective manner. There is also no mathematics on how exactly the ads are placed in the video games, one of the key "competitive advantages" that makes the company valuable.

So, what we have added — since I worked with "Massive Incorporated" with my Ph.D. student, John Turner — is a spreadsheet tool that has a stochastic, mixed-integer program model and solution all built in, for MBA "what if" use. A research paper on this topic (Turner *et al.*, 2011) has been published in *Operations Research*. John's PhD thesis, which had this paper as one of the three chapters, won the 2011 INFORMS Dantzig Prize for best doctoral dissertation. This spreadsheet adaptation satisfies items (S3) and (S5) of the previous shortcomings list, but not the others. For example, to address (S1), the class needs to add something more. One idea is to discuss the impact of corporate marketing of unhealthy foods on impressionable children and youth (mostly male, ages 18–34). For example, Kellogg's is facing these challenges: they want to create a healthy portfolio of foods, but Wall Street wants good returns in the short run, and many junk foods appear easier to sell and also have a higher profit margin. Is there an opportunity for an entrepreneur to create a company of healthy and tasty alternatives that Pepsi can acquire?

2. Another HBS case I really like is "Rent the Runway", also co-founded by two women (both MBAs from HBS).

Similar to the case above, we have created a spreadsheet with queueing and inventory models for MBAs that works with the case (satisfying S5). But how can MBAs discuss this business in the context of society (S4)? Perhaps it is worth introducing questions like: What is the role of fashion, unfettered desire for luxury, and the image of a "perfect woman" on the self-esteem of impressionable tweens (mostly girls)? What is the responsibility of corporate firms pushing their beauty products and fashion accessories at young audiences?

What about research papers? Vince Slaugh, my PhD student (joining Cornell this fall) was the TA for this course, and one of his thesis chapters studies on-line rental models with usage-based loss; this chapter has been accepted by *Manufacturing & Service Operations Management* (and was awarded Second Prize in IBM Service Science Student Paper Competition in 2015).

3. To address (S3) and (S4), I use the Darden Case (Wilcox and Yemen, 2011), now distributed by Harvard, on "SmartOps Corporation" (acquired by SAP). I was founder and served as the CEO for 12 years, from the beginning to setting up the exit. Thus, I can look at the various aspects of this firm over time, from a variety of perspectives — founder, angel investors, early employees, VC, competition, early customers, analysts, SAP, Accenture, McKinsey, non- SAP customers, later stage employees, engineers, pre-sales consultants, sales directors, marketing group, and so on — and I can connect them to standard topics in a text book. Of considerable interest to students is also how we created a win–win channel partnership — building an alliance and contract to ensure incentive compatibility — for a startup (SmartOps) with software giant (SAP). We co-innovated in enterprise supply chain software by bringing academic research in stochastic, multi-stage inventories and other analytics to market, and made our academic research widely used around the globe.

4. How about bringing academic technical papers (from *Operations Research* and so on) to the classroom? If we believe that complex mathematics is useful, then why not make it accessible to future practitioners? We take a paper by Cho *et al.* (2014) that helped design a portion of South Korean health care system, and that considers mathematically complex problems such as: How many trauma centers should there be, and where? Connected to that, what about the number and locations of helicopters (and heliports)? Should there be heliports at locations other than trauma centers? It is a complex problem to solve mathematically but has been done by my colleague Soo-Haeng Cho and his co-authors (2014). For class, we created a spreadsheet tool that MBA students can manipulate to understand the various tradeoffs. This "case" also offers the opportunity to discuss the role of public services, such as ambulances or fire engines, and thus elevates the discussion to the "optimal" role of government, and how to make our "public–private" society work effectively. Items (S1) and (S5) are thus covered. (This paper won the 2014 Pierskalla Prize.)

5. Let us revisit "OrganJet and GuardianWings", the HBS case on my social enterprise. This case can address both (S4) and (S1) by discussing an important inequality that exists in our capitalist society. I tie this to the broader discussion of societal inequality; for example, the *Foreign Affairs* article entitled "Capitalism and Inequality" by Jerry Muller (2013) is worth discussing in class. Additionally, to achieve (S2), the students are tasked with creating a Minimum Viable Product (MVP), the very fundamental basis of a service (or product) that is useful to some customer segment or improves the productivity of the firm, consistent with the "Lean Startup" view. A research paper on OrganJet (Ata *et al.*, 2016) that models the organ transplant system in the U.S. as a selfish routing game on a network of overcrowded queues with abandonment has been accepted in *Management Science.* (It was awarded the 2015 Pierskalla Award.)

Note that the four cases (other than the South Korean health care system design) are entrepreneurial in nature.

How can we further connect our classrooms with what is trending now? I have students connect to the Internet in class — yes, "classroom in the cloud" — to see what is happening with respect to the cases being discussed and topics of contemporary importance. For example, why Avis acquired Zipcar (one of the other cases in the course, co-founded by a female MIT Sloan MBA). How Uber's economics will change if driverless cars become a reality, and whether the freelance (or "gig") economy is further exacerbating inequality in society (Dai and Tayur, 2016). And whether the near future is all about "platforms" (by analyzing a CMU MBA alum's startup, ZenRez, which competes with an MIT alumna's startup, ClassPass).

Additionally, to discuss important OM issues in traditional, large companies, I cover (a) rapid-response supply chain design (Rao *et al.*, 2000) and supply chain flexibility (Tardif *et al.*, 2010) (b) operating a global supply chain with multiple stages and across enterprises (Keene *et al.*, 2006; Troyer *et al.*, 2005) and (c) optimal product portfolio design that trades off market share with cost of complexity (Yunes *et al.*, 2007). I also cover how EOQ models actually work in a real multi-billion dollar grocery chain (Erhun and Tayur, 2003), and how production planning is done at a multi-billion dollar consumer product food company (Mehrotra *et al.*, 2011). These help address shortcomings (S2) and (S4), and show the importance of enterprise information technology, incentive alignment across organizational silos and across enterprises, and the critical role of data.

I could go on, with examples from GE and others, connecting lean operations, kanbans, lead time quotation, and tying these to how private equity companies create value in our capitalist society, but I expect you get the drift.

7 The Role of Universities

Let me close with a quote by Alfred North Whitehead (1929):

> The justification for a university is that it preserves the connection between knowledge and zest of life, by uniting the young and old in the imaginative consideration of learning...The tragedy of the world is that those who are imaginative have but slight experience, and those who are experienced have feeble imaginations. Fools act on imagination without knowledge; pedants act on knowledge without imagination. The task of the university is to weld together imagination and experience...The task of the university is the creation of the future, so far as rational thought and civilized modes of appreciation can affect the issue.

I hope that this short essay opens the door to further discuss the topics that I consider relevant to MBA education in the 21st Century: (a) what is the role of business in society? (b) how can women and men be more equal participants? (c) how can HBS cases and "rigorous, publishable, mathematical" research work together? (d) how can imaginative ideas through entrepreneurial energy (including social enterprises) make our society better? And (e) how can we, as MBA educators, drive important changes in society and also train the next generation of Ph.D. students who will replace us as faculty. In this way, we may be able to achieve "higher aims" of our profession instead of simply creating another generation of "hired hands" (Khurana, 2007).

Bibliography

Ata, B., Skaro, A. and Tayur, S. (2016). OrganJet: Overcoming geographical disparities in access to deceased donor kidneys in the United States. *Management Science* (in Press).

Baptiste, J. L. (2012). *The Ultralight Startup: Launching a Business Without Clout of Capital*, Portfolio, New York, NY.

Battilana, J. and Weber, J. (2013). OrganJet and guardianwings, *Harvard Business School Case* 413-068, February 2013 (Revised April 2013).

Bok, D. (2009). *Universities in the Marketplace: The Commercialization of Higher Education*. Princeton University Press.

Cho, S.-H., *et al.* (2014). Simultaneous location of trauma centers and helicopters for emergency medical service planning, *Operations Research* **62**, 4, pp. 751–771.

Dai, T. and Tayur, S. (2016). POM and Manufacturing. In *Routledge Companion to Production and Operations Management (POM): Contributions from 50 Global Thought Leaders*, Routledge, London, U.K.

Economist. (2013). The feminist mystique. *The Economist*, 16th March.

Erhun, F. and Tayur, S. (2003). Enterprise-wide optimization of total landed cost at a grocery retailer, *Operations Research* **51**, 3, pp. 343–353.

Faust, D. G. (2009). The university's crisis of purpose, *New York Times*.

Keene, S., Alberti, D., Henby, G., Brohinsky, A. J. and Tayur, S. (2006). Caterpillar's building construction products division improves and stabilizes product availability, *Interfaces* **36**, 4, pp. 283–295.

Khurana, R. (2007). *From Higher Aims to Hired Hands*, Princeton Press, Princeton, NJ.

Mitra, S. (2013). Build a school in the cloud. TED. Accessible at https://www.ted.com/talks/sugata_mitra_build_a_school_in_the_cloud.

Mehrotra, M., Dawande, M., Gavirneni, S., Demirci, M. and Tayur, S. (2011). Production planning with patterns: a problem from processed food manufacturing, *Operations Research* **59**, 2, pp. 267–282.

Muller, J. Z. (2013). Capitalism and inequality, *Foreign Affairs* **92**, 2, pp. 30–51.

Rao, U., Scheller-Wolf, A. and Tayur, S. (2000). Development of a rapid-response supply chain at Caterpillar, *Operations Research* **48**, 2, pp. 189–204.

Sandberg, Sheryl. (2013). *Lean In: Women, Work, and the Will to Lead*, Random House.

Simon, H. A. (1976). *Administrative Behavior: A Study of Decision-Making Processes in Administrative Organization*, Free Press, New York, NY.

Slaugh, V. W., Biller, B. and Tayur, S. R. (2016). Managing Rentals with Usage-Based Loss, *Manufacturing & Service Operations Management* (in Press).

Snow, C. P. (1959). Two cultures, *Science* **130**, 3373, pp. 419–419.

Snow, C. P. (1963). *Two Cultures*, New American Library.

Tardif, V., Tayur, S., Reardon, J., Stines, R. and Zimmerman, P. (2010). OR practice — implementing seasonal logistics tactics for finished goods distribution at Deere and company's C&CE division, *Operations Research* **58**, 1, pp. 1–15.

Troyer, L., Smith, J., Marshall, S., Yaniv, E., Tayur, S., Barkman, M., Kaya, A. and Liu, Y. (2005). Improving asset management and order fulfillment at Deere & Company's C&CE division, *Interfaces* **35**, 1, pp. 76–87.

Turner, John, Alan Scheller-Wolf, and Sridhar Tayur. (2011). OR Practice-Scheduling of dynamic in-game advertising, *Operations Research* **59**, 1, pp. 1–16.

Whitehead, Alfred North. (1929). *The Aims of Education and Other Essays*.

Wilcox, Ronald, T. and Yemen, Gerry. SmartOps Corporation: Forging Smart Alliances? Darden School of Business Case. Available at https://cb.hbsp.harvard.edu/cbmp/product/UV5755-PDF-ENG.

Yunes, T., Napolitano, D., Scheller-Wolf, A. and Tayur, S. (2007). Building efficient product portfolios at John Deere and company, *Operations Research* **55**, 4, pp. 615–629.

Index

Printed in the United States
By Bookmasters